John Baines, a Winchester classical scholar and young Royal Engineers officer, was on active service in France and Salonika during the First World War. Throughout this time he wrote to his 'Dearest Mother' and to Honor, his younger sister. The letters give regular updates of his activities in an affectionate, amusing and relaxed way, while disguising the true horror, dangers and realities of war.

These letters have been brought to life by the editors, who are grandchildren of John Baines, in a refreshing and unusual way. Through careful research, many additional details of topics John writes about are included – individuals, articles, places, military aspects, family and also of his mother's life back on the Home Front. This book will therefore be of general interest to a wide readership.

Andrew Baines and Joanna Palmer are grandchildren of John Baines, and great grandchildren of Elizabeth Baines. Andrew followed in both his grandfather's and father's footsteps as a Wykehamist and Sapper; Joanna, in addition to being 'an Army child', is the widow of General Sir Patrick Palmer. So between them they have been able to combine and share their deep family knowledge and wide military experiences in editing *Dearest Mother* and making the letters accessible and enjoyable for all.

DEAREST MOTHER

First World War letters home from a young Sapper officer in France and Salonika

Andrew Baines & Joanna Palmer

Helion & Company Limited

Helion & Company Limited
26 Willow Road
Solihull
West Midlands
B91 1UE
England
Tel. 0121 705 3393
Fax 0121 711 4075
Email: info@helion.co.uk
Website: www.helion.co.uk
Twitter: @helionbooks
Visit our blog http://blog.helion.co.uk/

Published by Helion & Company 2015
Designed and typeset by Bookcraft Ltd, Stroud, Gloucestershire
Cover designed by Paul Hewitt, Battlefield Design (www.battlefield-design.co.uk)
Printed by Henry Ling Limited, Dorchester, Dorset

ISBN 978-1-910294-57-4

British Library Cataloguing-in-Publication Data.
A catalogue record for this book is available from the British Library.

For details of other military history titles published by Helion & Company Limited contact the above address, or visit our website: http://www.helion.co.uk.

We always welcome receiving book proposals from prospective authors.

CONTENTS

Foreword

General Sir Hugh Beach GBE KCB MC

John Stanhope Baines was born in 1894, passed into Winchester College as a scholar in 1907, and into the Royal Military Academy Woolwich in 1912 as a prize cadet. He was commissioned into the Royal Engineers just before the outbreak of the First World War. After a few months training at the School of Military Engineering at Chatham he was posted to a Field Company in France, arriving there in February 1915. In July a bullet wound in the hand brought him back to England for a few months. He returned to France early in 1916, this time as a staff officer (adjutant to the Commander Royal Engineers), but still actively involved in front line duties.

Baines spent the whole of the next two years (1917–18) in Salonika, again as a field engineer. This theatre of war is far less well known than the Western Front, but involved every bit as much gallantry and fortitude, confronting all the miseries of trench warfare with the additional torments of mosquitos and malaria, and involving the same dismal succession of British assaults against heavily defended positions. However the final success of the British, French, Serb and Greek allies in late 1918 contributed directly to the end of the First World War.

This book consists mainly of letters written by Baines to his mother and sister. They are in the artless style of a young man (a Wykehamist versed in classics) writing home. They are surprisingly up-beat, often saying how agreeable his living conditions are and how much he is enjoying life. This tone of voice will have been heavily influenced by his wish not to distress the family and by the deadening effect of official censorship, of which he fell foul on at least two occasions.

The book has been edited by Andrew Baines and Joanna Palmer, two of his grandchildren, with devotion and flair. Great care has been taken to explain the context in which the letters were written, to explain references which would otherwise be obscure and to include biographic details of some of the friends and colleagues Baines wrote about. The result is highly readable and will appeal to all who are interested in the human side of war. At a time of great popular concern about the First World War this book provides an original and timely snapshot of one young man's view of trench warfare, laced with humour, pathos and guts. As a Wykehamist and Sapper myself, I have found it a compelling read.

Preface

John was not famous; he did not win gallantry awards; he was not killed in action. Like millions of other servicemen, our grandfather served his King and Country throughout the First World War, never complaining and never wavering in his professional commitment to give of his best at all times.

In compiling his letters, and adding as much additional information as possible to bring them to life, we hope that readers will enjoy getting to know a brave, hard-working, typical young officer. We have tried to present a rather different view of the First World War – one which we hope is interesting and absorbing in its own way.

We also hope that the book might be an inspiration to anyone who is thinking of researching family links to the First World War. Start and you will never know where it will lead. You will never regret it.

On an editorial note, it may be helpful to explain that we have not altered John's letters in any way. 'We'ld' and 'he'ld' and 'its' and '&' are as written and all spellings, punctuation and grammar are his.

We would like to thank a number of people who helped us as we worked on Dearest Mother. These include: Bob Graham, a good friend and experienced investigative journalist, who encouraged us to launch the project at the outset; Suzanne Foster, the College archivist at Winchester, who has been unfailingly helpful in answering our many research requests; Nigel Jaques, a retired Eton classics master, without whose help John Baines' Greek would still be Greek to us; Meriel Sauvaget, our French friend, who did the critique and improved version of John's French poem; Didier Slock, living at Point X on the L'Epinette operation sketch map, who orientated us during our battlefield tour; staff at the National Archives, Imperial War Museum and RE Library for their valuable assistance; Duncan Rogers, our publisher, for his enthusiasm and support; Kim McSweeney, the typesetter, for her professional excellence; and finally Janet and Mike for their encouragement and patience at every stage of our project.

Andrew Baines & Joanna Palmer

Baines Family Tree

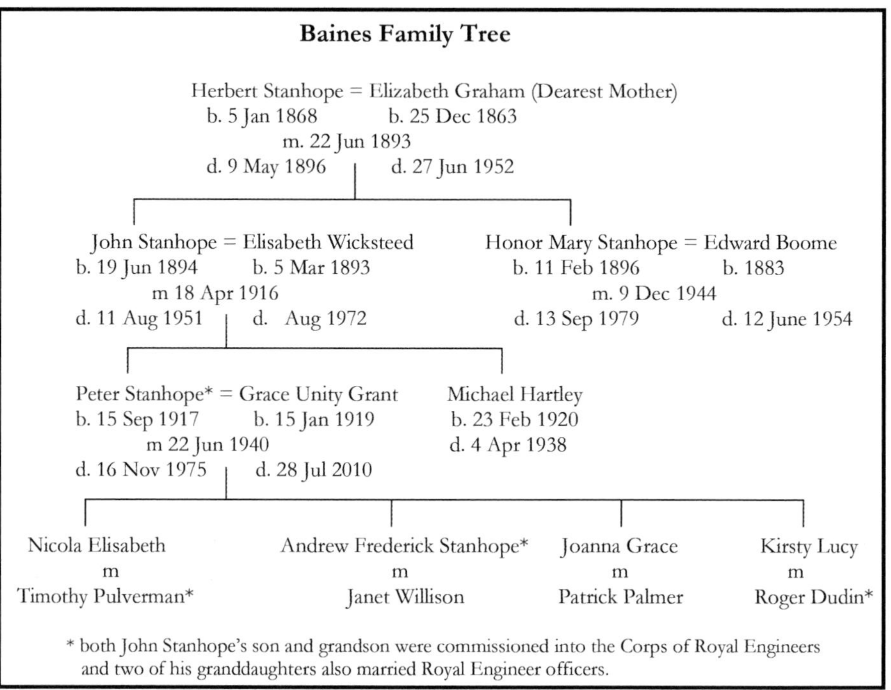

Baines Family Tree
Herbert Stanhope = Elizabeth Graham (Dearest Mother)
b. 5 Jan 1868
b. 25 Dec 1863
m. 22 Jun 1893
d. 9 May 1896
d. 27 Jun 1952
John Stanhope = Elisabeth Wicksteed
b. 19 Jun 1894
b. 5 Mar 1893
m 18 Apr 1916
d. 11 Aug 1951
d. Aug 1972
Honor Mary Stanhope = Edward Boome
b. 11 Feb 1896
b. 1883
m. 9 Dec 1944
d. 13 Sep 1979
d. 12 June 1954
Peter Stanhope* = Grace Unity Grant
b. 15 Sep 1917
b. 15 Jan 1919
m 22 Jun 1940
d. 16 Nov 1975
d. 28 Jul 2010
Michael Hartley
b. 23 Feb 1920
d. 4 Apr 1938
Nicola Elisabeth
m
Timothy Pulverman*
Andrew Frederick Stanhope*
m
Janet Willison
Joanna Grace
m
Patrick Palmer
Kirsty Lucy
m
Roger Dudin*
* both John Stanhope's son and grandson were commissioned into the Corps of Royal Engineers and two of his granddaughters also married Royal Engineer officers.

Who was Dearest Mother?

Elizabeth Graham was born on 25th December 1863 in Kilkeel, Co Down, Ireland, the first child of Letitia and Thomas Graham. At the time of his marriage Thomas was shown as a "Master at Workhouse" in Downpatrick. Elizabeth had five younger siblings: Isabella, Letitia (died aged 5), Anna, Thomas (died aged 1) and Letitia.

She was educated at Victoria College, Belfast, before entering Newnham College, Cambridge in 1888. Although women were first allowed to attend lectures at Cambridge University in 1868, Newnham College only received a full Charter as a Cambridge College in 1917. In 1888, therefore, it was still merely a boarding house for women wishing to attend lectures at the University, although they were not allowed to take the Tripos exam.

Elizabeth was a student of Classics. She studied Latin, Greek, Philiogy and Roman & Greek History. Records of her attendance at lectures show her to be a keen pupil. There can be no doubt whatever that it was at Cambridge during this time that she met her future husband, Herbert Baines. A fondly-worded letter from him dated Mar 1, 1890, detailing the last hours of his grandfather's life, reveal his feelings for her.

Herbert Stanhope Baines was the third child of Louisa Jane Haigh and John William Baines. During the 12 years of their marriage (until John's death in 1875) Louisa and John had eight children: Florence, Edward, Herbert, Ethel, Ella, twins Alexander and Hilda, and Charlotte.

He was educated first at Leeds Grammar School then London University. After matriculating he went up to Caius College, Cambridge where he graduated in 1889 with a BA Honors in Classical Tripos. He was a Member of the Debating Society and took part in sports, especially boating and football

Elizabeth and Herbert married on 22nd June 1893 and thereafter lived in Leeds, Yorkshire. Herbert became Editor of the Leeds *Mercury* newspaper (founded by his great grandfather Edward Baines), which had always held robust radical policies, and he stood as a Liberal candidate in local elections. When his cousin Talbot Baines appeared on the Unionist platform (breaking with the family Liberal tradition) and at the same time retired

Herbert and Elizabeth 1896

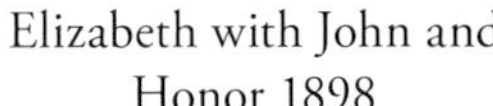

Elizabeth with John and Honor 1898

from running the *Mercury*, Herbert stepped into the breach. It seems he breathed new life into the newspaper.

Elizabeth and Herbert had two children John Stanhope (born 19 June 1894) and Honor Mary Stanhope (born 11 February 1896). In May 1896, three months after the birth of his daughter Honor, Herbert was "recommended to take a short sea voyage; not on account of any organic disease, but simply on account of some giving way of nervous force through overwork". He set off for the Canary Islands and for unknown reasons, instead of returning directly from there, he decided to go further south, down the west coast of Africa to Accra. Shortly before he reached Accra, however, he disembarked at Cape Coast (Ghana) to await a ship, the *S.S.Benin*, which would take him north again and home. During the week he was in Cape Coast he developed a fever (possibly malaria) and, although he boarded *S.S. Benin* to go home, he died the same day on board ship and was buried at sea – 9th May 1896.

Heartbroken, Elizabeth took her two children to stay with her mother-in-law at Windermere and it may be that this is when she came to love the Lake District and why she spent so much time there in later years. She never married again.

Postcards home from school

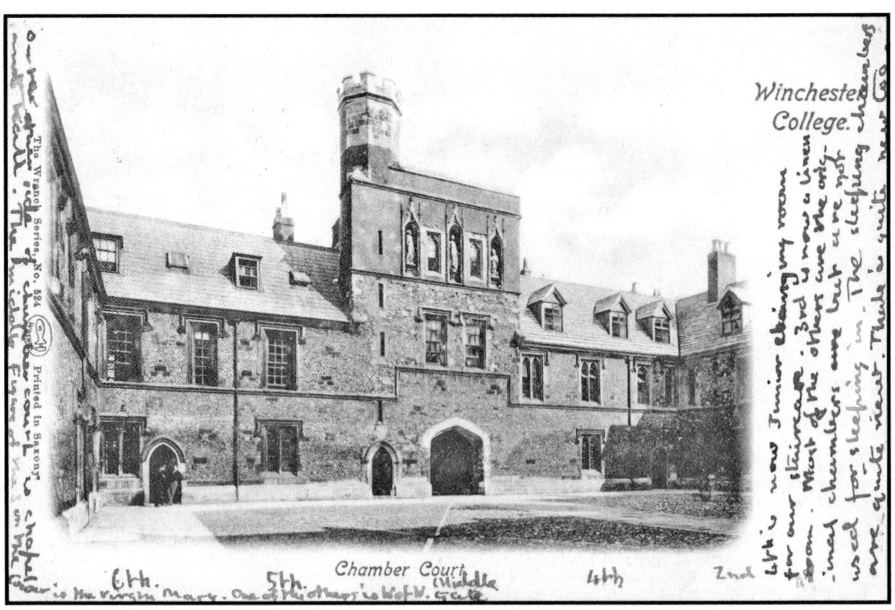

EARLY DAYS

Although not strictly within the book title, it seems appropriate to include some early letters which give an insight into aspects of John's character which come out more strongly as he matures.

John was a scholar at Winchester College, specialising in classics. Two letters written to his younger sister Honor show an early interest in politics and debating.

When John was asking advice about which regiment he should join, it must be remembered that in 1911 there was no inkling that a World War would start in 1914. He was thinking of a regular commission and a long term career in the Army.

Five letters written from Chatham, whilst undergoing young officer training prior to going to France, set the scene on the home front and show the particularly strong bond that existed between John and his mother and Honor. No doubt this had developed because his father died very early in his life, leaving him to grow up with a feeling of responsibility for the care of his family. These letters also introduce, though not yet by name, his future wife Elisabeth.

LETTERS FROM WINCHESTER COLLEGE

Miss Honor Baines
Switzerland

The College
Winchester

Nov. 10th 1910

My Dearest Honor,

Thank you for your letter. I am sorry you are having bad weather. We have it lovely here.

The Debate was quite amusing. I made a long and extremely dull speech which was entirely off the point. We lost by 26 to 37.

The last fifteen is today. Commoners beat us 10 – 2 and we were then beaten 10 – 5 by Houses who were very good. This afternoon Houses will probably not be as good as on Tuesday while we can't be worse than we were on Saturday. We shall probably be beaten but might make a good fight. I'll put in the score at the end.

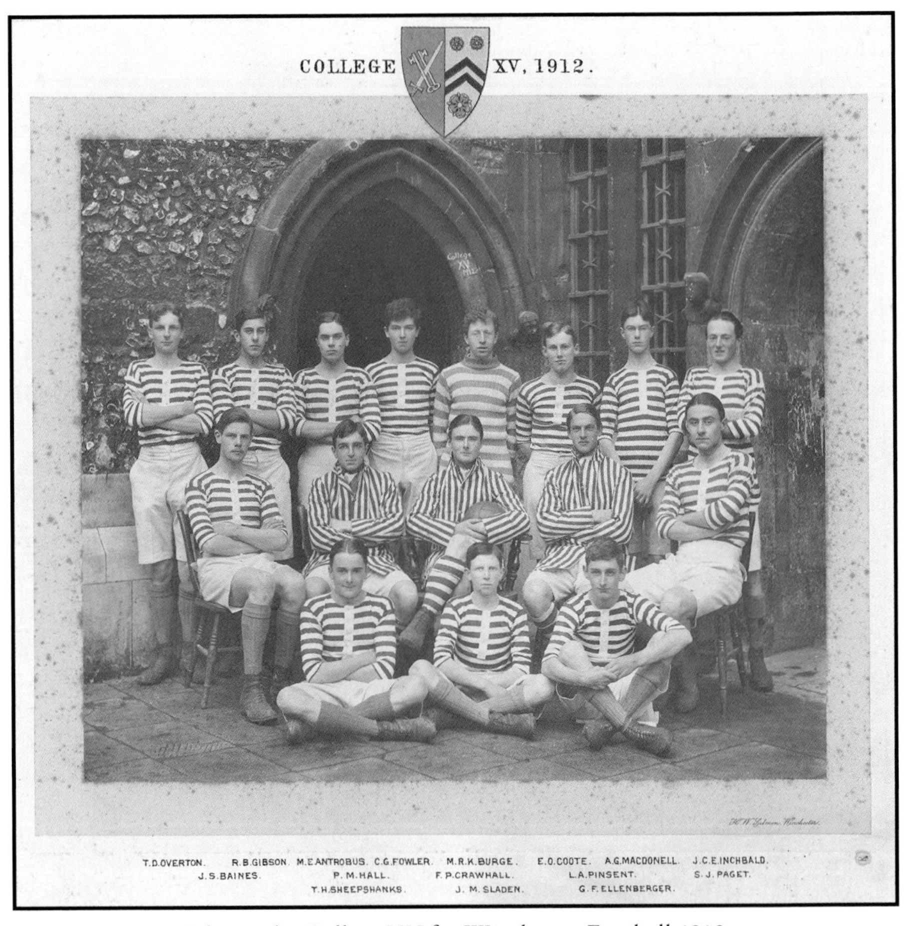

John in the College XV for Winchester Football 1912

It will be nice to have such a near relation at Neuchatel – the second cousin of the husband of the daughter of the husband of the great aunt of me – isn't that it? It takes us nearly back to Noah. I remember Shem telling me he had a cousin called Batten. He fell off the landing stage at Ararat, didn't he? Perhaps that was another member of the family.

How do you find your French? Is it holding out all right? – Pen of the stepson of my aunt's gardener – and that sort of thing. Eh what?? I expect it is 'orrid awkward at first. I am sure I shall feel a frightful fool coming out.

As I expected Houses beat us 11 – 5 but the game was not as uneven as the score seems to shew. Our "ups" and "hot watches" were quite able to hold their own but our kicks were outclassed and its the kicks who get most of the goals in a fifteen game. Had our kicks been able to take advantage of their chances the score would have been much more even.

When next I write to Irene I will give you her love. I may be able to see her at Leicester sometimes as it is only about 35 miles from Birmingham and is also on the Midland Main Line between Leeds and London.

I am feeling very sleepy now after two huge teas. We are going to have a fifteens grub to-night. The whole chamber will regale themselves on veal and ham pie, fruit salad and lemonade until late at night. I shall probably go continent after it. I have been thinking of doing so for the last few days.

I am quite ready for the holidays, 8 weeks of the half is quite enough. However, I suppose 14 is as good as from Christmas till the summer with just a fort-night at Easter which is what I shall have at Woolwich.

Love to Mother.

Your loving brother
John

The College
Winchester

Feb. 8th 1911

My Dearest Honor,
Many happy returns of the day. I hope that you will like these books. They are both, I think, quite interesting.

How are you getting on with your skating? Can you do a three yet? We had one day's skating but I was in sick house at the time. Most people fell in. One lady fell in and after many efforts four men got her out. They then stood smiling at the crowd but, as the ice was not fit to bear them all, the crowd began to smile instead.

The Suffragettes in February 1911

Although debates on women's suffrage had taken place in parliament almost every year from 1870, no decisions were ever taken on the matter. The suffragist movement started peacefully in 1897, when Millicent Fawcett founded the National Union of Women's Suffrage and sought to persuade men that women could be trusted to have the right to vote. After six years she seemed to have made very little progress, and some women were becoming angry and impatient.

In 1903 Emmeline Pankhurst and her daughters Christabel and Sylvia founded the Women's Social and Political Union, a group of women who became known as the Suffragettes. As their campaign of civil disobedience developed, and with no change coming from the Government, the Suffragettes became less passive. They were often manhandled out of meetings in a very rough and violent manner and they took to the streets with their message. They chained themselves to Government buildings; they broke shop windows in central London; they burned down churches; they organised marches on Parliament and attacked Members of Parliament on their way to work; they refused to pay their taxes or fines. When sent to prison, they went on hunger strike and were then force fed, which created an outcry as forced feeding was normally only used on lunatics.

This was the situation in February 1911 when 16-year old John spoke in favour of the Suffragettes at a school debate. It is a pity that we do not know the outcome of the debate.

The Suffragettes after February 1911

In 1913 the Government introduced an Act of Parliament, known as the Cat and Mouse Act, which stopped forced feeding. The Act let women in prison go on hunger strike, they were not force fed but allowed to grow weaker and weaker. When they were too weak to cause much trouble, they were released from prison "for the benefit of their health". This slightly took the wind out of the Suffragettes sails, but it didn't deter them. In 1913 a famous act took place when a suffragette, Emily Wilding Davison, threw herself under the King's horse, Anmer, as it raced in the Derby. She was killed and became a martyr to the Suffragettes cause.

When war was declared in August 1914, Emmeline Pankhurst, to her great credit, instructed the Suffragettes to stop their campaign of violence and pull together to support the Government in any way they could in the war effort. This they did and it was partially as a result of the invaluable work done by women during the war (which proved that they were just as capable as men in many aspects) that, in 1918, the Representation of the People Act finally gave women of property, over the age of 30, the right to vote.

Women only achieved full equality regarding suffrage in 1928.

I have been sabring this afternoon. It is quite hard to learn the art well and one's arm gets very tired at first as it is screwed round a good deal when it is in the right position. Nevertheless it is quite good fun.

I suppose that most of the people I knew had gone, except the Taylors who are, I suppose still going strong. "I should think so–a–o".

I am going to speak in a suffragette debate on Monday. I am going to speak in favour of them. Most people are speaking on the same side but I hope there will be room enough for me to get in "a few words to you tonight about…" as they say in books. I think the votes will go against us but I'm not sure whether my masterly eloquence may not win the day.

The other day the Prefect of Hall (who is also my senior prefect) went up with the Warden to see the opening of Parliament. Someone in the chamber said that it was so that people might have an opportunity to fear God as well as honour the King. But I am a good boy. I don't say such things. Oh shockin' shockin'!!

Grannie has written to ask me to go to Whitby at Easter in case I can't go abroad. I don't suppose Whitby will be very thrilling at Easter. However, it remains to be seen. We go down on April 5.

Your loving brother
John

CHOICE OF REGIMENT

Nov 10 1911

My Dear John,
Your letter gave me quite a shock. It seems to me a foolish plan. Suppose you don't get Sappers, still, if you go to Woolwich, you get R.A. and you had 50 times better be R.A. than R.M. Better class of men – better work – better openings for distinction – and it is still true, though someday it will be changed, better class of officers.

There are only two things that can be said for R.M.as against R.A., I think. (1) you might possibly live on your pay at an earlier date. I doubt it – the paper does not seem very encouraging. And (2) suppose you were in R.A. and had to go to India in order to live on your pay, you would be more away from your Mother than if in R.M.

From The Headmaster, The College, Winchester.

John Stanhope Baines has been under my charge as a Scholar of Winchester College during the last 3 years and I can speak very highly of his character.

(Signed) M. J. Rendall

Nov. 11. 1911 (Headmaster)

Culver's Close,
Winchester.

Nov. 13th 1911

I certify that J. S. Baines is a strong & quick swimmer. He has won the Winchester College quarter mile race & was a good second in the Drowning saving competition.

G. M. Bell.
(master in charge of swimming).

References for the Army authorities from Winchester College

Choice of Regiment

These three letters of advice to John reveal the minefield that potential young officers had to cross in choosing a regiment in the pre-First World War days. The system of purchasing commissions had been abolished 40 years earlier. By 1911 the process still involved a strong element of choice, but many other factors had to be taken into account.

Financial considerations clearly came high on John's list – being able 'to live on his pay'. It seems that the rates of pay for officers differed from regiment to regiment. Career prospects, including opportunities to go to Staff College, were also an important factor, but probably more so for those giving him advice than for young John receiving it.

There was also the matter of competition. Although John had narrowed down his choice to RE (Sappers), RA (Gunners), and RM (Marines), it is clear that Sappers were his first choice. Nevertheless he had some doubts about whether he would pass out of RMA Woolwich (*see next page*) high enough to guarantee a commission in the Royal Engineers. The alternative would then have been a commission in the Gunners, without any further choice. In the event, he followed the advice he was given and was successful.

In my opinion those 2 arguments don't at all outweigh the grave disadvantages of the Marine service – Policeman at sea! – better go into the Irish Constabulary or the Cape Mounted Rifles (? title)!

And then there is still the hope of Sappers. On that Mr Steel can advise you better than I can. But 18 months ago I thought him distinctly hopeful about it: "would not promise" etc.

So that I am dead against this idea; and prepared to take the responsibility of doing all I can to dissuade you from it.

You may show this to Mr Steel and the H.M. I am also writing to your Mother.

Do Marines ever go to the Staff College? If not that is still more against them.

Yours affectionately,
Winfrid V. Burroughs

I am sorry you were so badly beaten in your match. Good luck to you tomorrow. What does B.M.G. mean? I have not the slightest idea.

Nov 13th 1911

Dear John,
I don't recommend you to go in for the Marines. It is a small service which is always between two stools the Army and the Navy, and never really gets the best of either. The Staff College is open to them but the higher staff appointments are seldom filled by them & the Senior Officers never get any chance of handling large bodies of men & never therefore get employment either in peace or war.

You must go for Sappers, if you don't pass take garrison Gunners go to India & exchange into the Indian Army if you find you cannot manage the Gunners. Don't take Marines I say, a comfortable easy life it may give you but nothing more.

Yours sincerely
G A Gott

The Royal Military Academy, Woolwich

The Royal Military Academy (RMA), Woolwich, in south east London, was a military academy for training and commissioning officers of the Royal Artillery and Royal Engineers. It was founded in 1741 to produce "good officers of Artillery and perfect Engineers"

It was commonly known as "The Shop" because its first building was a converted workshop of the Woolwich Arsenal. It is believed that the expression "talking shop" came into common usage when officers of other regiments heard Gunners and Sappers talking in terms they could not understand.

Unlike modern day practice, where all officer cadets are paid and housed as full members of the Army, the parents of cadets at The Shop paid tuition and boarding fees, and also for the uniforms.

For each intake there were a number of cadetships (effectively scholarships) awarded on merit based on the results of academic exams. Those gaining the awards were known as Prize Cadets – and John Baines was amongst those in his intake.

RMA Woolwich closed in 1939. From then on all officer cadets were trained at the Royal Military College, Sandhurst, which had previously only trained Cavalry and Infantry. In 1947 the establishment changed its name to the Royal Military Academy, Sandhurst.

16th Nov 1911

Dear Baines,
I remember you perfectly well and I'm very glad that you wrote to me. I am sorry I could not answer your letter sooner but as I know a Marine officer I waited until I could get hold of him to ask a few questions. I will reply to your letter in the order in which you ask the questions or make remarks.

(1) Why are your chances of sappers not good? You told me you were good at maths and you ought to have no difficulty. It is of course the best paid branch of the service and I strongly advise you to go on trying for it. I don't recommend Gunners unless you can afford a field battery. Don't go in the R.G.A.

(2) Marines are not bad at all. The only draw back is that there are not many openings from them unless you come here and get a P.S.C. The pay is better and the expenses much less and you can go on £600 a year. Men in the Line never get beyond £420 after commanding a battalion so there is a distinct advantage there. Men and officers are a splendid lot and have never yet been found wanting. The officers do go to the Staff College, 2 every year, and often get billets at the War Office. 1 is there now (Captain Montgomery).

There is an awful block in the Gunners at present and there is little chance of active service.

If I were to advise you I would say the Indian Army is the best of the lot and one gets a great deal of leave, about double the pay and a pension of £750 a year as Lt. Colonel. (Cavalry is as cheap as Infantry). I put the corps down in the following order as to advantages, leaving out British Inf & Cav as you say you cannot afford them.

1. Indian Army
2. Sappers
3. Marines
4. Gunners (Field)
5. " (Garrison)

Wishing you every success in whichever you may choose.
Yours sincerely,
Austin C Girdwood

John was commissioned into the Corps of Royal Engineers

6304 THE LONDON GAZETTE, 11 AUGUST, 1914

Corps of Royal Engineers.

Harold Archer James Parsons.
John Stanhope Baines.
Alexander Vass Anderson.
John Drummond Inglis.
Nigel Duncan Ratcliffe Hunter.
Dennis Comins.
Eric Wingfield Pert.
Alec William Gordon.
Esmond Humphrey Miller Clifford.
Graham Lowe Reid.
John Kaye Tickell.
Edward Robert Luxmoore Peake.
Gerald Leigh Bleeck Fayle.
William Arthur Macdonald Stawell.
John Faviell Phipps.
John Reginald Carter.

John mentions that he forgot about the permit for his field glasses. This was probably a reference to an item in The Defence of the Realm Act which stated, among other things, that no-one was allowed to buy binoculars. The Act, first introduced on August 8th 1914, aimed to secure public safety and the defence of the realm and prevent persons from communicating with the enemy. It listed things that people were not allowed to do in time of war.

Defence of the Realm Act 1914

No-one was allowed to:

- talk about naval or military matters in a public place
- spread rumours about military matters
- buy binoculars
- trespass on railway lines or bridge
- melt down gold or silver
- light a bonfire
- fly a kite
- give bread to chickens and horses
- use invisible ink when writing abroad
- buy brandy or whisky in a railway refreshment room
- ring church bells

The Government could:

- take over any factory or workshop
- try any civilian for breaking the above laws
- take over any land it wanted
- censor newspapers

As the War continued more acts were introduced to DORA.

YOUNG OFFICER TRAINING AT CHATHAM

John decided to join the Corps of Royal Engineers. He attended The Royal Military Academy, Woolwich (The Shop) as a Prize Cadet. He then went for specialist young officer training at the Royal Engineers Headquarters, Chatham

The Train

postmarked Sheffield
6 Aug 14.

Dearest Mother,
I'm writing this in the dining car on the way to S. Pancras.

We handed Margery safely over to her father & Kenneth at Leeds & caught the connection quite comfortably.

We've been getting news gradually all along of the Belgian victory. It's a splendid effort. Now the Germans are going to declare war on Italy for not helping them. They are absolutely mad. I only hope they won't have been absolutely crushed till I can do it.

At the station I forgot about the permit for the field glasses. Will you send me a note, please, saying I may have them charged to my account.

With all love to Honor.

Your loving
J.S.

Brompton Barracks
Chatham
14 tel 482 Chatham

24 Sep 14

My Dearest Honor,
I'm so sorry for waiting so long before answering your letter. I've had a good deal to do this week and have been too sleepy after Mess to do anything but go straight to bed.

It will be great fun to have our week-end in Town. I can be fairly sure of getting leave and ought to be able to get up to Victoria by 2.40 which would probably give me time to meet you at King's Cross or Liverpool Street.

I finished my riding course yesterday and I'm rather glad on the whole. It was great fun at times but it was the same every day and the lecture part

Britain is at War!

1914: Theatre managers called an emergency meeting to discuss Theatres and the War. Sir Herbert Beerbohm Tree reported that he had already spoken to His Majesty King George to ask if the King wished theatres to remain open, but the King found it difficult to express an opinion. Mr Basil Hood felt that theatres should remain open, with authors and everyone reducing their fees (except those artists on very small salaries). Mr Cyril Maude did not like the idea of people being asked to take a cut in salaries. Mr Wyndham, of Howard and Wyndham, reported that several theatre companies had already cancelled their contracts for touring dates, blaming the uncertainties of the War, and he felt many managers were behaving in a panic-stricken manner. Mr H.B.Irving pointed out that since we had just embarked upon the greatest war that has ever been known, there might, perhaps, be some real cause for concern. The Managers decided that for the time being all their theatres would remain open, and that a Joint War Committee should be set up to help co-ordinate the entertainment profession during these difficult times.

(overthefootlights.co.uk)

Recruiting song is "Hit" of the season

1914: Paul Ruben's song "Your King and Country Both Need You So" is being performed at music halls and theatres all over the country. All the profits from the sale of published copies will be donated to the Queen's Work for Women Fund, which has started to provide work for those women who have lost their regular employment because of the War. The refrain of the song says: "Oh, we don't want to lose you, But we think you ought to go, For your King and your Country, Both need you so. We shall want you and miss you, But with all our might and main, We will thank you, cheer you, kiss you, When you come back again!" The publishers, Messrs Chappell and Co, were overwhelmed with the initial demand – W.H.Smith and Son ordered 13,000 copies for its London stores alone – and they have stopped all other printing so their presses can be dedicated to meeting the demand for copies. The song is said to be causing a massive increase in the number of men volunteering for recruitment into the Army.

(overthefootlights.co.uk)

lost some of its freshness towards the end. One or two of the horses were hunters or old troopers but the majority had spent their best years drawing cabs and had no more idea of jumping than of swallowing their own tails.

I'm doing Survey now and have spent all day playing with a theodolite. I found the river an excellent place to be taking angles to, as then I could watch all the shipping through the telescope.

I've heard that only about six of my batch will go to Signal Units and so I'm feeling better. Three or four applied for that and so I have now more chance of getting into a Field Company. I shall be awfully relieved when I know one way or another though if I do get a Signal Unit I shall probably twist up my toes and die.

I'm drilling a hundred of Kitchener's Army every morning for the next ten days. It was made harder this morning by the presence of a dense fog. Standing at one end of the company when it was in line you could only just see the other end. This caused such little surprises as suddenly finding a fence across your front when you thought yourself miles from anywhere. They aren't very smart but they think to some extent. That means that an order you give will be carried out though the way it is done might make generations of drill sergeants turn in their graves.

When we paraded alone it meant getting up at 6.30 or so to be clean and punctual but the British Tommy lives a more sheltered life and doesn't parade till eight. Thus I get 3/4 an hour more bed these mornings.

I'll find out about a nice theatre. I believe "Grumpy" and "My Lady's Dress" are quite good. Then we'll have supper at the Rendezvous or somewhere afterwards. I feel a bust will do me good. So it will you after your exams.

Let me know all about it and write to Aunt Letty. Will you go on to Wimbledon afterwards? I was there on Sunday.

Your loving brother
John

Honor in 1914 – aged 18

John's Aunt Letty designed and made jewellery and church plate.

This is a processional cross made by Letitia Graham for Wakefield Cathedral. The figures are silver, the crown fire opals and the evangelists are enamel cloisonné

30 Sep 14

My Dearest Honor,
I am so sorry about your exams coming at the wrong time. However, I hope we'll have better luck another time. As a matter of fact it is very doubtful whether I shall be able to get away this week-end as my turn for Regimental Duty is coming very soon. That takes three days as one is first "Supernumerary", then "Next for Duty" and finally "Orderly Officer". I will do my best, however, to get someone to change with me if necessary though it may not be easy. In that case I'll leave it open and will let you know later. I'll go to an hotel, I think, because then we shall be much more free to do what we like. We'll try for a theatre on Saturday and it may still be warm enough for the river on Sunday.

Let me know what your Cantab address will be if it's anything different from "Newnham College".

Your loving brother
John

Sunday 25 Oct 14

My Dearest Honor,
I'd have written sooner if I could but I've been doing a great deal in the last few days and so it is only now that I can write and thank you for your letter. It was just as nice a one as you could have written me.

She will be in Leamington for another month, but after she is back in Leeds I hope you'll be able to see something of her and get to know her because I'm sure you'll be great friends. Ask her to go with you to Coniston at Easter. I'm afraid I shan't be there too [I shall be most awfully sick if I am] but we have plenty of time before us for that to happen some other holidays.

There's a great scheme being formed in my brain so that I may see her one week-end. She might come up to Town just for Saturday afternoon or we might admit Aunt Letty into the secret and get her to write and ask her to stay the night. Then she could forward the letter to her Mother and demand permission.

I don't know whether she'ld get it because according to the powers that be this is not an engagement but an understanding fully approved, and it is to be very secret. That's quite right, but it leaves full powers to her Mother

John Baines newly commissioned
12 August 1914

Elisabeth Wicksteed 1914

Annexation of Egypt in 1914

In 1914 Egypt was technically under the sovereignty of the Sultan of Turkey, although Britain had had a military presence there for over 20 years. When the Ottoman declared war on the Allies in November 1914 action had to be taken to secure a British influence in Egypt. The main reason for this was to protect the Suez Canal, which was an important part of the route allied troops took when coming to Europe from India and Australia – and not just troops, but also horses and food supplies. Annexing Egypt allowed Britain to remain as advisors and defenders of a strategically important region without taking direct rule away from a Mohammedan sovereign.

and so we have to go subtly. I got very nice letters from both her people. Her father's was only a few words but one of the nicest I've ever had.

No, I've said nothing to Geoffrey yet. I didn't know where he was. Its rather amusing his being in Leeds. Give him my love when you see him again and ask him if it was his brother who got a D.S.O the other day (his elder naval one).

Congratulations on your exams and good luck in the ones to come.

With all love.

John

Dec 14

Dearest Mother,

At last I have an hour or two to call my own as I am on duty. It gives me a fairly free time from about 9.30 till 12.30 in the morning, though the night in Orderly Room is certainly a drawback.

A week to-day I shall be at home with you and there is at any rate this about a rushed existence – it makes the time go very quickly. I am very much afraid that I shan't be able to get a train from S. Pancras before 9.30 and that will mean getting into Leeds at 1.45 so that even were it punctual I couldn't be home till nearly half past two on Christmas morning, and allowing for the probable pace of the train on that date its more likely, I'm afraid, to be half past three.

You can't possibly wait up for me; nor can Honor, because we don't all want to be complete rags the next day, so will you post me the keys and I'll go straight up to my room. [I shall want the front door key too].

I'll leave my door unlocked so that you can come and wake me up as soon as you like. Its a pity that it can't be arranged better, but anyway its better than last year when I got in from the gasworks about four hours late, and it will be better than next year when I shall probably be one of the army of occupation, waiting in Germany until they can fork out.

I see to-day that we've annexed Egypt. I had been wondering when it was coming ever since we advised the two Egyptian princes to" travel for the sake of their health".

It really is adding insult to injury. Here I stick for months and months till even my grandmother gets active service before me. How are they all? I expect you've heard through the Aysgarth Press Bureau. I hope it hasn't given her a great shock. What rough luck it was on Uncle Edward that the

John's Grannie Baines lived in Whitby, as did his Uncle Edward who was a surgeon

German bombardment of East coast

In December 1914 a German naval fleet, commanded by Admiral Franz von Hipper, shelled the seaports of Hartlepool, West Hartlepool, Whitby and Scarborough. The bombardment lasted less than two hours but over 100 people were killed and almost 600 wounded. The coastal defence batteries responded, damaging three German ships, including the cruiser *Blucher*. Whitby Abbey sustained considerable damage in the attack. This bombardment came only a few weeks after the hospital ship *Rohilla* hit rocks within sight of shore just off Whitby, at Saltwick Bay, and sank with the loss of 85 lives.

HMS *Calliope*
Class of two ships (four ships of Cambrian-class were repeats) *Calliope* was built by Chatham dockyard, launched 17th December 1914 and completed June 1915. Weighing 4,228 tons she was 446ft long and was armed with 2-6in/1-13pdr AA/4-3pdr/2-21in torpedo tubes. Speed 29 knots. 368 crew.

injured were so unfairly divided. Whitby only had two and he can hardly have hoped to get 'em both.

By the way have you any rough clothes of mine at home in case there should be any skating or tobogganing. I suppose they are at Coniston. Could you possibly write for my Harris jacket and breeches and a pair of stockings?

I'm going to Wimbledon tomorrow to see Janet act in a French play. She sang me some of her songs last week and they were very pretty. Uncle Alec is in the War Office now as Private Secretary to the Director of Army Contracts (P.S.D.A.C.). It sounds very fine I think. It means very long hours and he can't always get off at week-ends at all, though he generally gets either Saturday afternoon or Sunday. I acted as butler on Saturday while he eat he dinner at about midnight.

We had our last day of pontooning yesterday and I'm rather glad, for they're heavy things to drag about. We got rather a good view yesterday of the launch of the Calliope – a new light cruiser – from the other side of the river. I've never seen a boat launched before and it was rather a pretty sight.

I heard from the McDowall's the other day about all that's going on at Winton. I shall try and get down there before I go, but their holidays don't end till Jan 27th so I mayn't be able to. I might look in on my way to Southampton on The Day.

With love to Honor.

Your loving

J.S.

WHY BRITAIN IS AT WAR

1.–TO SAVE HER GOOD NAME

Austria quarrelled with Servia. Germany made that an excuse to attack France. France is our friend, so we could not stand idly by.
Germany and Britain had by treaty promised Belgium safety and independence. Germany broke this treaty by making war on Belgium. Belgium asked our help. Had we refused to help Belgium our name for honour would have been gone.

2.–TO SAVE HER LIFE & HER EMPIRE

The German Emperor wants to "wipe out" France, strip Britain of Trade and Colonies and trample your rights and liberty into the mud, as he has done to the Belgians. In six months, if you don't wake up, you will be starved into slavery and have to take tamely any insults or ruin the German Emperor puts on you.

Millions of determined and unscrupulous German soldiers are in France only 20 miles from England, and any disaster to our Navy may let them come over here.

They will give you no quarter and no mercy.

3.–TO SAVE THE FREEDOM OF THE PEOPLE IN ALL EUROPE

In Germany the Emperor rules, the people have no power, there is no free speech.
The military class does what it likes.
If Germany wins, the progress of the people, the cause of freedom and equal justice and fair play for you will be gone for hundreds of years.

If your case is bad now, Germans will make it ten times worse.

You have a chance now, but you will have no hope if Germany wins.

The Russians are helping us. But, remember, Germany is very rich and strong and has made careful plans to crush first France and then Britain and defeat the Russians too. You can take no risks for your wives' and childrens' sake.

Our Colonies have seen at once what this war means. They have few people but are sending large numbers of men, enough to shame us.

Life perhaps seems to go on as usual. Do not be deceived, this is the most deadly peril Britain has ever met. You must strain every nerve or you will be crushed under the German boot.

Printed & Published by
David Allen & Sons Ld.
Harrow, Middlesex.

FIGHT THEN - FOR YOUR LIFE
FIGHT - FOR YOUR HONOUR
FIGHT - FOR FREEDOM
FIGHT - FOR MANKIND

EXTRACTED FROM **"THE TIMES"**

(IWM PST0948)

DIARY

I ALDERSHOT

I left Chatham on Saturday 23.1.15 for a week's leave before going out with Inglis and Hunter. We were given our orders and travelling warrants so that we could go straight from our homes to Southampton to embark the following Saturday, the 30th.

On Thursday evening however I got a wire saying that I was to proceed to Aldershot on the 30th to take a draft overseas. This was a nuisance in that it would prevent my journey being as irresponsible as it would otherwise have been, and since I thought "proceed on the 30th" might mean "better arrive on the 29th", it also meant destroying the plans I had made for spending Friday night in Town. Still I didn't expect it to make very much difference.

I reached Aldershot about 6.30 on Friday and drove up to the Mess, feeling very shy and lost. I was lucky enough to meet. Capt. J. Benskin, R.E. at the door as I got out of my taxi, and he shepherded me a little and introduced me to Capt. Egerton the regimental adjutant who knew nothing about me but was also very kind. Fortunately I had wired to Parsons to say I was coming and he had arranged for somewhere for me to sleep and as I had arrived in time for dinner I was at least sure of being able to exist. The Mess was very crowded and the usual single bedrooms had all 3 occupants, but I was lucky enough to have been put into a room with Morshead and Roseveare, two Wykehamists of the batch below me.

I was having breakfast at a reasonable hour the next morning (Sat 30th) when Inglis suddenly appeared. By this time I had more or less found my bearings for Egerton had introduced me to Capt Mariot, the Signal Depot Adjutant, so that we were able to start off together to sign our names in the various necessary offices – Regimental, Signal and the Chief Engineer's.

We found that the draft was to go on Monday and that Hunter was also to come but when he did arrive later in the day, he had seen in the C.E's office a note saying that we were not to go then.

We did not go on Parade on Saturday, but were told to stay in the Mess in case anything happened. Sunday of course there was again nothing to do. On Monday we attended the afternoon parade and henceforth we turned up at 8.45 am and 2 pm each day. As a rule there was nothing to do, though about twice in every three days we took them for a couple of hours of route march. We were fed up, the men were fed up; our whole spare time

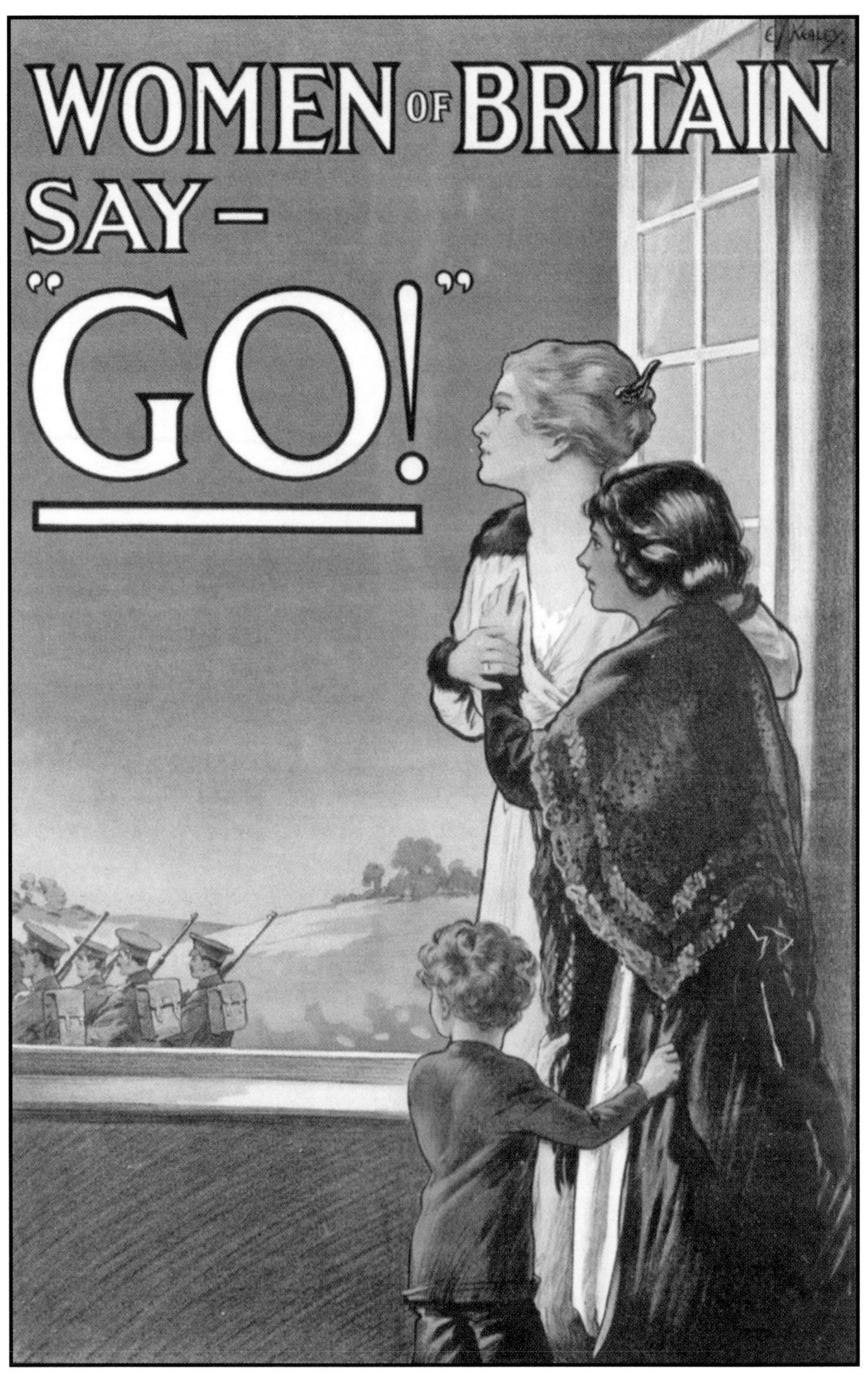
WOMEN OF BRITAIN
SAY –
"GO!"

was spent playing billiards, they were not allowed to leave barracks and in the meantime no news came through as to when the draft was to go. It was reorganised on the Monday and by Thursday "Records" had agreed to accept what could be sent, but that was all we knew.

It was difficult to deal with the men on these marches. We didn't know them or they us. They were signallers and we going to Field Companies. They had been got together by other people and we had nothing to do with them in their daily life. Individually they were very good fellows, but they lacked discipline and our dealings consisted almost entirely in saying "Don't" though in more forcible terms. Thus we were just tyrants to be circumvented and I think they were rather pleased in doing it, less for what they did than for the joys of being annoying. The kind of thing that happened was this. On one occasion I marched about 40 of them round to their rooms before a route march so that they might get their coats. I dismissed them and told them to be back in 2 minutes. About five minutes later I had 36 and no sign of any others. I had no NCO with me and knew none of their names so that I couldn't call a role. I might have taken the names of those present and afterwards tried to get hold of a complete list, but they were an odd 40 out of the draft of 64 and I chose the weaker path of pretending that I hadn't counted them. I wasn't very angry really because all through I've tried to keep thinking "What would I have done at the Shop?".

The time I did get really angry was on the same day. I had joined up my men to those of Hunter and Inglis and was marching at the head of the column with one of the others in the middle and one behind. We were marching easy so that the men were allowed to sing and to shout within reason, but one of two of them began to shout to a squad of recruits we passed a little way on, trying to confuse them with "About turns" etc. The NCO who was drilling them at once came to me though I had already halted the men. Of course I didn't know which men had done it for they were well behind me but I told them all a little of what I thought of them.

Still there were many excuses for them. They had by then been "on draft" for more than a fortnight and that meant that they had to stay in barracks all the time except when on duty such as route marches. A large number of them have come from the Post Office originally and are first class telegraph operators of course. They are all rather more highly educated than the ordinary recruit and therefore more independent and so harder to discipline.

One rather nice thing about them was their songs. Some of them got some really quite nice ideas and one or two were excellent performers on

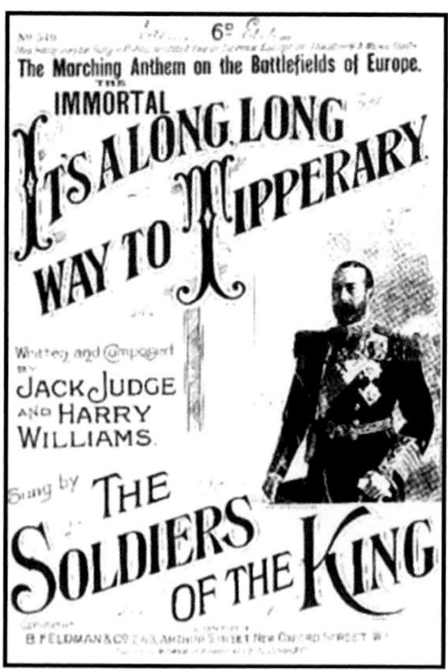

Mademoiselle from Armentières

Mademoiselle from Armentières, parlez vous
Mademoiselle from Armentières, parlez vous
Mademoiselle from Armentières
She hasn't been kissed for forty years
Inky pinky parlez vous.

Our top kick in Armentières
Soon broke the spell of forty years

She got the palm and the Croix de Guerre,
For washin' soldiers underwear

From gay Paree we heard guns roar
But all we heard was "Je t'adore"

The Colonel got the Croix de Guerre
The son-of-the-gun was never there!

You didn't have to know her long
To know the reason men go wrong!

You might forget the gas and shell
You'll never forget the mademoiselle

Inky pinky parlez vous.

mouth organs. One day I discovered a new direction to march in and as we turned down that road I heard just behind me, to the tune of the second half of "Who's your lady friend?" this:-

Hurray, hurray, we're goin' a different way.
We're goin' a different way this afternoon.
It's not the way we went this morning,
Hurray, hurray, we're goin' a different way.

They have also a large number of hymn tunes. To the tune of "Holy, holy, holy" they gave:-

Marchin', marchin' marchin'
Always bloody well marchin'

I couldn't hear the rest. They had an annoying way of mumbling the words whenever they came to anything which was particularly evil. One humourist was always shouting out silly things such as, "Upon my daughter's wedding day Ten thousand guineas will I pay". He was once really quite funny. I had let us in for taking a short cut across very slushy ground on Laffan's Plain and I heard sung just behind me the first line of "We are but little children weak". At the time it sounded priceless and brought the house down. They had of course all the ordinary topical comic songs and silly things like – "We're here, because we're here because etc" to the tune of Auld Lang Syne and also "Here we are, here we are again". They had one shout with which to greet the end of any song "More!" pronounced something like "Mo – o – ah!" I can't write the correct way of saying it but you must understand a very sarcastic note in it. There were others too but I can't mention them all. Anyhow my life was pretty well divided between billiards and route marches with songs to enliven the latter and damnings to make them depressing.

["Mo – ah" was a general comment on anything and was frequently heard on the boat – when a motor-bike was hoisted on board for instance].

***Boy Scouts** did a lot of useful war work in Britain. John came across them helping in the docks as troops embarked on ships bound for France, but that was just one of many tasks they took on nationwide*

(IWM Q30596)

A Boy Scout military despatch cyclist at work in UK.

(IWM Q30604)

Boy Scouts on guard by a railway bridge and train track.

(IWM Q30606)

Boy Scouts collect eggs from a maid to be given to wounded people in UK.

(IWM Q30598)

Boy Scouts load mangelwurzels onto a horse-drawn cart on a British farm.

II THE VOYAGE

On Tuesday 9.2.15 we arranged to break life's monotony a little by going to the theatre

At 6 o'clock – as we were arranging for an early meal we at last got a message to say that we were to go off early the next morning for Southampton. We were all three in the billiard room at the time and the accumulated sense of relief was tremendous.

The theatre, "Oh I Say", went splendidly. I found I had seen it before with James Welsh in it, at the Criterion, but I enjoyed it none the less. It isn't a play to take all one's relations to and therefore we enjoyed it tremendously. We managed to get a cold supper when we got back and spent the rest of the evening playing pool – about six of us.

As I got into bed about one, I was not particularly glad when my servant called me as instructed at six, but I didn't have any too much time for packing, breakfast and paying mess-bills etc before getting on an 8.30 parade in "Christmas Tree" order. Our draft, 185 strong, was then inspected by the C.E. (Chief Engineer, Brig-Gen J.A. Gibbon) and we marched down to the station.

I was very glad when the train had drawn up and my men were safely on board for a platform is an awkward place to leave men standing easy for long. They keep slipping out of the ranks to buy things from the newspaper boys and so were hard to keep absolutely in hand, but still we managed to steam out at about 9.45 without leaving anyone behind.

We got down to Southampton in about an hour and a half and were handed over to a Boy Scout who led the way from the Docks station to our berth. We marched into a large shed on the quay and the men were allowed to fall out. They were not allowed to leave the shed and sentries were posted at all entrances to prevent this. They were also not allowed to smoke, but there was a coffee bar in one corner where they could buy cake and coffee.

I was kept on the run for a bit by three fellows who wanted to go to the Dockyard gates to see their wives or fathers and I had of course to get their passes signed by the Embarkation Officer. What struck me most was the extraordinary good temper of this class of person. The two at the station and those on the quay were as kind as could be though I should have expected their kind of work to have ruined the temper of an archangel.

We got on board towards two o'clock and I was led to a room between decks right aft where my men had to go. There looked about enough room for 40 men but the Marine who led me there assured me he'd had 250 in it.

Blackout in World War 1

> **BARWICK VILLAGE**
> Two special constables have called from door to door demanding that the night lights in the cottages shall not be allowed to illumine the streets even if they were powerful enough to do so. As a consequence, quite a number of dear old ladies (some, mothers of real men, not specials) are living in constant dread of mythical Zeppelins. Accidents, collisions, and other deeds of darkness are more serious than any probable depredations by the Germany enemy. In villages where light is so scarce that not one single street-light is afforded, the act of the "specials" is the result of mis-interpretation of the Government order.
>
> *Skyrack Courier*. 25th February 1916

The first ever bombing of civilians in Britain took place on 19th January 1915. At the time biplane design did not lend itself to carrying and dropping bombs, but the German Zeppelin airship did. Zeppelins floated silently, high over their target and, on that first raid, dropped twenty four 50kg high explosive bombs and a number of smaller incendiaries onto Great Yarmouth and the King's Lynn area. People were shocked. There were no air raid shelters at that time or any form of air raid warning but it was soon realised that, as the Zeppelins came in the dark hours, it could baffle their pilots if there was no light showing on the ground. So a system came into place where, as soon as a Zeppelin was spotted on the coast, a message was sent to local authorities who took the steps needed to plunge their district into darkness although lights were only dimmed and not dowsed completely.

Bully Beef

Although the soldiers often complained that meals, supposedly 'hot', were cold by the time they received them, great effort was made to have food for the troops prepared as close to the lines as possible, without smoke or smell attracting enemy attention. But there were times (when a battle was raging) and places (on board ship) when it was impossible to get a freshly cooked meal to the soldiers. This is when a tin of corned beef, or bully beef as it came to be known, came into its own. Bully beef was made by soaking brisket of beef in a brine solution with spices for a good length of time and mixing it with bread-grains before sealing it into tins. It was not a specially healthy food on its own and so it was only issued as an emergency or stand-by ration. But it could be eaten straight from the tin or easily heated up on a small stove with a stock cube and water to make a stew into which the men would crumble some hard biscuits.

Any how it was all my 185 had and they tucked themselves in somehow or other. I next found where they could get hot water to make tea and shewed it to one of my N.C.O.s and told him to issue the mens' rations for dinner. Then I was able to find my own cabin and at last get rid of my own equipment. In order to lighten my valise, wh. weighed about 70 instead of 35 lbs, I had carried a maximum of weight and my shoulders weren't at all sorry to be rid of it all.

There was a fairly comfortable saloon which we shared with a Remount subaltern, who was bringing over a lot of horses, and with two Territorial subalterns who had about 140 men. One of these was a Lieutenant and so was O.C. Troops.

We were too late for lunch, but the steward managed to raise some cold meat for us with some tea. Then Tanglis and I went down to see how the men were getting on. We found they'd got plenty of bully beef and biscuits and some cheese and jam, and they were going to get some tea presently. We just trotted round asking the fellows if they had enough and chatting a little with them. It was the first chance we had had of talking to them and I was very glad to get it, because it's rather difficult to command men who don't know you. By shouting enough you can get the things done but it's nicer to have them done willingly.

Afterwards we found some chairs and sat on the Quarter Deck. It was a lovely sunny evening and might have been in May. There were half a dozen hospital ships in the Water. They are white with a green band round them and with the sun falling on them they were lovely.

We made afternoon tea for ourselves and had a high tea at six, the latter just after the boat started. After we had got out of the Water all lights had to be covered, the ports having brown paper as well as the ordinary blinds. No smoking was allowed on decks and I followed the advice I gave to the men, by turning in early.

There was a slight swell when we first got into the channel (where our Destroyer escort joined us) but otherwise the sea was like a duck pond and at the slow rate we steamed there was no vibration at all from the engines.

I'm afraid I was too comfortable in my sleeping bag (reinforced by the three ship's blankets) to get up for the sunrise, but I was awake enough to see that we got into Havre about 7. We passed one ship that had been submarined but had sunk in quite shallow water and also the hospital ship which the Germans fired at and missed.

We had got into Havre about an hour late and so had missed the tide and could not go on to Rouen at once. The horses on board and some

Censorship of letters

Letters to and from the front were important for the morale of the troops. Writing them relieved boredom and was a distraction from the horrors going on around them; receiving them lifted their spirits.

Censorship of every letter written by soldiers from the front line was generally thought to be to prevent the enemy from finding out secrets. In fact it was more to keep bad news from reaching those at home, whose continuous support for the war was vital. It was forbidden to say where you were, anything about suspected enemy movements or about your own future plans of action. Bad news, such as the death of friends, was also censored. The censors, who were usually junior officers in a unit or army chaplains, used coloured pencils to scribble out banned information and sometimes chunks of letters were torn or cut out.

'Wizz-bangs', or Field Service Post Cards, were a quick way to get a re-assuring message home during periods of heavy fighting when there was not time to write a full letter and, as they did not need to be censored, they travelled more quickly. They carried a series of simple messages that could be deleted or retained, but nothing else was to be written on them. By the end of 1917, 285,000 wizz-bangs a day were being sent from the front.

Censorship of the Press

At the beginning of the war there was blanket press censorship. The government formed its own Press Bureau, which censored even military communiqués before they could be publicised, and newspaper reporters were threatened with the death penalty if they did more than write articles based on releases from the Press Bureau.

This couldn't last long as 'the real story' began to be told by wounded soldiers returning from the front. In 1915 a handful of correspondents were given permanent accreditation to go to the front, on condition that all their stories were run before the censor, and were then shared for general distribution to all news outlets in the United Kingdom and abroad. The fact that censorship was still very strict and under the control of the army, meant that stories could change dramatically as they passed through the hands of senior officers at the front and then officers at the War Office before they reached the national newspapers.

Correspondents were very unhappy and frustrated about this situation, but most of them accepted that having even limited access to what was really happening at the front was worth the loss of some professional integrity. However, after the war ended, some were ashamed at the truths they had hidden and refused to accept knighthoods from the government, which they saw as a bribe to keep their silence.

Ordnance stores we carried were therefore leisurely disembarked while we hung about with nothing to do. I tried to get permission to take my men for a route march as some exercise wd not have done them any harm and they were keen to have a look at the town, but the Landing Officer would not allow it. Tangles and I however got away and had a good lunch and got our hair cut. We also changed our money, but did nothing else as the Town seemed rather dull. We also wanted to get back in time to let Hunter get away. He went with one of the Terriers and we commissioned them to get chocolate and éclairs so that our tea was a great success.

The day of course was punctuated by saying sweet nothings to the men. In the evening I took over all guards from the Terriers and posted a sentry over the store, arranging for others over gangways at Rouen to prevent men leaving the ship without orders. The men had had rather a rough time the night before; it was too hot and crowded inside their quarters and too cold on deck, so that whichever place they chose they didn't sleep much, but this second night there were no horses and some of the men went and took their places, thus being more comfortable themselves and also making more room for others.

We left dock about six, but the pilot refused to take us up the river by night as he said it was going to snow (it didn't), so we anchored for the night in the river. I was very glad for several reasons. I wanted to have the trip up the Seine by daylight and also I didn't want to reach Rouen at 2 in the morning. We shouldn't have disembarked till daylight, but I'd have had to be up to see that sentries were posted and I should never have known when the landing officer would appear.

I went down to the men to tell them, amongst other things, that they would not have to get up in the middle of the night. Just after I finished one invisible voice shouted out "Will there be any passes on shore tonight Sir?". This raised a laugh as we were anchored about a mile from land, so I shouted back "Have you passed out in swimming yet?" It wasn't a very brilliant repartee, but fortunately it raised a counter laugh.

Thanks to the pilot I again had a comfortable night in pyjamas and did not see the start of our voyage at about 6. I got up, however, at about 7.30 to see that my sentries were properly posted.

After breakfast I arranged for the fatigue-parties needed for things like unloading stores and cleaning up when we got to Rouen. I also had all the men called together and read them the regulations about postage and the censorship. From the remarks in some letters I censored myself later on at

The "lost battles of 1870", which the old French fellow in blue might have been thinking of, would have been during the Franco-Prussian War.

Franco-Prussian War 1870–71

The Franco-Prussian War or Franco-German War often referred to in France as the War of 1870 was a conflict between the Second French Empire and the German states of the North German Confederation led by the Kingdom of Prussia. The conflict emerged from tensions caused by German unification. Prussian chancellor Otto von Bismarck planned to provoke a French attack in order to draw the southern German states—Baden, Württemberg, Bavaria and Hesse-Darmstadt—into an alliance with the Prussian dominated North German Confederation

Bismarck adroitly created a diplomatic crisis over the succession to the Spanish throne, then rewrote a dispatch about a meeting between king William of Prussia and the French foreign minister, to make it appear that the French had been insulted. The French press and parliament demanded a war, which the generals of Napoleon III assured him that France would win. Napoleon and his Prime Minister, Émile Ollivier, for their parts sought war to solve political disunity in France. On 16 July 1870, the French parliament voted to declare war and hostilities began three days later. The German coalition mobilised its troops much more quickly than the French and rapidly invaded northeastern France. The German forces were superior in numbers, had better training and leadership and made more effective use of modern technology, particularly railroads and artillery.

A series of swift Prussian and German victories in eastern France saw the French army decisively defeated; Napoleon III was captured at Sedan on 2nd September. For the next five months the German forces fought and defeated new French armies in northern France. Following the Siege of Paris, the capital fell on 28th January 1871. The German states proclaimed their union as the German Empire under the Prussian king, Wilhelm I, uniting Germany as a nation-state. The Treaty of Frankfurt of 10th May 1871 gave Germany most of Alsace and some parts of Lorraine, which became the Imperial territory of Alsace-Lorraine.

The unification of Germany upset the European balance of power that had existed since the Congress of Vienna in 1815; Bismarck maintained great authority in international affairs for two decades. French determination to regain Alsace-Lorraine and fear of another Franco-German war, along with British concern over the balance of power, became factors in the causes of the First World War.

Rouen, my discourse must have been very impressive. They held the Censor in very great awe.

I spent a good deal of the rest of the day packing my valise up again, but I had plenty of time to look at the river. There were hills three or four hundred feet high on both sides which had a steep slope. According to the way the river curved, there would be flat meadows on one bank for half a mile or so, and very often cliffs coming right to the water's edge on the other. In some cases the chalk had been cut away inside so as to make houses, windowed properly, right inside the cliff. The whole was extraordinarily pretty and all along the stream were little villages, where man, woman and child turned out to welcome us. They were old men though and it was more than touching to see some old fellow, in that blue they always wear, leaping up and down and waving a Union Jack or Tricoleur, cheering wildly the fellows who were coming over to help them to avenge the lost battles of 1870 which he had probably taken part in himself.

There is one little village where the pilot is dropped and the Naval Transport Officer told me that there, in August, all the girls used to come out with bunches of flowers, which they threw to the troops, who wore them marching through Rouen. Now there are no flowers to throw, but they still line the banks crying "Vive l'Angleterre" and sometimes "Are we downhearted?"

We reach Rouen about 2 p.m. on Friday 12 .2.15 and got the draft lined up, less a fatigue party to get our bits, the spare rations and the ammunition into the Transport Wagon. I told them off and we followed in the train of the Terriers. We started off with a quick short step about 100 yards behind them and I felt very proud marching at the head. Unfortunately we soon caught them up and for the rest of the three or four miles had to crawl behind them. We did our best to keep our original step but it meant stepping so short that we gradually got into their long slow crawl which takes all the life out of a march and makes it very tiring.

Army horses being loaded on board ship.

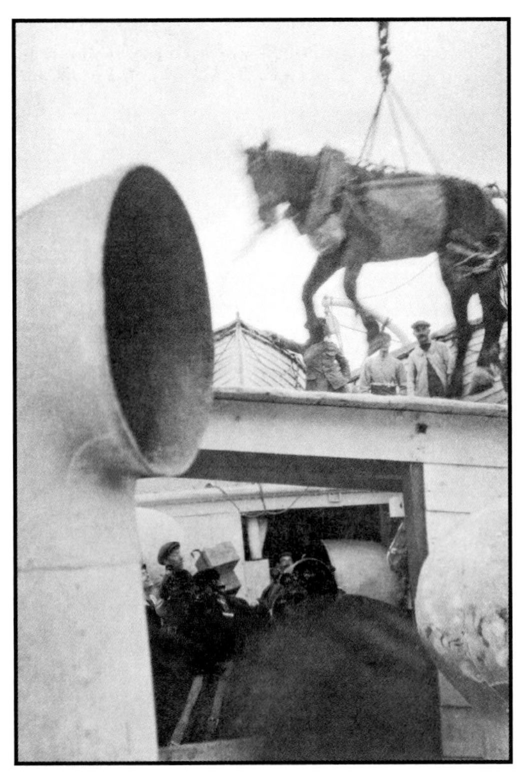

(IWM Q51470)

(IWM Q33310)

Sappers taking their horses away after disembarkation in France.

LETTERS FROM FRANCE

No 2 Cav Camp
No 6 General Base Depot
Rouen

Sun 14.2.15

Dearest Mother,
I've not written before because I've only just got rid of my Draft and that left very little continuous spare time. What writing I have done has been in a diary wh. I've begun and wh. I will try and keep up-to-date from time to time. I'm arranging it, not by days but by chapters, such as I Aldershot, II Voyage, III Rouen

We managed to get the draft here without losing anyone and I enjoyed the journey. We left Southampton on a delightful sunny evening and got into Havre about 7, where we unloaded some horses and spent the Day. The men were not allowed off the ship but Tangles & I went and had a good lunch in the town. We anchored for the night in the river and came up the Seine to Rouen the next morning. It was fine weather and the river was awfully pretty. The villagers came out to wave flags and cheer all along the way and it was very stirring to see them, women, children and old men.

The draft were awfully good really. They were horribly crowded but were really very cheerful. We got lots of chances of going and talking to them and there was no grousing.

I've been censoring most of their letters and they nearly all take their discomforts as all in the day's work. I was rather bucked at one man saying "We are lucky in having such good officers who up to the present have shewn us every consideration". I suppose he guessed I should censor his letter.

We had two tents given for the three of us so Tangles and I went together. We have managed to get a certain amount of furniture rigged up out of packing cases – a washstand, a table with a shelf below it and two small benches. We've had a trench dug round to keep the place dryer and some gravel laid down in front of the door. Above all we've got a biscuit box with holes knocked in the sides which sits on a slab on the floor and holds a charcoal fire. We've a crosspiece put onto the tent-pole to hang things from

Land and Water was a weekly journal formed in 1914 by Jim Allison, advertisement manager of The Times newspaper. It was intended for country gentlemen and dealt exclusively with the war and immediate post-war events. Supported by many advertisements it became very popular, selling over 100,000 copies a week soon after its launch, and only ceased publication in 1920.

Hilaire Belloc was at first the military correspondent of Land & Water and then became the editor. He had very forthright views and wrote stirring articles (it is said that he was not always entirely truthful with his facts and figures) which John appears to have much enjoyed. He makes several references to Belloc; in a letter written towards the end of his time in Salonika he says, "I'm going to be a Belloc in the next war. His methods are perfectly easy but at the moment they're unique. He's the only military critic who can intelligently read & explain a map. Why the others don't do the same thing I can't imagine".

Hilaire Belloc 1870–1953. Born in France to a French father and English mother, his father died when he was two years old and he was brought up in England. He did, however, do military service in France before gaining a first-class honours degree in History at Balliol College, Oxford. He was Liberal Party MP for Salford South from 1906–1910 and editor of Land & Water from 1914–1920.

In 1896 he married an American, Elodie, and they had 5 children before she died in 1914. Hilaire and Elodie's son Louis joined the Royal Flying Corps and was killed in August 1918 while bombing a German transport column.

Well known as a writer, poet, satirist and political activist and admired for his debating skills, he was also, in later life, an accomplished sailor. Hilaire Belloc died in 1953, having never fully recovered from a stroke he suffered in 1941.

and we've three excellent blankets apiece issued on loan. We are thus very comfortable.

The mess is rather full of S.R. & T. C. officers, practically only the senior officers being regulars but the food is good, run by a French contractor.

Our draft has gone on to its own base in charge of Hunter and we are waiting here doing nothing until needed at the front. There is only one of Pank's batch left here so that I shouldn't have long to wait.

Will you send me Land & Water to this address & it will be forwarded if I've gone. I saw the one for Sat 5th at Aldershot but have not seen it since.

I've not yet had any letters except Aunt Flo's Weekly Times for the 5th wh. arrived here before me. They'll have got a little astray through my having given Havre as an address.

Will you give Aunt Flo my love and this address please.

I'm very fit and very comfortable.

With love to Honor,

Your loving

J. S.

One of the letters I had to read was to Polly Steel's maid – a most loving one.

17.2.15

Dearest Mother,

Will you please hand these on to Elisabeth when you've read them. If she can do anything with them, so much the better, but I'm afraid they are rather old news. [You might correct any bad spelling mistakes]. My name of course mustn't be given.

If anything is taken I'ld like to see the cutting.

Anything I can raise in the course of the war can go to a "Bust Fund" for when I come back.

Your loving

J.S.

SOLDIERS AND SAILORS' STORIES.

COLDSTREAM GUARDS' FINE WORK.

24 FEB

HONOURS FOR A BRAVE DEED.

An officer at the front, who has sent to his home in Leeds a portion of his diary, writes:—

I am trying to retell some of the experiences of my soldier servant, a private in the Coldstream Guards, who fought from Mons to Ypres. He was wounded in three places during the attack by the Prussian Guard. He has told me of many little incidents in the retreat and afterwards, and of being in hospital for a few days after being buried alive by the earth thrown up by an exploding "coal-box"; but I shall only try to give a few of his stories. I only wish I could do so in his own words and phrases.

In the part of their line north of the Aisne, which was opposite the Coldstreams' trench, the Germans one night lessened the monotony of fighting by means of one of their national brass bands. They annoyed our men by singing their own National Anthem, which has, unfortunately, the same tune as ours. This, together with the possibility of finding the German sentries taking part in the choruses, persuaded a Coldstream subaltern (one of the only two officers left to the battalion) to go out to reconnoitre their trenches. He did this with such success that he ordered his company to parade at 7 o'clock next evening, two platoons armed with rifles and bayonets, and the other two carrying picks and shovels, so as to be able to fill in the German trenches. It was still too light at seven, so they paraded again at nine, and moved silently off through the narrow gap in the wire entanglement in front of them. They crawled forward towards the German trenches, whose loopholes, with the lights behind them, looked like the portholes of a ship by night. No alarm was given, and when about a yard from the parapet the officer gave the arranged signal to charge. He touched the man next to him, who passed it on until it came to the last man. This man then stood up, and the whole leapt forward with a shout. The Germans in the bottom of their trenches could do nothing. "They were like pigs in a boiler," my story-teller told me, and they were stabbed from above as fast as they tried to get out. The parapet was being destroyed and the trench filled up when the German supports counter-attacked. Men left behind stood at the gap shouting, "This way the Coldstream Guards," and they got back with very slight losses. The result was a D.S.O. for the officer and a V.C. for one N.C.O. The men were inspected and congratulated by the General.

His description of the charge of the Prussian Guard was not very full, as he was wounded in three places, and did not see the end of it. In the evening there was a light mist, which favoured the grey clothing of the Germans, who crept up to within a few yards of the trenches. This had been remarkably well done, for they had avoided the listening posts in front of the trenches without disturbing them at all, and by night a man in a dangerous position is far more likely to hear too much than too little. Had they got a little further unseen they could have caught our men from above with almost no chance of escape. But a close watch was being kept, and a rapid fire was brought on to them, which drove them back. Again and again through the night the Germans advanced to the attack, but were driven back. The reserves they brought up fared no better Our men were told to get out and lie down behind their trenches, so that these would form an additional obstacle to the enemy's rush. When the latter came on, however, we leapt forward over the trench and met them bayonet to bayonet, and so this hand-to-hand fighting went on through the day. By the evening the Coldstreams had lost all their officers, and the remains of the battalion—52 men—were commanded by a lance-sergeant. Their places were taken by the London Scottish. These, as is, of course, well known, continued the fight, and by midnight the German attack had completely failed.

The article John asked his Mother to pass on to Elisabeth appeared in The Times *on 24th February and we hope his "bust fund" did benefit.*

It seems likely that the Coldstream Guardsman concerned, having sustained injuries in 1914 in the early stages of the war, was an orderly to officers in transit in Rouen on their way to the front. This is where John could have heard his story.

P.T.O.
I am having 3 notebooks sent out from England & I told Gale & Polden to send you the account as it's hardly worth my while to send a cheque (wh. needs special envelopes). I hope you won't mind doing a few of these now and again. I'll settle up with you when I come back if you'll keep the receipts for me.

J.S.

Rouen

18.2.15.

Dearest Mother,
While I was shaving this morning the Adjutant came round and told me to "stand by" as I should be going up to the front to-day or to-morrow. The letters go at breakfast time and I just had time to put a postscript into a letter to Elisabeth, telling her I was going to the 12th and asking her to tell you.

I have done a preliminary packing so that I can be off at quite short notice but as I've heard nothing further I'm not likely to go today.

At lunch Tangles and Hunter were also warned. The latter will be a bore again as he'll insist on joining in the conversation, but I'm glad I shall be going off with Tangles. We shall be going to different divisions, I think, as he goes to the 38th (Hunter to the 56th). It will seem rather odd not to find ourselves together for once.

It takes two days, I think, to get to the front, as the trains seem to travel only by night. We shall probably report at 4 o'c to-morrow to the R.T.O. (Railway Transport Officer) and have our carriage allotted to us, and then go away into the town for dinner and come back for the train at 8. We spend the next day at Boulogne and then go on again wherever we are going. (It will probably be Boulogne, but we don't know of course).

We're trying to get leave to go down into the Town this afternoon. Except for the two days I was on duty it has always rained lately and so I've not yet seen the Cathedral, except the second evening when we dined at the Café Cathédrale which is just by it. Still you can't see much by night and we didn't try to go in.

I'm glad to get away from here, for though I'm very comfortable, yet one gets sick of doing absolutely nothing for any length of time.

6th Division deployed to the Western Front in September 1914. In February 1915, when John arrived, it was holding a section of the front line between Armentières and Lille.

The Division consisted of four Brigades and Divisional Troops. Although the engineers supported all the units in the Division, it is clear from the letters that 12th Field Company was frequently engaged with 17th Brigade.

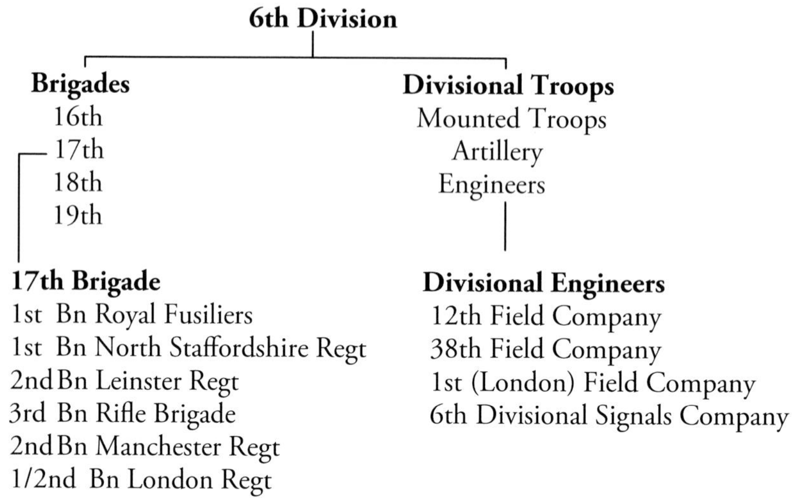

Ronald Scobie

Ronald Mackenzie Scobie played centre for Scotland Rugby XV in three home internationals in 1914 against: Wales at Cardiff on 7th February; Ireland at Dublin on 28th February; and England at Inverleith, Edinburgh on 21st March.

After that no more rugby internationals were played until 1920 on account of the First World War.

Ronald Scobie died in Aldershot on 23rd February 1969.

My address is:- Royal Engineers
12th Field Co. R.E.
British Expd Force.
I'll write to Honor again in a day or two –

Your loving
J. S.

P. S. I thought it wasn't possible. Tangles and I are going to the same division after all. The 12th and 38th are sister-companies in the 6th division, so that its all according to precedent. I don't know where the 6th is and I suppose that after I've left Rouen I shall have to be more careful about what I say, so that you won't know for some time where I am, unless one of the Dispatches or Press Bureau Communiqués says something about the 6th. I'm not sure even which Army Corps its in but I think the 3rd.

You can add to my address under 12th Field Co R.E. «6th Division». That will make the letter come a little quicker I expect, (please tell Lisbeth that).

We managed to get down to Rouen all right and saw the Cathedral and St. Ouen. We also had an excellent tea of brioches and meringues as we did the first time we went down.

We missed the tram going down so we stopped a motor lorry and got into that with three cavalry subalterns. Thats a thing you wouldn't often see in England – half a dozen young officers sitting on the side of YMCA lorry.

I met a fellow called Scobie to-day – a Scotch Rugger international – whom I knew at the Shop and Chatham. He's been in the 1st Field Squadron and got knocked out by a hand grenade which he was throwing himself. He's fairly fit again, however, & is going back soon.

Your loving
J.S.

Smoking

Before the first World War 'real men' smoked cigars or a pipe while smoking cigarettes was considered a bit effeminate for men and was somewhat frowned upon for women. That changed dramatically in 1914. Men of all ranks at the front became avid cigarette smokers and cigarette advertising at home took off as people sought a brand which they thought best depicted their man. It was noted, for example, that officers preferred different brands to other ranks. Cigarettes were known to give great comfort to the troops – they calmed nerves and suppressed the appetite – and in 1916 tobacco was introduced into rations for front line troops.

Knowing what we do now about the serious health risks associated with smoking it is amazing to learn that the most popular items sent to the troops by war charities were tobacco and cigarettes. The Weekly Despatch newspaper set up a Tobacco Fund and raised over £200,000 to send tens of millions of cigarettes to the front. Princess Mary's Christmas Gift Box sent to all troops in 1914 contained a packet of cigarettes.

12th Field Coy,
6th Division
B.E.F.

23.2.15

Dearest Mother,
I went up last night into the trenches with Playfair who takes alternate nights with me. I just looked around and came back and to-night I'm taking up my own section. These trenches were evacuated, because of the wet & they're scarcely habitable now. We're trying to make them bullet-proof and put some sort of flooring down in the worst places. There are boards in most places but they're well underneath. Those long waders of mine are splendid things. I got a certain amount of mud over the top of them, but my feet stayed as dry as a bone.

This is my first evening's work and of course most of the arranging has been done for me but I think that in a little I shall settle down all right.

Your loving
J. S.

I wonder if from time to time you could send me something eatable as the messing system exists a good deal on extras sent out from home. The kind of cake I like best is that sort which consists almost entirely of currants & with a brown background. Sweets too are acceptable and perhaps you could send me 50 Abdulla cigarettes No 16. I don't smoke them but other people will. I don't much mind what I get. I just want to appear to be doing my share. I should also like a couple of pairs of long stockings (without tops). I think there are some in my drawers upstairs.

We've got a piano here and one fellow (Playfair) plays extremely well so that we can shout lots.

Everything is very quiet here still.

Your loving
J. S.

P.S. Urgent. If my British Warm comes from Chatham will you please send it at once. Am writing to Chatham too.

1st Battalion North Staffordshire Regiment Christmas 1914

Official Unit War Diary

24 Dec Quiet. Germans ask for armistice for Xmas. Sing songs in turn from opposite parapets. Germans win prize at this.

25 Dec Not a shot fired. Germans bury their dead. Our men go and help. Baccy and cigars exchanged and our men walk about in the open together!! Return to trenches at 4 p.m. Peace reigns till midnight.

26 Dec Germans still anxious to continue peace. No shots fired. Rain in torrents.

(National Archives WO95/1613/3)

Extracts from a letter to the Times by an officer of the Battalion

(*Christmas Eve*) We had been calling to one another for some time Christmas wishes and other things. I went out and they shouted "No shooting", and then somehow the scene became a peaceful one. All our men got out of their trenches and sat on the parapet, the Germans did the same and they talked to one another in English and broken English. I got on top of the trench and talked German, and asked them to sing a German Volkslied, which they did; then our men sang quite well, and each side clapped and encored each other. I asked one German who sang a solo to sing one of Schuman's songs, so he sang "The Two Grenadiers" splendidly. Our men were a good audience and really enjoyed his singing.

Then I walked across and held a conversation with the German officer in command … I gave permission to bury some German dead who were lying in between us, and we agreed to have no shooting until midnight tomorrow. Then we wished one another good night, a good night's rest, and a happy Christmas, and parted with a salute. I got back to the trench. The Germans sang "Die Wacht am Rhein". It sounded well. Our men sang quite well "Christians awake", and with a good night we all got back into our trenches.

(Christmas Day) This morning after reveille the Germans sent out parties to bury their dead. Our men went out to help, and then we all both sides met in the middle and in groups began to talk and exchange gifts of tobacco, food, etc. … The Germans are Saxons, a good-looking lot, only wishing for peace in a manly way, and they seem in no way at their last gasp … I wonder who will start the shooting … tomorrow we shall be at it hard, killing one another.

24.2.15

Dearest Mother,

I was very glad to get your letter today – the first I've had from you since I got out here. I got Land and Water at the same time. Thanks very much for it. It is interesting to know what he thinks about the Russians as they seem to have taken a fairly good knock.

I took my section up last night and we did a certain amount to our trench – putting hurdles to hold the walls up, footboards to keep above the mud and some dug-outs.

Everything is very quiet here as the Saxons are opposite us and they're rather old friends. They had a truce here at Christmas and it lasted quite a long time. Both sides used to come out and work in the trenches by daylight. When the powers on both sides heard about it they were rather sick and we got Prussians for a time. That's all stopped, of course, but still there is nothing more than sniping and you're quite safe walking about at night. We do no day work in the trenches, but each section is out every other night.

I'm glad that you've been getting away to Thomer and to Whitby. Please give my love to all of them there.

I don't think there will be much news to give for some time.

We're quite comfy in the Asylum. We have two living rooms and I share a bedroom with two other subalterns, (Playfair and Jackson).

We get the papers a day or two late and letters take three days or four.

Your loving

J.S.

26.2.15

Dearest Honor,

You needn't be sorry for me any longer, as I have had letters now for the last three days. Thanks so much for yours and for Land & Water.

You needn't pity me at all in fact, for I'm not overworked. By day there is nothing to do except to prepare material and I don't have anything to do with that except in so far as that I may look into the workshops once a day or so.

I've been doing quite interesting work by night, turning into a palace what used to be the worst trench in the line. Now that it's very largely done,

Trenches

There were many different types of trenches at the front line, including fire, communication, supervision, shell and trenches with living dugouts. All had to provide the maximum protection from enemy direct fire and shelling, but none more so than the fire trenches.

The Sappers' main duty was the construction, repair and improvement of trenches, mainly working at night and sleeping by day in billets close to the front lines. Their work also included wiring and mining in no man's land, with all the dangers involved.

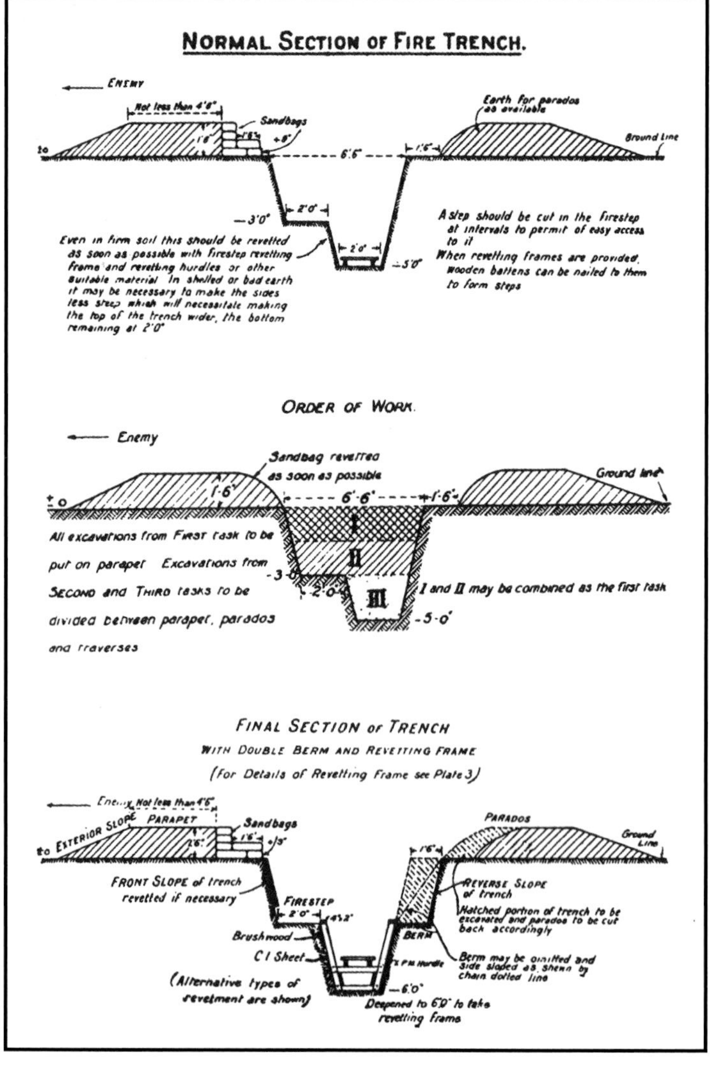

(War Office Manual of British Trench Warfare 1917–1918*)*

we hear that this trench is going to be abandoned for a breastwork just behind. It's rather disappointing.

It's just as well, as a fact, to get out of the place where I was working yesterday. It's full of dead Germans and they stink horrid. Still it was becoming a jolly nice trench.

I'm afraid that the parkin is stuck at Havre. All Rouen things will be forwarded eventually but I don't know about the others. I'll write to the P.O there about it.

I wonder if you would send out my Songs of Two, Savoyards, the Hermann Lohar book, my Pelissier song books and Maguire. (Only the H.L. portrait album – not the green coloured one. I think Lisbeth has it). We have a piano and Playfair is very good on it.

I'm sitting over a lovely hot fire now in an armchair and the table by me has cards and a glass of hot rum on it. I've been playing racing demon and poker patience.

We do our messing at about a franc a day as the only extras we buy are eggs, milk and beer. Everything else is ration (including the rum. You don't get very much of it).

I'm sending this to the High School, as I don't know whether you're at Aysgarth or Shire Oak.

I'm very comfy here.

Your loving brother,
John.

Sunday 28.2.15

Dearest Mother,
It is over a month now since I left Chatham and am settling down quite comfortably now.

I was up in the front line again last night putting up breastworks. The work is very interesting because such lots of little things turn up, such as putting a small footbridge across a dyke or putting a box-drain (a drum pipe made of four planks) down before the earth of the breastworks is put on, so that where the ground slopes forward, a drain can be made through it.

Breastwork

Here John describes a breastwork, which would be constructed when the ground was too wet to allow trenches to be dug and occupied. Instead of digging down, the vital protection had to be built above ground level.

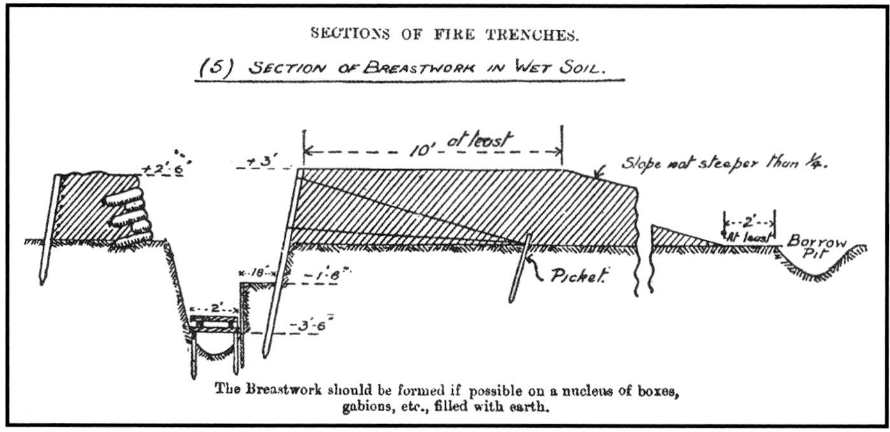

(War Office Manual of British Trench Warfare 1917–1918*)*

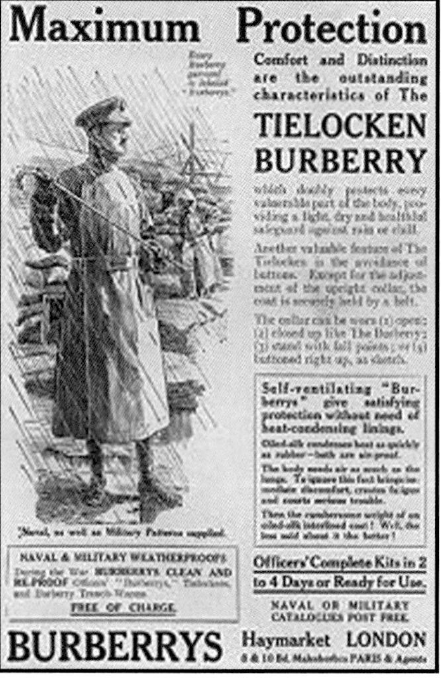

A section of a breast work is something like this:

Just behind the firing step is a lower step for walking along and this has foot boards on it to keep the mud away. Below again is the drain. Behind is the parados which protects against the back burst of shells. At intervals we put dug-outs in the parapet for the men to live in.

At night all the bullets fly high except where the enemy fix rifles by day and fire them at night along certain approaches. There was one road I come by which they shoot down the middle of but they can't quite cover one side of it so that you can walk along quite safely and hear these things missing you by about a yard.

The trenches themselves as I've said are as safe as houses by night because they can't see to aim properly and so all their shots go very high.

I'm really having a very good time – good billets, good food, not too much work and that very interesting.

Please give my love to all at Whitby.

By the way, things like tongues and potted meat are quite acceptable here.

Your loving
J. S.

9.3.15

Dearest Honor,
You've been simply splendid in sending things out. Thank you so much. I think the only thing I need now is my Burberry and some writing paper, if you could get me some rather like this. I shall probably send my greatcoat home, for its too long for the mud. I only use it now for my bed. Did I ask for two small bath-towels and some socks?

There, I think I finished asking for things. It's very hard to do it gracefully, so I'm afraid I haven't tried.

Carrying Parties

In the course of time, as the necessity for skilled work in making dug-outs, in mining, revetting, trench boarding, etc., became more and more pressing, the infantry were required to do the simple trenchwork without the assistance of engineers, except for laying out the trace and for the supply of tools, etc., and also to wire their own front, the engineers being kept for work which the infantry could not do. Even then the engineers required reinforcement by temporary working parties from the infantry for the unskilled work such as carrying up materials, the removal of spoil from mine galleries, etc. This work was much disliked by the infantry who believed they were being exploited for the benefit of the RE and was called “RE fatigues”. The arrangement was also not liked by the engineers who often had to work with unwilling and resentful infantry officers and men, who had never been taught that the work in the execution of which they were required to assist was for their own security, and that it was not unreasonable to ask them to lend a hand in it. Later the practice was adopted of attaching an infantry working party to each field company, with whom they were billeted and fed. This arrangement worked much better. The infantry soon learnt to do the work required of them and became efficient at it; they made friends with their RE partners in toil and were willing and contented, but it was not very satisfactory to the infantry battalion commanders who lost a considerable number of their rank and file for a long time.

(The History of the Corps of Royal Engineers, Volume 5)

(IWM Q1338)

Pack mules fitted with special saddles for carrying shovels.

I'm getting a great critic of letters, for every evening we have to censor the company's letters. I used to trouble sometimes to try to write good letters, but in future I shan't, for I see now how very ordinary mine are. The only thing at all original which I seem to do is to omit from mine the phrase "as it leaves me at present". I think I shall have to start doing that too.

I've had quite a slack time to-day as I was out last night. I just had to look after a carrying party of 150 infantry, but as all the stuff was the same it was not much trouble. One of the Infantry officers was a fellow called Herbert-Smith who was at Winchester with me. He was skipper of Houses VI and about two years senior to me. It was odd meeting him in the dark because I met him one night in Rouen while waiting for a tram and these are the only two times I've seen him since I left. He was at the Varsity & got an S.R. commission in the Rifle Brigade at the beginning of the war.

That little piece of news was quite accidental for I began this letter before going out and I didn't expect to have any news to tell. Even that's not very thrilling but its all that I've got to give. You see after I've settled down here there is nothing more to say. Its really only journeys that give much to write about.

At present I'm working on a communication trench. In the Autumn the trenches here were lovely and you could walk for miles without shewing yourself. Now of course those are full of water and people can only move about much by night. The kind of communication trench I'm building is a shallow thing about 2'6" deep. About 4 yards on each side of it another trench is dug which is about 3' deep and the earth from them is heaped up on both sides of the middle one so as to give cover. These also act as drains.

We had made such good progress reclaiming the other trenches I was on that when the general saw them he changed his mind and let us finish them. They're really very good now and when we've finished the present job we're going on to some others which are nearly as bad.

I got a message from the Brigade Headquarters the other day telling me to go to one of the companies in the line and "assist and advise about demolitions". I found some walls of a farm-house which were going to fall down and they wanted them brought down at once for safety. My learned advice was to take a rope and pull them down. See what it is to be a Sapper!

Your loving
John

17 BRIGADE OPERATION ORDER NO 11

Secret
Copy No 4

ARMENTIERES
11 March 1915

Reference :- Attached Sketch

1. The 17th Infantry Brigade will during the hours of darkness tonight seize and make good the line W. X. Y and Z on the accompanying map.

2. The line from W to X will be held by 1 Coy 2 Leinster Regt under Capt E.H.Murphy. Separate instructions have been issued to 2nd London Regt who will provide working parties under Lieut E.F.Tickell RE. All work in this line will cease at 11.45 p.m. when working parties will be withdrawn.

3. At 12 midnight the 1st N.Staff Regt will seize and make good the line X (exclusive). Y. Z. 12 Coy RE and 1 Coy London Regt is placed under OC 1st N.Staffs for this purpose.

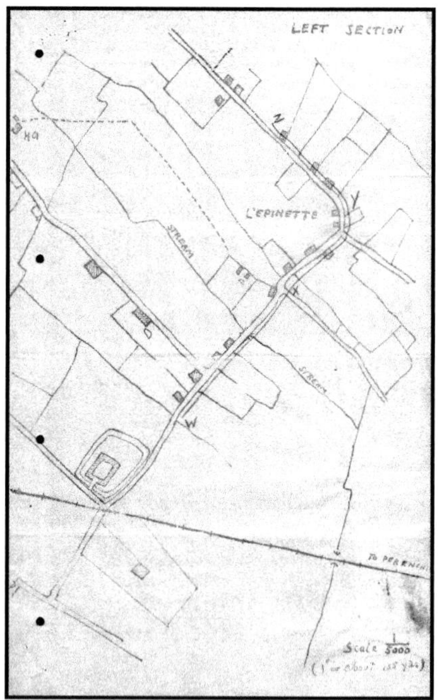

(National Archives WO 95/1613/3)

4. Artillery support will be furnished under arangements made by Lieut Col C.E.Lawrie CB Bde RA. Artillery fire will not be opened during the night unless the enemy prevents the carrying out of the work. A prolonged bombardment of the hostile L'EPINETTE re-entrant will be carried out at dawn.

5. 2 Leinster Regiment will man their trenches by night and be prepared to support the 1st N.Staff Regt by fire from their trenches.

6. All Troops detailed to occupy the advanced line will take with them 2 days rations, 220 rounds S.A.A.

Reports to B.H.Q at normal place.

Signed Capt Bde Major 17 I.B.

Further details about this operation are at Appendix 2

Sunday 14.3.15

Dearest Mother,
I've not written for the last few days because I've got in just in time for breakfast the last three mornings and with starting off at 6 in the evening there's not much day left after sleeping and eating are over.

I've been reading the headlines of yesterday's papers and seeing "Gallant British Army wins another Splendid Success" and "3rd Corps Capture Another Village" with maps shewing its position. Unfortunately they've got hold of another of the same name and the one they shew isn't in the firing line even. Its quite true that the third corps was the one, but it was not the whole corps or anything like it.

The "splendid success" was won by the 1st North Staffords and the 12th Company R.E. who gallantly stormed an advanced German position held by six snipers, who decamped in great haste.

Now I'll tell you what happened.

The village is a group of 12 houses from which the Germans used to snipe and there were two communication trenches running back to the German lines from them. They were about 100 yards from their trenches and 300 from ours and it was decided to advance our line so as to go through them.

We started out at midnight, wearing white tape round our necks in case the Germans counter-attacked and had to be bayonetted in the dark. Our advanced parties, mostly R.E., cut the wire and removed the snipers, filling up part of their communication trenches afterwards. The main body, 2 companies, advanced under fairly hot fire from their German trenches but almost everything went high and they had very few men hit. My section was with the supports who came on immediately afterwards. As soon as they arrived the Infantry began to dig themselves in along the new line and we set about loopholing the houses and filling up the windows and doors with sandbags full of broken brick. We also did a little digging to join up places in the line which were not actually to be used as fire-trenches. We got back with a loss of 2 Sappers wounded. The Infantry had 18 wounded.

The sniper's Post in my part of the line was very snug. It was just above a cellar where he could get down and be safe from anything but large high-explosive shells. He had evidently just begun his evening's correspondence, for we found letters from his girl and his people and a post-card congratulating him on their "glorious victory" whenever that was. There was also one he had just begun to write to the lady and his pay-book so he had evidently been in rather a hurry.

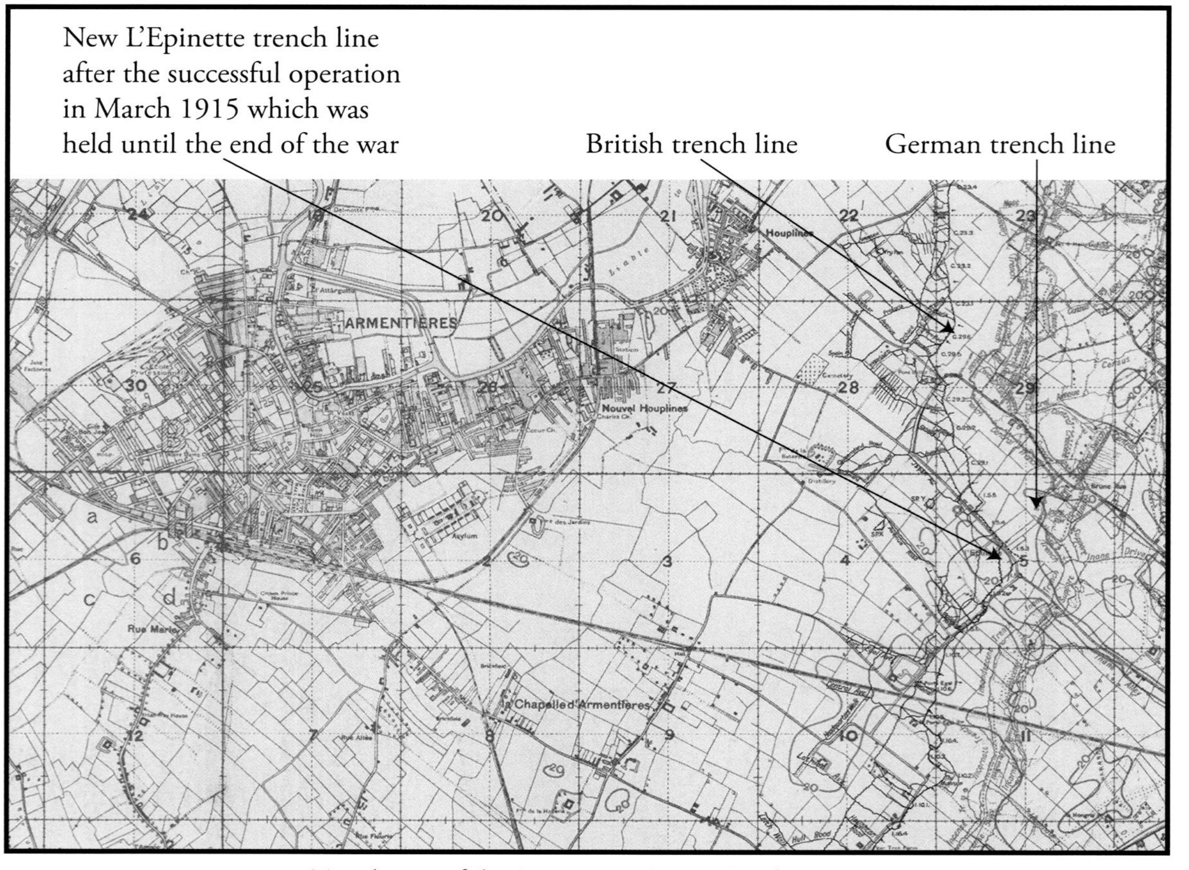

Trench map of the Armentieres Sector, October 1917

As there had only been about 4 hours for digging before daylight and the Infantry had had a fairly large rum ration before the start the trenches were not very far progressed and the losses were very heavy when the Germans began to shell the place by day. We were working there all that night finishing the houses, wiring the front and putting in a few shrapnel-proof shelters. The Infantry were also digging and we made much improvement. We had to stop working for a bit as they shelled us for 10 or 15 minutes. They shot very well, using their searchlight very prettily to mark the bursts, but at the bottom of a trench you are pretty safe and there weren't more than half a dozen casualties, only one Sapper.

It was my first shelling and I expected to be rather frightened. I was pleasantly surprised to find I wasn't. I suppose really bad shelling is awful, but shrapnel at night is quite pleasant. You can stand about till you see the flash of the gun and then you've heaps of time to sit down before the thing arrives. I was in a house when they began, and as there was a little mortar flying about I moved out and into a trench. Personally I far prefer it to rifle or machine gun fire, because with the latter the bullet is on you so much quicker.

We scuppered a German bombing party that night. The Sappers of Jackson's section were out doing wire, Jackson saw a bomb lit and thrown towards one of our machine-guns. He loosed off with his revolver and then got into a trench. As soon as the bomb exploded the machine gun fired a belt at them. We brought in three of them (2 Infantry & one Pioneer) and found nine dead. The prisoners said they were the only three left out of twenty but probably the other eight had had time to get into the communication trench between Jackson's effort and the machine gun's and so get away.

As the result of our work there were fewer casualties the second day. That night we spent putting up shelters. At intervals along the trench we put a roof across and then the Infantry made it shrapnel-proof by covering it with a foot of earth. This earth also protects the trench to the right of the shelter as the shelling is all from the left. We didn't get shelled this third night. The rifle fire was hotter than before, but we had no men hit (no Sappers at any rate).

Here you have something of the true account. It wasn't a general advance by the 3rd Corps but just a local advance of 300 yards along a quarter-mile front. Its object is more to frighten the Germans than anything else.

They've had quite a big show to the south as you've seen. I'm glad the Indians have done so well. After their division had taken about 400

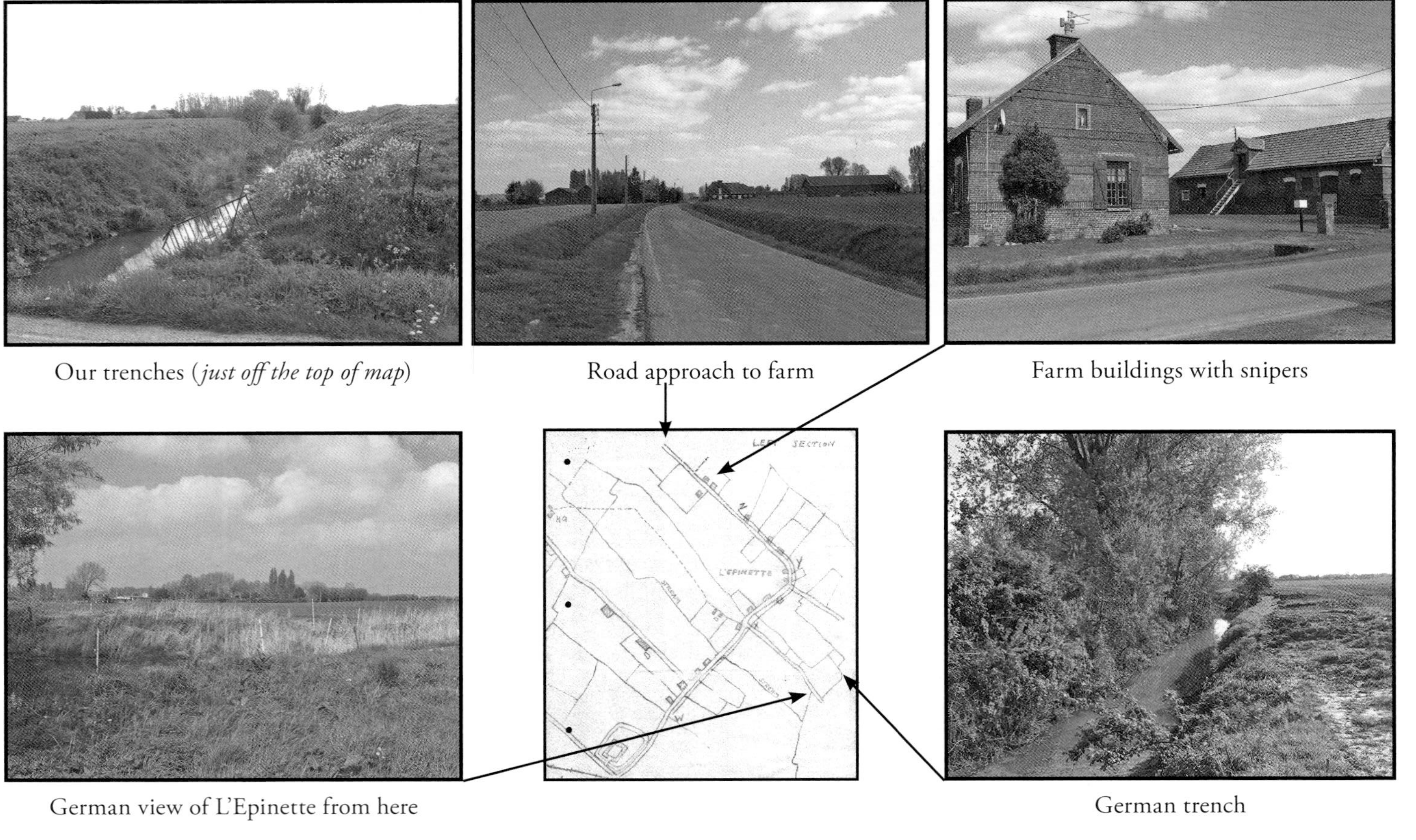

Our trenches (*just off the top of map*)

Road approach to farm

Farm buildings with snipers

German view of L'Epinette from here

German trench

L'Epinette photographs taken by the editors in April 2014

prisoners they found them a nuisance to look after and didn't take many more! There's not much love lost between them and the Germans, and when they are going strong I'ld just as soon not be opposite them.

In one place a man came across a dummy figure in the dark. He knocked it down and it went off & wounded him.

Will you please pass this letter on to Elisabeth as it will save me writing the same thing twice.

Please thank Honor very much for her excellent sweets. I'll try and write to her to-morrow.

Your loving
J. S.

If ever you send humbugs or any very sticky sweets will you put them in a tin. There is one kind of humbug which doesn't run about much.
J. S. Baines

Fri 19th March

Dearest Honor,
Thanks very much your letter which came today. I'm very sorry to hear about Toby. The Neuve Chapelle losses have been rather heavy I'm afraid. Three of the 10 of Pank's batch have been killed, but I think before that time.

I've been up to L'Epinette "consolidating" most nights since we took it. We parade about 6 and get back about six so that its a fairly long night. To-night, however, I may with luck get back sooner. Our work has done good for in the last few days they've had hardly any casualties there, though they've had their share of shells.

I had a most amusing time yesterday. A heavy battery has just arrived close to us commanded by a Major Rowan-Robinson who used to be chief instructor in artillery when I was at the Shop. He came in yesterday and found me alone. He wanted a better observation post for shelling a certain village so his late pupil, who now has nothing to do with guns, suggested a certain factory chimney and undertook to take him to look at it. I got him up inside (there was a ladder of sort) and there was a small shell hole just below the top when he could look out delightfully without being seen. I then advised him about what to shoot at, told him he might as well begin and register to the church as he couldn't do anything wrong by knocking

"They've evidently seen me."

(2015 Estate of Barbara Bruce Littlejohn)

that down and then let him begin as soon as his telephone had come up. I never came out here with intention of running a 4.7 battery, still less of doing it for Rowan R.

I heard one rather pathetic remark. It was the 17th and I was "consolidating". The Leinsters hold the place and I had a few of them to help me. I heard one voice in the darkness saying: "Sint Pathrick's Day, an' me fillin' sand-bags".

I rather like the Leinsters though they have their faults. If they think its doing the R.E. a good turn (or anyone else really) you can get a lot out of them. If they look on it as just work they're as bad as the worst. Their officers are a cheery lot and very hospitable on a cold night. They know the right way of serving rum which is with lemon in it (hot of course).

I've taken their tip and bought lemons for our mess. I'm responsible for the catering but its not much trouble. Rations come automatically and all I have to do really is to order beer when our supply runs out. The rum is a ration.

If you have time some day we should love some of that soft toffee. Elisabeth sent me some that a friend of hers made & it went in a flash.

I've just got to gulp my tea before going out so I'll ring off.

Your loving brother
John

21.3.15

Dearest Mother,
I'm afraid I must ask you not ever to send any more of my letters to the papers as I got into trouble a little over my description of our advance. I wrote in a very indiscreet way, and as rather a lot had been made of the shew the Brigade H.Q. were rather sick and the General gave me a little speech all to myself. I don't know how the thing got past the Press Bureau, but anyway I've got only myself to blame for writing the way I did, and in future I want you to keep on the safe side by publishing nothing at all. If it happened again I might get into serious trouble. All that's happened now is that I have to have my letters censored by the Major. Will you please let Elisabeth know this too. So much for things serious.

I feel much inclined to burst into Journalese about the birds twittering on the branches etc. for in more than date its the first day of spring. Its a lovely sunny morning and I'm practically out of doors as I write in the window. And the night before last I marched my section home in a snow-storm.

Military Chaplains

Throughout the war military chaplains, better known as padres, were attached to medical units behind the lines where their pastoral care was much needed among the wounded and dying. They had the time, that medical staff did not, to help soldiers write letters home, to read letters from home and listen to things they had to say, to administer the last rites and to undertake burial services.

In 1915 the army had the idea of attaching a padre to a specific unit or battalion. The padre then moved wherever that battalion went – up to the trenches and back for a rest behind the lines. Padres, who were always volunteers, never carried weapons, and in the trenches worked tirelessly to maintain the morale of the troops, assuring them that God was on their side. They frequently put themselves into great danger by going into no-man's land to comfort the wounded and they were never far from the aid posts, which were the first place wounded men were taken in the trenches. Whether in the trenches or behind the lines, services were always held on Sundays and additional services were often held the day before a battle was to take place.

Neville Talbot

Padre Neville Talbot was the senior military chaplain in the area around Ypres, Armentières and Poperinge in 1914/15. He was not a blood relation of John's, but, through marriage, they had a cousin in common. The son of a clergyman (who became successively Bishop of Rochester, Southwark and Winchester), Neville had served in the army in the Boer War for 4 years before going up to Oxford University. He was ordained in 1908. His younger brother Gilbert was killed in the Ypres salient in 1915 and it was in Gilbert's memory, as much as because of the great support from Neville while it was being set up, that Talbot House (Toc H) took its name.

Toc H

Instructed by Neville Talbot to set up some sort of rest house for the troops behind the lines, Padre Philip (Tubby) Clayton rented a house in the town of Poperinge and in December 1915 Talbot House was opened. Talbot House became known first as TH then as TocH (using radio signallers' shorthand of the day). Tubby Clayton's idea was to create not simply a church club, but a place where every man could feel welcomed, of whatever rank or religious conviction. He put rugs on the floor and vases of flowers on tables to make men feel at home; there was a library of books to be read in the quiet room; there were concerts and debates for socialising; and, of course, there was a small chapel where religious services were held on a regular basis. Many men were confirmed and took their first communion in Toc H, and hundreds more benefitted from the solace gained in the peaceful and comforting atmosphere created there.

That same night I went out in front with the Infantry company commander to see how much still needed filling in of an old German communication trench and we got three Deutscher rifles from close to it. They had belonged to the bombing party I told you of. I brought one back, but I believe I'm not allowed to keep it.

Since I began this letter I've had one from you. Thanks for what you say about the food. As a matter of fact I think the pie would get crushed and our cook is rather good at pies but if you could send some tinned things – sardines, tongue, sausages, or marmalade – they would arrive quite well and be very welcome. We have got a great many humbugs, but ordinary chocolates go very quickly.

I forget whether I said that I had sent back the waterproof stockings. They would almost have gone on over my boots. What I want is a small medium size. I told about that however & asked them to send the right size. They seem to be excellent things.

If we get a few more days like this it will dry the place up wonderfully. Its just the sort of day for the Lakes – bright sun and a few clouds just level with the peaks, and a slight haze in the distance so that you can only see the outlines of the far hills; a little cold on the water but just the day for a Tarn Hows picnic. I'm glad you are going there soon. When is Elisabeth going to join you? At the beginning?

I'm fairly well off for clothes now though perhaps I could do with another pair of pants and a vest. Its just in case I get wet through while one pair is being washed.

The Padre here is Talbot – the very tall one. We had a service here this morning in the Asylum Church. For a church it's very little damaged but some of them are pretty knocked about. There are two rather war-worn villages here just opposite each other.

After some months of shooting the Deutschers on Friday brought our steeple down. This put our guns on their mettle and yesterday we smashed their tower into little heaps.

After church this morning I introduced myself to Talbot, saying we possessed a common cousin in Freddy, and walked with him to where his next service was. He got a slight hit in the leg the other day though not enough to go home with. I heard someone saying that it would have got any ordinary man in the head.

I had some of the West Yorks as a carrying party the other day and asked one of the officers if theirs was Captain Riall's battalion. He's quite close to

Postal Services to and from The Western Front

Initially mail for units on the Western Front was sorted in France, but in December 1914 the Post Office built a Home Depot in Regent's Park, London. From there mail was shipped to Le Havre, Boulogne or Calais where the Royal Engineers Postal Section sorted and delivered it on to postal orderlies of individual units. On average it took only two days for a letter to reach the Western Front area, unless it was held up by the censor.

In order to avoid revealing information on the location of troops, letters to them were addressed only by name, military number and unit c/o GPO. To further disguise the location of units and ships "dumb" postmarks (cancellation stamps) were used which voided the stamp but didn't disclose a place name.

The public were invited to hand in, at any Post Office, books or magazines and small gift parcels to be sent to servicemen abroad. These were sent free of charge and were much appreciated by the recipients.

Between 1914 and 1918 the volume of mail increased from around 700,000 items to around 13,000,000. This meant that postal deliveries within Britain were cut from the pre-war level of 12 a day (in some areas) to 6 a day in London and 4 or less in rural areas. They never returned to pre-1914 arrangements.

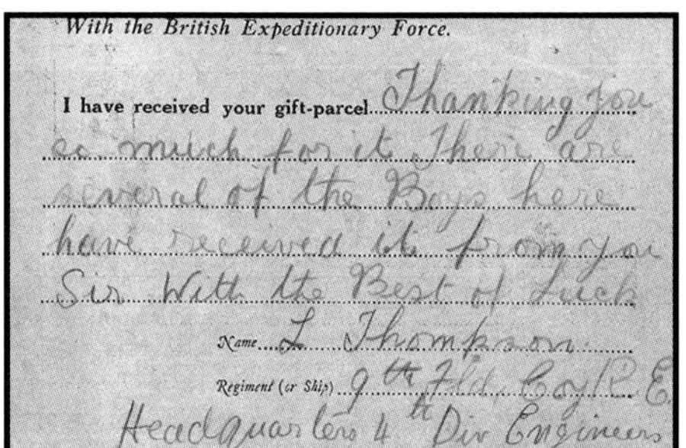

With the British Expeditionary Force.

I have received your gift-parcel. Thanking you so much for it. There are several of the Boys here have received it from you Sir. With the Best of Luck

Name L. Thompson

Regiment (or Ship) 9th Fld Coy R.E.

Headquarters 4th Div Engineers

R 114

POST CARD.

ARMY PO

Lieut. J. Stanhope Baines R.E.

Brompton Barracks

Chatham

PASSED BY

No 1389

CENSOR

me (in the same division) but I'm not very likely to see him as I don't generally have anything to do with his brigade. That once was an exception.

When do Honor's holidays begin?

Your loving
J. S.

P. S. The Major says he's not going to censor this after all. I'm sorry I've caused this trouble. I ought to have warned you not to do anything with that one, but it didn't occur to me that the Press Bureau would let it pass. J. S. Baines

Wed 24.3.15

Dearest Mother,
I'm sorry if my last letter seemed rather abrupt. I thought that it was going to be censored by the Major. It was silly of me to write the other quite as I did without telling you that you mustn't publish it, but everything has blown over now I think.

The day after my chat with the General I heard the Colonel was coming over about something and wanted to speak to me. I felt that two tellings-off were about as much as the flesh could stand, but I brushed my hair & put on my cleaner coat & met him.

He was quite friendly about it & simply advised me not to describe other actions quite so fully and not to allow anything to be published, because it was easy to put other people's backs up when one only could give one's own impressions. Why he was so mild was that the General had had no right to tell me off. The General is the Brigadier of an Infantry Brigade and the Colonel is C.R.E. (Commanding R.E.) for the Division and I come under him. It's like this:

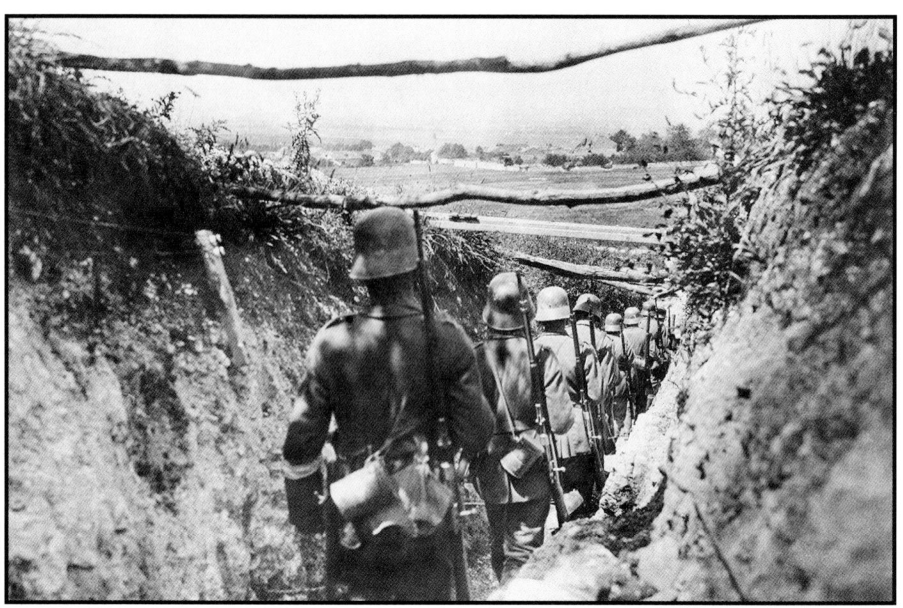

(IWM Q23940)

German infantry file down a communication trench on their way to the front line.

(IWM Q6183)

British cavalry unit crossing a bridge over a communications trench.

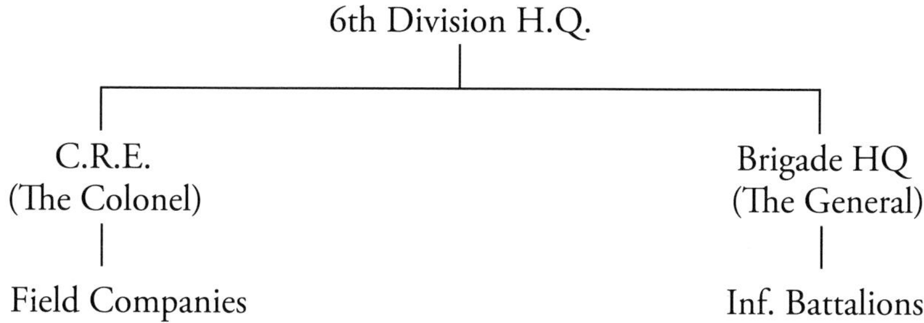

There's a god known as Chain of Command. If the General wants to tell me off he has to tell the Division to tell the Colonel who either sees me direct or tells the Major. In practice we do take our orders straight from the Brigade because it saves trouble, but in theory they should come through the C.R.E.

The Pork and Mince Pies arrived yesterday quite uncrushed. There are seven of us in the Mess (one Captain attached to the company pro-tem) but one fellow didn't like mince pies so there were two apiece. The Pork Pie was excellent and as I happened to have bought some oranges and grapes in the town I really provided the whole meal last night.

On Monday I had fairly interesting work. I had a small bridge to carry a sandbag barricade across a ditch and we put up a good deal of wire in front of the line. I also did my first blowing up job.

When the Germans were here they had one or two communication trenches running back to their main line wh. is 150 yards or so away. We have a machine gun at the top of one but about 40 yards down it was a traverse i.e. a wiggle which stopped us firing right down it. They wanted it destroyed so we brought up a box of guncotton, and exploder etc. The Infantry sent a patrol of 4 men to see that the coast was clear and they lay down about ten yards in front. We came along and found the traverse was held up by plank hurdles, but that the planks didn't come right down to the bottom. We burrowed a hole into it, put in the guncotton with the leads attached, rammed in the earth & went back to our line. Here we fastened the leads to the exploder, blew a whistle to tell everyone to get their heads down and I rammed down the handle of the exploder. There was a perfect hail of loose earth some of which hit our parapet about 200 yards away. I didn't go down to see, but I guess there wasn't much traverse left.

What amused me most was that there was a German wiring party out in front of their trenches and we could hear them talking and working as we prepared the charge. They must have got most of the old traverse on top of

The Seige of Przemyśl

The longest siege of the First World War began on 24th September 1914, when Russian troops set out to overwhelm Austrian forces dug in at the Austro-Hungarian city of Przemyśl (now in Poland). With only a few days respite, the ensuing battles and siege lasted until Przemyśl capitulated on March 13th 1915. During the intervening winter months, ill-prepared in summer weight clothing to sustain the raging snow blizzards and increasingly short of rations, both armies suffered enormous casualties and hundreds of men froze to death on the battlefield before they could be treated.

(Winchester College Archives)

Sunday morning in Chamber Court.

them. I expect they thought the end of the world had come, though I don't suppose it hurt any of them. It would be in too little bits.

I don't really get very much time for writing now because we have a good deal of work to do just at present, so you mustn't be anxious if you sometimes have to wait 3 or 4 days for a letter. I'm not out every night for a long night but I very often have to go out for the early part of the evening so that I don't get a chance of sitting down to a letter. I will try however to let you or Elisabeth hear from me 3 or 4 times a week.

Yes I think I should like a book now and again. Thanks very much.

Please thank Honor for her letter. I will try & write to her tomorrow or the next day.

Your loving

J. S.

Sunday 28th March

Dearest Mother,

I've not been doing anything very thrilling lately. Its still the old farm being turned into a minor Przemyśl (except that it could hold out longer). Its called Waterwheel Farm because on the remains of one wall are bits of an old dog-wheel. [Dogs out here are used for all sorts of things. It seems strange to us but they seem to love working].

I wasn't out last night, so I went to church again to-day. Its again been a lovely sunny Sunday though cold. We're having frost again at nights but the sun is lovely. I did "Stables" this morning and as I came back to breakfast it made me think of Sunday mornings at Winchester. I don't know why unless perhaps it was that in Chamber Court the white stones and walls always used to make the sun very bright on a clear day such as this even with great cold.

The trouble about the letter has blown over all right. In fact most people are rather amused. You see the Brigade made the most of it, the Division backed them up, it was in French's despatch as an advance by the 3rd Corps and Kitchener mentioned it in the house of Lords. Then the next day my thing talked of the 6 German snipers & that annoyed them some. When the General told me off, which he did very well, the only time he exposed the joint in his armour was when he said "How did you know it was held by six snipers?" I didn't say anything, for of course I didn't know the exact number.

Rum Ration

A rum ration for troops in the front line was introduced in the winter of 1914 to combat the cold and damp in the trenches. A rum jar held one gallon. A teaspoonful of rum was issued twice daily, just after dusk and dawn, and extra rations were often issued as a nerve calmer just before troops went over the top or as a reward for completing particularly hazardous or tiring tasks.

The popularity of the rum ration is best described in the words of a soldier: "... it is not compulsory, and no man need take it unless he wishes ... our commanders and the army surgeons believe that rum as a medicine, as a stimulant, is necessary to the health of the soldier, therefore the rum is issued. We take this ration as a prescription. We gulp it down when half frozen, and nearly paralysed after standing a night in mud and blood and ice, often to the waistline, rarely below the ankle, and it revives us as tea, cocoa or coffee could never do. We are not made drunkards by our rum ration."

Of course some temperance societies objected to the issue of rum, but abstainers often used the rum to rub on their feet.

John writes, "They are stopping the rum ration which is a bore". In fact this only ever happened for short periods. When the Commander of 33rd Division, General Pinney, banned the rum ration it caused such a furore in his Division that it was soon reinstated. Captain Alexander Stewart expressed the views of many when he said:

"The finest thing that ever happened in the trenches was the rum ration ... yet some blasted, ignorant fool of a general – damned in this world and the next – wanted to stop it and, for a time, did. The man must be worse than the lowest type of criminal, have no knowledge of the conditions in which troops exist, and be entirely out of touch with the men who are unfortunate enough to have him as their commander. He should have been taken up to the line and frozen in the mud. I would have very willingly sat on his head, as he was a danger to the whole army. Curse him. Those who have not spent a night standing or sitting or lying in mud with an east wind blowing and the temperature below freezing may think that I am extravagant in my abuse of the man who denied the soldiers their rum rations. Those who have will know I am too temperate."

I saw two delightful pictures yesterday by the Brigade-Major of the other Brigade we work for (who of course thought it funny). The first is the thing as imagined by the British Public. The Governor of Epinette is seen in a place full of great houses & factory chimneys handing over the keys to the G.O.C. 17th I.B & Staff (General Officer commanding 17th Inf. Bde.) The second is "as described by a subaltern of the 12th Co. R.E. in a letter to the Times". It shows four men with fixed bayonets charging a very ruined cottage and in the background is a German sniper going Hell for leather down a road. They were very well done.

There were some Russians here the other day and "Uncle" (the G.O.C. 17th IB) was very polite about the fall of Przemyśl. The Russian replied "Ah, but I must also congratulate you General upon the capture of L'Epinette."

This of course is a very indiscreet letter too so be careful about who you shew it to, won't you?

They are stopping the rum ration, which is a bore. As one Leinster officer said to me. "It's enough to make a dog hit its father." It makes a great difference on a cold night to be able to look in on some fellow in his dug-out & get something hot. Also to have it when one gets in in the morning.

I'm glad you're going to Coniston because I always think of it as home more than anywhere else & I'm very glad Lisbeth is going to be there. I like to think of her there with you where I know all the country so well.

With love to Honor

Your loving

J.S.

3.4.15

Dearest Honor,

I'm not sure whether I'm right in addressing this to Coniston but as far as I can judge from your "only x days more" its on Monday that you're going there. I don't exactly wish I were going there too because I'm much too happy here. It's rather that I look forward to the next time I shall be there. Sometimes, when there's nothin' much doin' and its a sunny day, I rather wish I could be dropped onto the hills for a few hours.

Lately there's been nothing very thrilling – just the ordinary thing. On Thursday I improved a path by filling up shell-holes and put down a lot of foot-bridges just behind the breastworks. It was rather a good evening because we did a lot of valuable work and it was quite a short night too. Last night I was also in fairly early but I had rather a worrying job. I had about

Aerial Propaganda

Sir Campbell Stuart KBE in his book "Secrets of Crewe House" states that in October 1914 Lieutenant-Colonel Swinton prepared a propaganda leaflet (*translated below*) with the aid of Lord Northcliffe's Paris Daily Mail organisation, and distributed it by aeroplane among the German troops. "But," says Sir Campbell Stuart, "the Army chiefs at that time did not show any enthusiasm for the innovation, and Colonel Swinton was unable to proceed with the project." He paid the cost of printing out of his own pocket and recovered this from the Army authorities later.

NOTICE
NEWS FOR THE GERMAN SOLDIERS

It has come to notice that the German soldiers have been informed, that the English have treated their prisoners in an unmanly fashion. This is a lie.
All the German prisoners of war have been well treated, and are looked after by the British just as if they were men of their own.
This opportunity is being taken to enlighten the German soldiers on a few points which have so far been treated as confidential.
The German army has never reached, or taken, Paris, but since the 5th September have retreated from there.
The English army has neither been captured nor beaten. It is being reinforced day by day.
The French army is not beaten. Totally in the reverse, the Germans received a severe defeat at MONTMIRAIL.
Russia and Serbia have defeated Austria in such a manner that she plays no further part.
With the exception of a few cruisers neither merchandise nor warships of the German fleet are to be seen on the sea.
The English and German fleets have both had heavy losses, but the German losses have been by far the heaviest.
Germany has already lost several colonies, and will in a very short while lose the remainder. Japan has declared war on Germany, Kiau-chiao is at present being besieged by the British and Japanese.
The rumours spread about in the press to the effect that the English colonies in India are in mutiny against England is totally untrue. In the reverse, these colonies have sent many troops and supplies into France to help their country.
Ireland is allied with Great Britain, and is sending soldiers from the north and south; they are fighting with great courage by the side of their English comrades.
The Kaiser and his Prussian ministers started this war against all interests of the Fatherland. In secret they prepared themselves for it. Germany alone started the war, to which cause the following facts are due. Now we have ceased our victorious advance. Supported by the sympathy of the whole world, who were dead against any such war as this, Great Britain, France, Russia, Belgium, Serbia, Montenegro and Japan are bent on carrying through this war until their end is attained.
These facts are being brought to the general notice in order to throw some light on the truth which has been kept in darkness so long.
You are not fighting to defend your country as no one ever had the wish to attack it. You are fighting to satisfy the war lust of the military parties with the idea that it is all in the true interests of the Fatherland. It is simply infamous!
At first view these facts will seem doubtful to you, but it is now up to you to compare this with the news published in the newspapers during the last few weeks.

THE RUSSIANS GAINED A GREAT VICTORY IN EASTERN PRUSSIA ON 4th OCTOBER. GERMAN LOSSES NUMBER OVR 70,000

(www.psywar.org)

400 yards of communication trench to dig by means of rather unskilled Terriers. It was pitch dark and raining and they worked in two reliefs of 3 hours so that I had to wait a long time before I could get the second lot started & go home. They were fellows who had only been here about two days & weren't much used to night digging esp. without a moon.

We had a Deutscher dropping bombs on the Town on Thursday (our first) & the last thing he let go fell in our garden. It was a cylinder about 8 ins long with a cork in one end and fastened to it a long piece of cloth (about 5 feet) divided into red, white & black portions and across the white was printed Flieger – Meldrung [Flight – Message]. Inside the cylinder was a German message form with "Ostergrüsse von Ignatz v Havel" (Easter greetings from Ignatz). We have it pinned up on the wall of the dining room.

Did I ever tell you about the two horses in my section who are exactly alike. They're called Kate & Duplicate.

I'm out to-night for a short time but only superintending the carrying up of some of our stores, so that I shall be in fairly early.

It's odd how little one realises the time of year. I got a frightful shock last Sunday when Neville Talbot said it was Palm Sunday. And tomorrow is Easter Day. It's rather odd. I wonder if this shew will be over by next Easter.

Thank you so much for all the parcels you've sent me. You're being simply splendid. Thank Mother too for the Way of an Eagle. I've read it as a matter of fact but some of the others haven't.

I'm afraid this sheet is in rather a mess. I had to cross out a lot of one letter I was censoring and thoughtlessly had it on this sheet (which I had only just begun) & of course the other side all traced through.

Let me know what you do at Coniston & I'll picture it all. The primroses ought to be rather good there now.

Your loving brother
John

John's passion for the Lakes

John inherited three strong links with the past from his Baines forbears: Leeds, politics and the Lakes.

For four generations his family had lived in Leeds and been proprietors of the Leeds Mercury newspaper. His great great grandfather and great grandfather, both called Edward, had also been Liberal MPs for Leeds.

However, one senses from John's letters that it was the third inheritance that meant the most to him – the Lakes. Edward Junior (later to be Sir Edward) wrote one of the first guidebooks of the Lakes in 1829 with the title 'A Companion to the Lakes of Cumberland, Westmorland and Lancashire; in a descriptive account of a Family Tour and Excursions on horseback and on foot, with a new copious and correct Itinerary'. There is no doubt that his great grandfather's book, with its extraordinary sensitivity for the beauty and uniqueness of the Lakes, must have inspired John to get to know the area equally well.

Dearest Mother spent much of the war at Coniston; at the same time it is clear, through John's letters home, that his deep affection for the Lakes often gave him the inner peace he so badly needed.

Howhead Cottage, Coniston in 1914 and 2014

15. 4. 15

Dearest Honor,
Thanks for your long letter & the cake both of which were very enjoyable. I'm glad you've gone to Coniston, because the times when one thinks of England aren't suggestive of any town – even old Leeds. We've been having a few showers lately but for the last week there's always been a still clear evening and its then that one feels like "home and a garden". You couldn't ask for a much better garden than the Lakes.

I'm glad all those people have been remembering me. Give them my love or respects or whatever you think suitable – Cohens, Cowmans, Priestleys, Proctors, the glad-eyed Miss Fleming. My special friends are of course Mrs Henley William & old Irwin. Ask after the latter for me if you don't see him. I hope he's not ill. Perhaps you'd better leave out Miss Fleming. I nearly forgot the Fells. I don't know about Joe Tyson. I don't know him well enough perhaps. Anyhow, those'll be enough to go on with.

I'm still on the same old communication trench. It's a splendid sight & I'll bet my bottom dollar it'll still be there two thousand years hence (most of the lines will). It'll be no trouble to future historians to make military maps of this country. We've got a new Terrier company here so I shall be back with my old Brigade next week. They've been in a good deal of fighting & are quite a good lot.

Do you know whether Mrs Mayo did send me a second parcel. I don't know that I've got it unless I mistook it for something Mother had sent.

I'm sorry you've got a cold. I hope its not going to last long. You'll have to walk it off.

I don't remember much about the new cottage. Its pink, isn't it? A little more space will certainly be an advantage.

I've just re-read The Way of an Eagle. It's a jolly good yarn. I always take your Fragrant Weed to my bath.

With love to Mother and Lisbeth.

Your loving brother,
John

J. S. Baines

Recipe for Hawkshead Wigs

This is a traditional English recipe for a classic lenten bun made from a basic bread dough enriched with lard and flavoured with caraway seeds. They were usually only made during the season of Lent, although up until the 1930s the village of Hawkshead in Cumbria used to bake them regularly. They are seldom baked these days, however.

Ingredients

900g strong white bread flour
1 tsp salt
1 tsp caster sugar
1 packet active, dried, yeast
1 tbsp caraway seeds, lightly crushed
1 tbsp olive oil
600ml warm water
200g lard, softened
milk for brushing
granulated sugar for dusting

Method

Combine the flour and salt in a large bowl.
In a cup, mix the sugar, yeast and 100ml of the warm water. Cover and set aside for about 10 minutes, or until the mixture is frothing
Form a well in the flour and add the yeast mix and the oil.
Stir to combine then add enough of the remaining warm water to form a soft dough.
Knead the dough thoroughly for at least 15 minutes then turn out onto a well-floured work surface and knead well for another 5 minutes.
Grease a bowl, form the dough into a ball then place in the bowl and cover with a damp cloth. Set aside to rise in a warm place for about 40 minutes, or until the dough has doubled in volume.
Knock the dough back and turn out onto a floured work surface. Add the softened lard and knead into the bread dough along with the crushed caraway seeds. Once the lard and seeds have been evenly incorporated, divide the dough into 40g portions.
Shape these into oval buns and arrange on baking trays. Set aside to rise again for about 40 minutes, or until doubled in volume.
Glaze the tops of both loaves with milk and scatter over some granulated sugar. Transfer to an oven pre-heated to 220°C and bake for about 20 to 25 minutes, or until cooked through and golden (when ready, the base of the loaf will sound hollow when rapped. Serve slightly warm.

(www.celtnet.org.uk)

18. 4. 15

Dearest Mother,

A Hawkhead cake arrived to-day for which many thanks. I haven't begun it yet though I've had a nibble at the Gingerbread. A parcel came from Powolony's two days ago with two boxes of sweets and a dozen buns which were very good. Was that yours or do you think it was Mrs Mayo's? I wish people would put their names on the things because I don't want not to thank them.

Have you got the new cottage yet? I'm sorry in a way to leave the other, but the extra room and the garden and view will make an enormous difference. You must take that £1.14.0 of the Times' towards getting it nice. It's no good to me here, and I can't think of a better way of spending it. Will you, please? You must let me know too if it wants much doing to it, because I'm getting piles & spending nothing. The cottage will be a splendid investment.

The weather is keeping good and we've only had one wet night this week. You can have no idea what a difference stars and a clear sky make when there is no moon. On a black night you don't get a third of the work done. Now, however, we're beginning to get a moon again.

I did stables this morning. There wasn't a cloud and for once I really enjoyed having got up early. After breakfast I went for a ride. My horse is rather a slug and tries to shy at anything along the side of the road. He hasn't, however, sufficient energy to get really excited about them. Still I enjoyed the run, for it was an absolutely perfect morning.

I believe they had quite a successful little shew somewhere north last night – blew up a German trench and rushed it. I haven't heard anything very definite yet though we heard a little of the noise in the distance. *Have* you seen French's comments on our show! I'm afraid he can't have seen my letter!

If you don't call that kitten "Wiggs" I shall run away to sea, join the Turkish navy, defend the Dardanelles & become Emperor of Smyrna. I mean it.

Your loving
J.S.

J. S Baines

(IWM Q27633)

A rare air-to-air photograph showing a Royal Flying Corps BE.2C aircraft in flight over trench lines in the Grand Bois area. The aircraft has an aerial camera mounted on its starboard side below the pilot's cockpit. The BE.2C was an ideal photographic platform because of its stability in flight. However it was slow and unmaneouverable, rendering it vulnerable to German attack. At this time, British reconnaissance aircraft were accompanied by at least three fighters on missions over the Western Front and were also forced to carry out their mission at greater altitude.

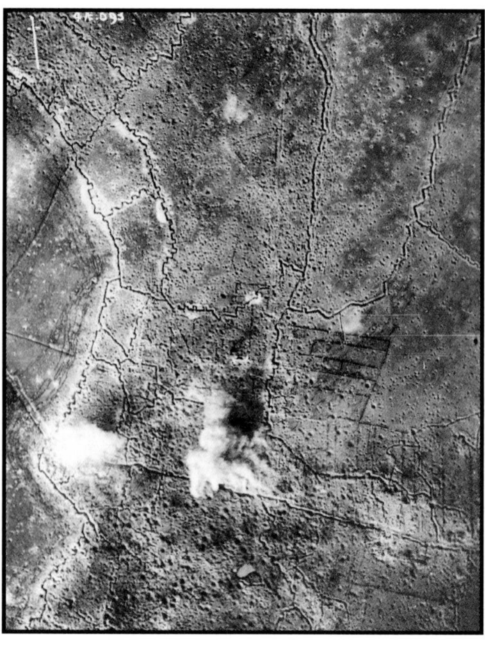

German front line and support trenches at Thiepval village , while undergoing bombardment by British artillery 25/9/15.

(IWM Q63740)

26. 4. 15

Dearest Honor,
Thanks for your nice Lakey letter which took me away for a minute to a place which isn't flat. Here the streams don't run down the paths – they sit there. There's just one stream I know which really flows. Its between steep banks and there's a plank pathway right down the middle of it for about half a mile. Except on dark nights its as good a communication trench as you could find.

You might ask Planchette how long were going to sit here but I suppose she'ld say till late in life.

I've pretty well finished my map and I've got a very good aeroplane photograph less than a week old to help me to put the last few touches on. I'd got our line practically right but there are one of two extra German saps which I hadn't got in before.

I don't see anything wrong in the prophecy. If you're married at 23 you'll still I hope be engaged to him at 24!

The toffee was delicious. I'm awfully glad you didn't eat it all before it got posted which is certainly what I should have done myself. The violets too were very nice to have.

I'm so sorry about Aunt Flo. I wrote to her yesterday. I hope Mother will have found her better. I had a letter from Aunt Hilda mentioning the illnesses of all the family. We do seem to be a bit run down, don't we?

Everything is still quiet here and even of the battle at Wipers we get most of the news from the papers. I suppose we shall hear something soon of the Turkish campaign. That ought to liven things up a bit.

With love to the Lady & to Mother when she comes back.

Your loving brother,
John

This has been rather a dull letter but somehow to-night mine doesn't seem to be the pen of a ready writer.
J. S. Baines.

Those Tubular Trenches

"Is this right for 'eadquarters?"
"Yes, change at Oxford Circus"

(2015 Estate of Barbara Bruce Littlejohn)

Theatrical entertainment (Follies and Fancies)

Entertainment was arranged for the troops behind the lines at rest camp sites and central depot. Each division would audition for musicians, singers, actors and even female impersonators to make up a concert troupe. Many of these men would have been entertainers of some sort before they enlisted, so their talents were much sought after. Concerts always contained a lot of singing, both rowdy and sentimental, and having a good laugh at humorous sketches released tension. As units within one division moved to another, the make-up of the troupe would change and there was a certain amount of good-natured competition between divisions regarding the superior quality of their particular troupe at any one time.

2. 5. 15

Dearest Mother,

The Powolony parcel came two days ago and was very good. I wonder if sometimes you could send me out some Eiffel Tower Lemonade or something of the kind as one gets very thirsty in the hot weather. It's been cooler as a matter of fact for the last few days and to-day is trying to rain, but most of last week was delightfully summery.

I've again changed my brigade and am back with the one where we made the big communication trenches (known as Park Row and Shaftesbury Avenue). There's a branch out of Park Row called College Green. They're official names, painted up at the ends, not just jokes.

Playfair and I are running the shew on our own. One of us goes round to the Brigade each morning and settles what work & materials are needed. It's much more fun than just being told what to do.

We're on a kind of support line just behind the firing line, and it's going to be fairly interesting I think.

As usual there's nothing new to say. The Follies and the Fancies have gone away but we've got a Cinema instead. I've not been to it yet but I hear it isn't bad.

I've been getting one or two quite nice rides lately. Unfortunately one has to walk a fairly long way before getting a decent place for a canter because the roads here are beastly and you can't trot on them. They're what's called pavée which means the sort of thing some of the Leeds streets are – beastly stone sets.

I've just finished the Inviolable Sanctuary. I had read it before but it stands re-reading as all his things do.

I hear the French did well yesterday at Ypres but you'll have seen that by this time in the papers. They're at it hard at the present moment to judge by the sound.

With love to the Lakes.

Your loving,

J. S.

(IWM Q1048)

Royal Engineers with a pontoon.

(IWM Q6632)

British horse-drawn transport wagon crossing a pontoon bridge.

5. 5. 15

Dearest Honor,
I had tea to-day with the Leeds Rifles. They are just to the right of our division and so I rode over to their billets. They have been in the trenches in one or two places under instruction and now are going in properly to-morrow night. I saw Graham chiefly and also congratulated Hartopp. Edwin Roberts was there and Dell Bousfield who is Graham's Coy. commander. I found out yesterday where they were, as I had to go over quite near them to see about a pontoon bridge. I'd heard that the West Riding Division were coming there and I asked about them.

I told you I'd gone to a new brigade. Well I've changed again without even ever having taken my section out there. I don't know how long we're with this one for. It's not the old original one, but the other one I was with before for a few days.

It began raining just as I was saying goodbye to Graham and I got soaked coming home. Its an awful nuisance 'cause I'm going out to-night and it'll be pitch dark. I've got 250 yards of barbed wire to do (not in the front line) and on a light night it wouldn't take long. Now they'll all tie 'emselves up in it horribly & won't be able to see to hit it in the posts.

I'm sorry this is short but I've only been in a little & I've got to go & have dinner now.

With love to all.

Your loving brother,
John.

16.5.15

Dearest Mother,
There's again nothing much for me to write about. By the way I haven't had a letter from you for some time I wonder if one got lost.

I'm still working in the same place but mostly by day – one night in four only. Its an interesting bit of line but I can't tell you much about it.

I hear again to-day that we've done well south. There's been no actual fighting here, only "frightfulness" i.e. making a noise to frighten the enemy. Sometimes its quite successful.

Are they doing all you want in the cottage? I wish I could be there for a minute to see it.

Internment of German civilians

If 'Schoody' was German then it is most likely that he was interned. At the start of the war all foreigners living in Britain had to register at their local police station, as did any British women married to foreigners. After the sinking of the Lusitania by the Germans in May 1915 anti-German feelings were so strong that the government moved all German civilian men of fighting age (18–50) into internment camps, as much for their own safety as anything else. Almost the whole congregation of one German Evangelical Church in Birmingham, including their pastor, was sent to a camp on the Isle of Man.

Whereas military prisoners of war were expected to work on the land, civilians were not expected to work at all and life was very boring for them in the camps. A lot of the men turned to education to pass the time.

When the camps closed at the end of 1919 the internees were deported to their home nations, often most unwillingly if they had British wives and had been well settled in Britain pre-war.

Move to Ypres

By the time John wrote home on 6th June the whole of 6th Division, including 12th Field Company, had redeployed to the Ypres Salient. We know from the 12th Field Company war diary that the unit marched from Nieppe to Bailleul on 28th May; then on to Winterhoer on 30th May; and then to one mile north west of Ypres on 31st May. The move is also recorded in the Division's war history as follows:

'On the 27th May 1915 began the relief of the Division by the 27th Division, and on the following days its move northwards to join the newly formed VI Corps. On the night of the 31st May/lst June the Division took over its new front in the Ypres Salient, commencing its long tour in that unsavoury region, and trench casualties almost doubled immediately.

It continued in the Salient up to the end of July 1916, with three periods of test, each of about a month's duration: the first spent in the neighbourhood of Houtkerque and Poperinghe, in November and December 1915; the second in the Houtkerque-Wormhoudt area, with one brigade at a time back at Calais from mid-March to mid-April 1916; and the third again in the Houtkerque-Wormhoudt area from mid- June to mid-July 1916'.

If you get the Daily Mail for Saturday 15th you will see some photos of parts I've worked on or near. The "Rhine" bends round & cuts our trench again. I didn't do the bridge you see there but I did one like it at the other place. I may have mentioned the farm that picture came from. It's the one where they have a piano & where their cat got shot.

I wish they'ld push in K's army now. We'ld be on trek again soon if we'd a few more men to break the line with. I dare say it won't be very long now . Everyone's fed up with the Deutschers. Will Schoody be interned? I suppose not. It'ld be rather bad luck on them.

We've got a Cinema here now. Our two theatrical companies left us – one permanently and the other on tour. Tomorrow however, "having successfully terminated its provincial tour", as its posters say, its returning with "new songs, new dresses, new theatre".

We had Neville Talbot to cricket & dinner last night. He's a very good fellow. I wasn't able to hear his sermon this morning as I had to go out. We're not getting all our Sundays off now but day work isn't bad. I got quite a good lunch to-day after I'd finished my own.

With love to Honor and remembrances to Coniston Old Man.

Your loving,

J.S.

This looks a most awful scrawl but I've been trying hard to think of something to say & there's nothing at all.

6 Jun 15

My dearest Honor,

Wotcher bin a doin' of? Here I am with trenches to fall into in the dark, barbed wire to get tied up in, shell-holes to drop into, smells to fly from and every other imaginable joy and yet I don't fall off my bicycle – or hardly ever. Not coming down hills anyway because there aren't any. You silly old thing. I'm glad though that you're not knocked up badly but it was sickening for you anyway. I suppose that your next design will be a blue and gold reproduction of the stars you saw. You can use the lace for bandages.

We're not back in our old billet, but are in huts for the time being. I believe however that we shall be able to be "inmates" again in a few days. The huts aren't at all bad though they're less luxurious. The only real trouble is that the butter runs horribly and the meat once came up

(Harrods Ltd)

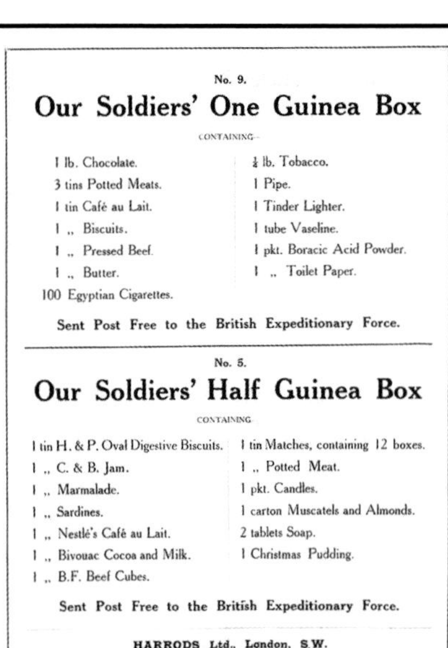

No. 9.

Our Soldiers' One Guinea Box

CONTAINING

1 lb. Chocolate.
3 tins Potted Meats.
1 tin Café au Lait.
1 „ Biscuits.
1 „ Pressed Beef.
1 „ Butter.
100 Egyptian Cigarettes.
¼ lb. Tobacco.
1 Pipe.
1 Tinder Lighter.
1 tube Vaseline.
1 pkt. Boracic Acid Powder.
1 „ Toilet Paper.

Sent Post Free to the British Expeditionary Force.

No. 5.

Our Soldiers' Half Guinea Box

CONTAINING

1 tin H. & P. Oval Digestive Biscuits.
1 „ C. & B. Jam.
1 „ Marmalade.
1 „ Sardines.
1 „ Nestlé's Café au Lait.
1 „ Bivouac Cocoa and Milk.
1 „ B.F. Beef Cubes.
1 tin Matches, containing 12 boxes.
1 „ Potted Meat.
1 pkt. Candles.
1 carton Muscatels and Almonds.
2 tablets Soap.
1 Christmas Pudding.

Sent Post Free to the British Expeditionary Force.

HARRODS Ltd., London, S.W.

2

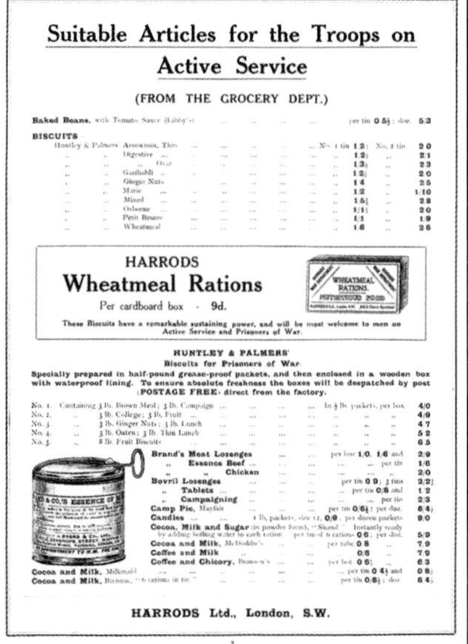

Suitable Articles for the Troops on Active Service

(FROM THE GROCERY DEPT.)

Baked Beans, with Tomato Sauce (Libby's) ... per tin 0 5½ ; doz. 5 3

BISCUITS

Huntley & Palmers' Arrowroot, Thin	No. 1 tin 1 2	No. 2 tin	2 0
„ „ Digestive	1 2½	„	2 1
„ „ „ Oval	1 3½	„	2 3
„ „ Garibaldi	1 2½	„	2 0
„ „ Ginger Nuts	1 4	„	2 5
„ „ Marie	1 2	„	1/10
„ „ Mixed	1 5½	„	2 8
„ „ Osborne	1/1½	„	2 0
„ „ Petit Beurre	1/1	„	1 9
„ „ Wheatmeal	1 6	„	2 6

HARRODS
Wheatmeal Rations
Per cardboard box - 9d.

These Biscuits have a remarkable sustaining power, and will be most welcome to men on Active Service and Prisoners of War.

HUNTLEY & PALMERS'
Biscuits for Prisoners of War.

Specially prepared in half-pound grease-proof packets, and then enclosed in a wooden box with waterproof lining. To ensure absolute freshness the boxes will be despatched by post (POSTAGE FREE) direct from the factory.

No. 1. Containing 3 lb. Brown Meal ; 3 lb. Campaign	In ½ lb. packets, per box	4/0
No. 2. „ 3 lb. College ; 3 lb. Fruit	„ „ „	4/9
No. 3. „ 3 lb. Ginger Nuts ; 3 lb. Lunch	„ „ „	4 7
No. 4. „ 3 lb. Oaten ; 3 lb. Thin Lunch	„ „ „	5 2
No. 5. „ 8 lb. Fruit Biscuits	„ „ „	6 5
Brand's Meat Lozenges	per box 1/0, 1/6 and	2/9
„ **Essence Beef**	per tin	1/6
„ „ **Chicken**		2/0
Bovril Lozenges	per tin 0 9 ; 3 tins	2/2½
„ **Tablets**	per tin 0/8 and	1 2
„ **Campaigning**	per tin	2/3
Camp Pie, Mayfair	per tin 0/6½ ; per doz.	6/4½
Candles	1 lb. packets, size 12, 0/9 . per dozen packets	9/0
Cocoa, Milk and Sugar (in powder form), "Shand" Instantly ready by adding boiling water to each ration	per tin of 6 rations 0 6 ; per doz.	5/9
Cocoa and Milk, McDoddie's	per tube 0 8 „	7/9
Coffee and Milk	0/8 „	7/9
Coffee and Chicory, Branson's	per bot. 0 6½ „	6 3
Cocoa and Milk, Milkmaid	per tin 0 4½ and	0 8½
Cocoa and Milk, Bivouac, "6 rations in tin"	per tin 0/6½ ; doz.	6 4½

HARRODS Ltd., London, S.W.

3

extremely gamey. Still there's not much to grumble at in getting fresh meat every day on active service. It's only once that the heat has overcome it.

I get a cold bath every morning. After I've finished washing in my canvas bucket I get on the grass and pour it over myself. One wouldn't do that before as there were female caretakers about.

My valise has some flax under it. It's not as good as ordinary straw but now that I'm wearing the lumps into the right places it's not so bad. Capt Riall and Guy Stockdale are in the next hut to mine. It's rather funny the way I've kept coming across them lately. Douglas Stott is sick, but will probably be back again soon. There's a fellow here who was one of the Pip-Toc instructors at the Shop and a jolly good fellow. He's commanding a company now. He's only an acting Captain now but will get the rank soon. It's quick promotion. He was gazetted some time after me but he's a first-class officer and deserves it. Most of these Sergeants and Sergeant-Majors do make extremely good officers.

I haven't yet fully designed the new coal-house. I must wait till I've examined the site and seen what timber Coward can produce. There won't be the least difficulty in running up a shed for it. I shall have to get a few tools but they'll be ones that its always good to have about.

I'm going to sleep now.

Your loving brother,
J.S.

I wonder if you could send me another writing pad.
Any old thing of Irwins will do.
Do you think there's anyone in Coniston who could pack eggs. We pay 1½d each for them here and a proportion are bad. Probably it wouldn't be much more expensive to have them sent out. I'd order a dozen a day for the Mess if I could get them. I wonder if Harrods could be trusted to send fresh ones.
J.S. Baines

Bruce Bairnsfather
Dear
"At present we are staying at a farm . . . ."

(2015 Estate of Barbara Bruce Littlejohn)

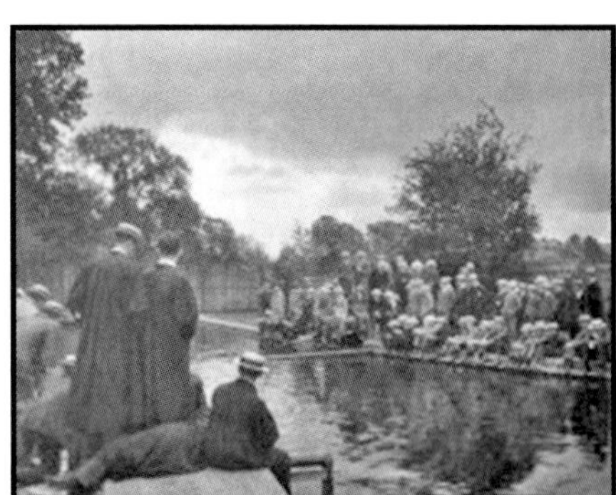

(Winchester College Archives)

Gunners Hole,
the College swimming pool.

(Winchester College Archives)

School Shop, at the junction of
College and Kingsgate Streets.

10.6.15

Dearest Mother,

We have just moved out of our huts into another billet. It is quite a comfortable one, has good water for the horses and has no civilians in it, though it has all their furniture, crockery, linen etc. There's a cat too whom we've called Gaby. She was rather shy at first and then became wonderfully affectionate even before she'd had any milk. She is swelling visibly.

It's extraordinary how these silly beasts stick to their homes. You get them hanging on at places which are just a mass of charred ruins – not wild ones but pets who come and rub themselves up against you and purr. They'll let you do what you like with them until you try to take them away. Heaven alone knows what they live on.

Gaby, however, is fairly fortunate because her house is now inhabited again. She's almost a kitten and won't be so bad when she filled out a little. A dog came and called on us this afternoon. She had him out again in no time.

So far we haven't got a piano but we are negotiating with a Curé with a view to getting his.

Tangles is back here again. His company left this division some time ago but now his division are back resting and he's up here working on some rear line or other as he knows the country. He got five days leave a short time ago, lucky fellow. Still, you don't get leave without being in a pretty beastly hole first and I think that division had enough to go on with for a time up north.

The Deutschers haven't attacked anywhere for a long time. As soon as we'd all got respirators their tails went between their legs with a click.

I ran across Medley the other day. He was in my Shop my last term in college. So was F.A.F. Baines. I was awfully sorry to see that he'd been killed the other day. So was Crawhall. I missed his name but Medley told me. I also saw Beart, who used to swim against me. We had the following conversation (both in shirt-sleeves and melting in the shade)

– I wouldn't mind Gunners Hole now.

– God! Wouldn't it be topping. And then the longest lime-juice that ever was, at School Shop.

– And ices, strawberry and chocolate.

– And iced coffee.

Use of bicycles in World War 1

During World War I, cycle-mounted infantry, scouts, messengers and ambulance carriers were extensively used by all combatants.

Italy used bicycles with the Bersaglieri (light infantry units) until the end of the war.

German Army Jäger (light infantry) battalions each had a bicycle company at the outbreak of the war, and additional companies were raised during the war bringing the total to 80 companies, a number of which were formed into eight Radfahr-Bataillonen (bicycle battalions).

The British Army had cyclist companies in its divisions, and later a whole division became The Cyclist Division.

Black & White is a blended Scotch whisky. London-based James Buchanan created the brand in the 19th century and it was originally called House of Commons. On his way back from a dog show, around 1890, James conceived the idea of a label depicting a black Scottish terrier and a white West Highland terrier. Black & White soon became the nickname for the whisky and was eventually adopted as the official brand name.

I shouldn't mind a plunge in the Lake now and again these days. I should have to stay down there, for it is far too hot to walk back up the hill again. I'm glad Lisbeth was able to come up to you again. Please give her my love and Honor too.

Your loving,
JS.

20.6.15

My dearest Honor,
Thanks ever so much for your splendid parcel and the cream. One end of the tin had got squashed on the way, but that only affected a very little of it.

I had rather a busy birthday. When I got home in the small hours I found some letters and your cream. I didn't get up till lunch and then I was out off on a bike till dinner. I expected to have the evening in but I had to gulp down my food & go out again to tape out a new trench in front of the line. I had a bike, however, and so got home before midnight in time to get your parcel, still on my birthday.

I expect that my leave will be June 30th till July 4th. I expect I shall be able to get away in time to catch the afternoon boat on the 29th. In that case I can reach Coniston at 9:25 a.m. on the 30th if the trains are still as they used to be. I shall have to leave Victoria at 2 p.m. on the 4th. I'm afraid that will mean leaving on the night of the 3rd. You bet I'm looking forward to it all some.

I managed to get some strawberries yesterday afternoon in the intervals of running about. I'm afraid that seven of the eggs got broken so that with the postage and everything it will hardly be worth having them sent out. Thank you very much, however, for those that did come. They were very good.

I'm much looking forward to seeing the new cottage. I shall be too early to be in it. I'm not sure, however, that I shan't prefer being in the old one. This is only a sort of scribble, but now that I'll so soon be home letters seem silly.

Your loving brother,
John

PS Please get a bottle of Black & White & some syphons. I haven't had a whisky & soda for months.

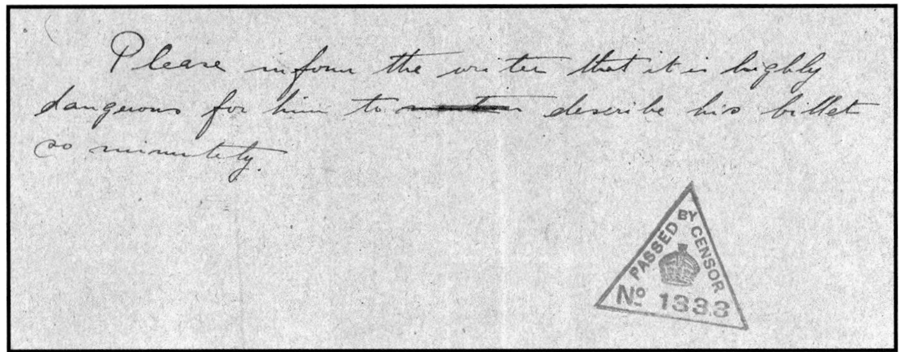
Please inform the writer that it is highly dangerous for him to ~~mention~~ describe his billet so minutely.

PASSED BY CENSOR
No 1333

Censor's note enclosed in letter

The contrast between Gunners and Sappers

Gunners are peculiar people. When professionally engaged, no men could be more retiring. They screen their operations from the public gaze with the utmost severity, shrouding batteries in screens of foliage and other rustic disguises. If a layman strays anywhere near one of these arboreal retreats, a gunner thrusts out a visage inflamed with righteous wrath, and curses him for giving his position away. But in his hours of relaxation the gunner is a different being. He billets himself in a house with plenty of windows: he illuminates all these by night, and hangs washing therefrom by day. When inclined for exercise, he plays football upon an open space labelled – Not to be used by troops during daylight. Therefore, despite his technical excellence and superb courage, he is an uncomfortable neighbour for establishments like Hush Hall *[N.B. Hush Hall is what Ian Hay calls Brigade HQ].*

In this respect he offers a curious contrast to the Sapper. Off duty, the Sapper is the most unobtrusive of men – a cave-man, in fact. He burrows deep into the earth or the side of a hill, and having secured the roof of this cavern against direct hits by ingenious contrivances of his own manufacture, constructs a suite of furniture of a solid and enduring pattern, and lives the life of a comfortable recluse. But when engaged in the pursuit of his calling, the Sapper is the least retiring of men. The immemorial tradition of the great Corps to which he belongs has ordained that no fire, however fierce, must be allowed to interfere with a Sapper in the execution of his duty. This rule is usually interpreted by the Sapper to mean that you must not perform your allotted task under cover when it is possible to do so under fire. To this is added, as a rider, that in the absence of an adequate supply of fire, you must draw fire. So the sapper walks cheerfully about on the tops of parapets, hugging large and conspicuous pieces of timber, or clashing together sheets of corrugated iron, as happy as a king.

(Extract from Carrying on after the First Hundred Thousand *by Ian Hay 1917)*

Envelope (EXAMINED BY BASE CENSOR)

1 July 15

Dearest Mother,
Me voiçi enhammock with the sun shining on me. I wish you could see our present quarters. We are in dug-outs in our advanced billet and it's simply topping …

(CENSORED – *some crossed through and the whole bottom half of the page cut out. This also cuts out the part of the letter written on the other side*)

… opening onto this are the two officers dug-outs and the mess. These are cut into the bank at the back & have front and side walls of sandbags and a strong roof covered with earth and planted with flowers . The mess …

(CENSORED … *other side of cut out page*)

… glass doors. The dug-outs are named "Whizz" and "Bang" & after them comes the Mess. Mine is Bang. It's about 7 feet square, 5 to 7 feet high, has a bed, table, chair, carpet, 8-day chiming clock & a large mirror. The walls are covered with green waterproof canvas.

I shall be here till I go on leave. We keep two sections here and two in our back billet with the headquarters section and horses. I only wish I could be always here for the difference, after a long night, between half an hour through fields and an hour and a half over cobbles is enormous.

I hope to get home by that first train on the 8th.

With love to Honor

Your loving

J.S.

CENSOR'S NOTE Please inform the writer that it is highly dangerous for him to describe his billet so minutely.

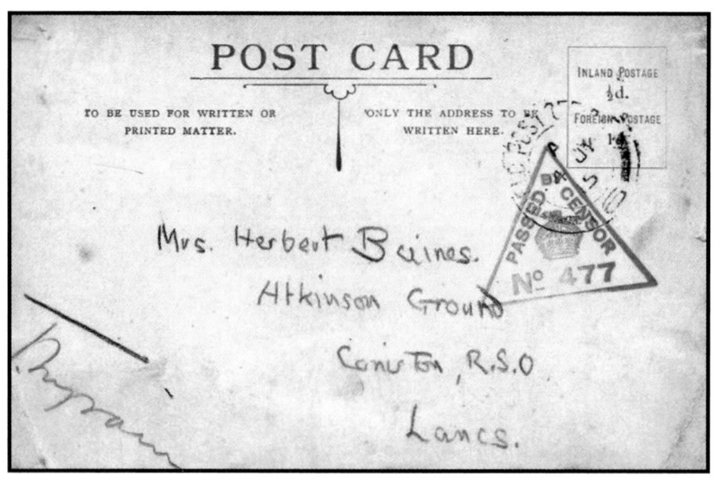

POST CARD

TO BE USED FOR WRITTEN OR PRINTED MATTER.

ONLY THE ADDRESS TO BE WRITTEN HERE.

INLAND POSTAGE ½d.
FOREIGN POSTAGE 1d.

PASSED BY CENSOR
No 477

Mrs. Herbert Baines.
Atkinson Ground
Coniston, R.S.O
Lancs.

2.7.15.

Half an hour ago a beastly Deutscher put a small hole in my right hand. The M.O. is very happy about it. It'll be quite a short affair. I'm now enjoying whisky, cake & a cigarette.

S.D.

I have just done him up. He has a clean bullet wound through the palm of the right hand. He will have perfect use of his hand in a very [illegible] time. T.J.

POSTCARD
2.7.15

Half an hour ago I beastly Deutscher put a small hole in my right hand. The M.O. is very happy about it. It'll be quite a short affair. I'm now enjoying whisky, cake & a cigarette.

J.S

(post script by MO)
I have just done him up. He has a clean bullet wound through the palm of the right hand. He will have perfect use of his hand in a very short time.

T.J.

3.7.15

Dearest Mother,
I expect y. have now got the p.c. I sent off last night, saying that I had got a gentlemanly scratch on the right hand. Hence the awkward writing. I got it just at the right time. I'd brought up my section and carrying party to just behind the trench with my pickets & coils of wire & I went out with my sergeant to shew him where to wire. I'd just finished explaining to him & was telling the officer of the covering party where I'd be when the thing hit me. I got a Field Dressing on and walked down to the Dressing Station whence I got a car to the Field Ambulance. I came on here in a car this morning & may get a train to Boulogne this afternoon. I'll send you my address when I get to Town. I hope to be up in the Lakes in a fortnight & have nothing to complain of.

Love to Honor.

J.S.

JS Baines

Medical Services

(IWM Q1348)

A soldier wounded in the trenches would first be taken to a front line aid post for rudimentary treatment. These were manned by a unit Medical Officer and sited at regular intervals along a line of trenches.

Relays of stretcher bearers and men trained in first aid would then take the wounded back, along designated evacuation routes, to the nearest Field Ambulance unit. Those who were lightly wounded were quickly treated and returned to their unit, but the more seriously wounded received emergency treatment in an Advanced Dressing Station, before being moved several miles further back to a Casualty Clearing Station. Transport from a Field Ambulance unit to a Casualty Clearing Station took various forms – stretcher bearers on foot, horse drawn wagon, motor vehicle (ambulance or lorry) or light railway on carts pulled by horses.

Casualty Clearing Stations were often tented camps, a few miles behind the lines and usually on a railway line. They were well staffed and could undertake surgery, including amputations. Apart from looking after men wounded at the front, the Casualty Clearing Stations also cared for soldiers suffering other illness or infection such as venereal disease and trench foot.

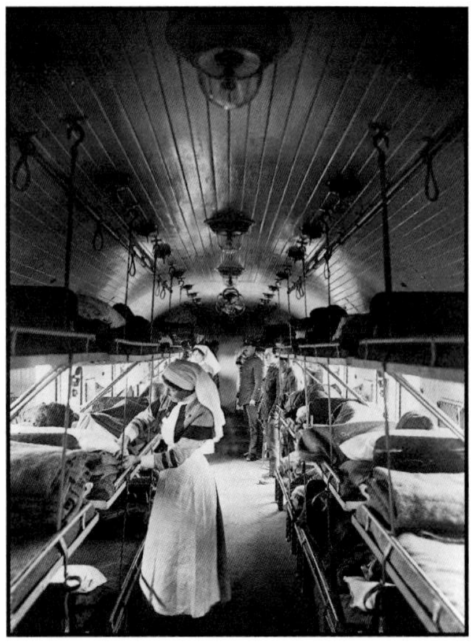

(IWM Q8749)

From the Casualty Clearing Station a wounded man would be taken by specially equipped train, either to a Base Hospital in France or directly to a channel port, usually Boulogne, to be transferred onto a ship and taken home to England. These hospital trains were specially marked as such to protect them from enemy attack and, typically, each one had aboard three medical officers and four nurses. They had different compartments for 'lying down' patients and 'walking wounded'; they had electric light and steam heaters to keep their patients warm and some of the Red Cross hospital trains had operating theatres.

Above right: Transporting wounded by horse-drawn light railway 1916.
Above left: British hospital train.

No 2 Red X Hospital
Rouen

4.7.15
Sunday

Dearest Mother,

Here we are again! I'm at Rouen and the doctor has promised me the next boat home – probably on Tuesday, perhaps to-morrow.

As I told you I was sent back in a car to the Field Ambulance where I was antitetanussed and given a bed. Before I left, at 10, the Major (he's really a Lt-Col now) came along to see how well I was & to say Goodbye. My kit also arrived and so I went off contented in another car to the Clearing Station whence in the afternoon I was "evacuated" by Queen Mary's Hospital Train. It's a lovely train – three layers of beds each side all the way down, perfect springs and the white paint of the thing making it more like a ship than a train. It was a bit hot with the sun full on it in spite of the electric fans but they did us very well. I was particularly proud of my success in eating a boiled egg with one hand. I had a little help now and again, but the main work was my own. We didn't get into Rouen till 1 o'clock to-day, but then we came straight up here. It's a college for priests turned into an officers' hospital.

My wound is quite the right kind – clean through and broke nothing. A rifle bullet is always much the best thing to have. It makes quite a small hole and it goes so fast that it automatically cauterises the wound by the heat its got going through the air.

Would you please forward this & my last letter to Elisabeth. I've written to her but life isn't long enough to write all these circumstantial details twice.

Love to Honor,

Your loving

J.S.

27 Grosvenor Square, Belgravia, London W1
Robert Fleming Hospital for Officers

At the beginning of World War 1, when casualties began coming back from the front in large numbers, there was not enough room in existing military hospitals to accommodate them all. A large number of auxiliary hospitals were set up all over the country, some in large buildings such as town halls and many in smaller private houses, cottages, garages even stables. Some of these auxiliary hospitals could deal with bed patients, needing considerable nursing, while others cared for the 'walking wounded' and convalescents. John must have been in the latter category.

Robert Fleming and his wife Kate provided an auxiliary hospital for convalescent officers at their London home, 27 Grosvenor Square. It had 14 beds. Auxiliary hospitals were not initially paid very much for occupied beds and nothing at all for unoccupied beds. This was probably not something which worried a wealthy financier such as Robert Fleming unduly.

Robert Fleming was born in 1845, the son of a shopkeeper in Dundee. He worked in a local textile firm where he learned about investment procedure and by 1873 was knowledgeable enough to launch one of the first Scottish investment trusts, Scottish American Investment Trust, and then to form his own investment bank, Robert Fleming & Co. In 1909 the headquarters of the bank moved to London and Robert became widely respected as an international financier in America as well as at home. Robert and Kate had two sons Vincent (father of Ian Fleming, author of James Bond novels) who was killed in France in 1917 and Philip, and a daughter, Dorothy, referred to by John as Miss Fleming.

The house which stood at No 27 Grosvenor Square no longer exists. It was on the west side of the square, which is now occupied by the American Embassy built in 1960.

('Collage' database: 131459)

27, Grosvenor Square. First floor dance hall and billiard room. London Metropolitan Archives, City of London.

27, Grosvenor Square

Telephone.
Mayfair 3475

6.7.15

Dearest Mother,
I left Rouen yesterday morning and had a topping run down the Seine and across. We saw the coast of Blighty just after dinner. They "unloaded" us this morning and tacked the Hospital van onto the end of the 11 o'c Waterloo express & I got here with another fellow in time for lunch.

This is a topping house – a private one with one floor turned into a hospital for Officers. There are two very jolly wards, and a sitting room and the ball-room for us to play about in. There are three trained nurses helped by Miss Fleming & two others (its Mrs Fleming's house). I shall see the doctor to-morrow and shall then know how long I shall be here. It won't be v. long.

You've not got to be in the least worried about me. I've got the cushiest one possible. A little either way & it might have hurt a bone but as it was it just slipped through. My first & second fingers are little stiff, but only temporarily and only as is to be expected. It went in about an inch behind my knuckles and came out of my palm near the heel of my hand.

I'm going to let Aunt Letty know I'm here as we can see people from 2.30–4.30. As a matter of fact I shall probably be allowed out most of the day.

It's hardly worth your while to trouble to come down & see me because I shall soon be up in the Lakes. If you did come, however, for a couple of days I could take you to a theatre or two & we might see a few things. Try, however, to give me time to get some clothes. I can get hat, puttees, boots, a cane and gloves to-morrow and be measured for the rest. Hawke can probably do them pretty quickly.

Love to Honor,

Your loving,

J.S.

Mining

Although we do not know the location of this incident, it seems clear that John was an observer, probably with his CRE, not an active participant.

The complex two-stage mine operation, so graphically described, must have been planned in great detail to achieve the required deception. Almost certainly the first 'baby mine' would have been planted by combat engineers working by night in no man's land. Meanwhile the 'enormous charge of guncotton' must have been the work of sappers in a Tunnelling Company.

These companies had been formed early in 1915 and were largely made up of men who had been miners in civilian life. Tunnels would be constructed from our front line trenches out beneath no-man's land. At serious risk of being buried alive, drowning, suffocation and gas poisoning, these brave men prepared the mines and packed them with explosives. The explosions would be designed to destroy enemy trenches, or to create large craters which would then be occupied and fortified as forward positions in no man's land.

(IWM Q88093)

German stormtroopers waiting in a mine crater for the signal to attack.

The Germans also engaged in these operations, so the danger of detection from the opposing tunnellers was ever-present. Work had to be carried out silently, and great emphasis was placed on listening for enemy mining, with highly trained listeners using sensors designed for the specific purpose.

Bantams

Two new battalions were formed in November 1914 specifically to take men under the height of 5ft 3in (160cm) which was the standard requirement of the army at the time. They were called Bantam battalions, a name probably taken from the category of bantamweight used in boxing. Recruits were between the heights of 4ft 10in (147cm) and 5ft 3in (160cm). Recruiting took place in mainly industrial and mining areas where there were large numbers of short men used to hard physical work. They fought hard alongside other infantry battalions.

After being evacuated to England, there are no letters from John for four months. He spent the time recovering from his wound and in staff training at Bulford, after which he returned to France in a completely different role, as Adjutant on the Chief Royal Engineer's (CRE) staff. It must have been at this time that he became engaged to be married to Elisabeth Wicksteed.

23.11.15

My dearest Honor,
I'm in quite a nice billet these days with some very decent French people. At present we have just our four in the mess but we hope soon to join up with the Signallers.

I went round part of our front line yesterday. There was one quite interesting bit going through a mine crater which we made a day or two ago.

It was a low and subtle mine. We had an enormous charge of guncotton which would wreck everything for distance round – all the German mines would be blown in but we didn't want them to occupy the crater. So we had a baby mine above which went off and the German bombers occupied the crater. Our bombers gave them enough attention to draw plenty of Huns in and then retired. There were about 50 of them there when the big mine underneath was let off. One of the 50 jolly nearly killed a man 200 yards behind our line. I don't know where the others went.

Give Ernest and Lydia my love when you see them. I suppose as he's in the Bantams he won't have got very much leave for being married and so they'll have quite a short honeymoon. Will he be able to get a house for her near his station? Several of our crowd had their wives at Amesbury which is as close as they could get to Bulford and I used to have tea with Mrs Jackson quite often. Jackson is a junior Captain who did 9 months in the Cameroons & was returned sick in July. He wired to his wife from Madeira & she had the Banns already going strong when he landed. With two months sick leave to follow they had quite a nice honeymoon. I used to envy him his luck a good deal when he used to be able to trot down to her at all sorts of times. He's about 9 years senior to me but as we were the only two fairly junior Regulars we came together a good deal.

Wire Obstacles

Barbed wire obstacles in no man's land were used throughout the war, by both sides, as their main form of defence. These were created in many different ways, including: low wire entanglements, using single strands of barbed wire at around knee level; apron fences, making fences of the barbed wire in varying complexity; and concertinas, large rolls of barbed wire stretched out to make the obstacle. Often these different forms of wiring were combined in elaborate configurations. In all cases, pickets of varying lengths were required to support the wire.

The design of new wire obstacles was often the responsibility of the Sappers (see John's letter), as was their construction, assisted by infantry working parties. Once in place, the obstacles were frequently damaged by enemy artillery shelling, so constant repairs and upgrading were necessary. This was highly dangerous work in no man's land, invariably carried out at night.

Whilst our own wire obstacles and those of the enemy were designed for defensive protection, they also had to be taken into account when sending out reconnaissance patrols and forward listening posts, and recovering our wounded from no man's land. Whenever possible, the wire had to be silently cut – another highly dangerous job, as the risk of being seen or heard was high. However, such preparations were rarely possible ahead of major offensive operations launched across no man's land from our forward trenches, because of the wide frontages involved. In these cases, artillery barrages were relied on to destroy the wire obstacles just before the assault. In the event, they often made the situation worse for the infantryman as they threw the barbed wire into an even more tangled and impenetrable mess.

Major-General (addressing the men before practising an attack behind the lines). "I want you to understand that there is a difference between a rehearsal and the real thing. There are three essential differences: First, the absence of the enemy. Now *(turning to the Regimental Sergeant-Major)* what is the second difference?"

Sergeant-Major. "The absence of the General, Sir."

(Punch)

I'm glad you had a good time in Edinburgh. Did you see submarines or bombs or anything interesting?

How's the school of art going? Are you making large numbers of pictures for next year's academy.

With love to Mother

Your loving brother,

J.S.

Tuesday 14th Dec 1915

Dearest Mother,

I've been very bad at writing lately but I've had a pretty strenuous time. We're in "rest" now (vide this week's Punch) and though there is a good deal to do its not quite so bad. Some days last week I was in my office from 8:30 a.m. till 9:30 p.m. with half an hour after lunch at 3 o'clock – and I came out with the guileless idea that an Adjutant had nothing to do. It's all jolly interesting however and is a wonderfully valuable experience.

I've had a better time for the last day or two & I've got quite an interesting little job on. The other day the Staff told the C.R.E. that they wanted a wiring drill. I suggested my old 12th Co way, which I've always considered a special child of my own although I didn't invent it but merely did a great deal of it. I explained it to the C.R.E. & the Staff approved at once & said I was given two days to collect material & to train a squad and the General would see it. So yesterday I had a lorry & found some excellent brushwood for pickets where no one was looking & I also collected a lot of wire. To-day I gave a lecture and did a few yards quite slowly in the morning and this afternoon I was very pleased with them as they put me up 40 yards in 15 minutes which is a very good time. It was only the second time they'd tried it. If the General likes it I shall probably have to go & instruct infantry officers in doing it, which will be another day out of the office.

Thanks ever so much for your parcels. None ever came at a better time. Yesterday I invited two fellows to dinner without knowing in the least what we had and when I came in I found your hors d'oeuvre, crème de menthe, fruits and all the needs of civilisation. About 10.30 everyone went to bed & our guests were getting up to go but I kept the conversation going and then brought them back again & we talked till 12. They were Jackson and Williams whom I think I've mentioned before. Jackson's a sapper who's been on the coast and the other fellow commands the Signal Coy & has

Elisabeth Wicksteed

Elisabeth was the fourth daughter of Joseph and Mary Wicksteed. Her father was a mechanical engineer and inventor of many mechanical appliances, including vertical and horizontal testing machines, two-spindle radial drills, double cutting tool-holders and hydraulic plate shears. He was President of the Institution of Mechanical Engineers in 1903–04.

Her uncle, Charles Wicksteed, founded Wicksteed Park at Kettering, Northamptonshire, in 1913 'to create an open, safe park land area where families and children could play'. At that time, many homes had no garden, forcing children to play in the street. Charles also owned an engineering company, that supplied park equipment far and wide; some of this equipment can still be found in Wicksteed Park today. As the park developed, excited crowds were drawn in from all over to see attractions like the Train, Charabancs and the Waterchute. Wicksteed Park was one of the first ever leisure parks in the UK and still brings pleasure to visitors of all ages to this day.

the Boer War & Zulu rising medals & has knocked all over S. Africa & Australia having gone out to the war as a Senior Scholar of John's & having left a prejudice in the minds of the Dons against his coming back. (That sounds the sort of yarn a man would tell but I think it's true). Anyway he's a first rate fellow and I never want a better evening than hearing two of that kind of fellow topping each others lies & then going one further with a preface of "Now this is true".

I'm really most awfully happy these days. You see I've got plenty of work and its both valuable & interesting and it means a great step educationally and then above all there's Elisabeth.

Although I know how much it pained her yet I'm awfully grateful to that incident last August. Of course if my nerves had been quite right it wouldn't have happened & yet without it I doubt if we'ld have come as close to each other as we have. For one thing it got rid of that reaction which is I suppose bound to come for a minute to every man when he feels that he is bound & wants to be free. Well I've spat all that up once & for all & she understands. And then it cleared up all sorts of other little things. I felt that she admired me an awful lot & I couldn't help feeling that it was the good she saw in me she was loving and emphasising and that she mightn't care so much about me if she realised that I wasn't a hero after all. Well now that's all gone and I know that we both love just for what the other is. I felt too at that time that the having to work for money to marry was an extra burden which would cramp me. Now I know that that's all rubbish. Work which was a burden wouldn't be good work: but now although it sounds the same the point of view is quite different. Its not that I've got to marry & therefore have got to work: I'm going to marry & therefore I'm jolly well going to work.

Little Mother, you mustn't let what happened then make any difference to your loving her. I think it did a little and somehow that made me feel a little reserved. You must love her all the more Mother because of the great love we have between us.

You can think how I used to envy Jackson. He came home sick from the Cameroons and as he had been able to wire that he was coming his lady had the Banns half through by the time he arrived. Then he got two months sick leave & a topping honeymoon and came down to Bulford. I used to lend them my room when she came up to the Camp because at first he hadn't one with a fire. She was a nice little thing – just the right woman for him & they'd had a three years engagement. I'd half a mind, almost, to take a week-end leave and a special licence & bring my Betsy down to the plain.

L'Emprunt de la Victoire

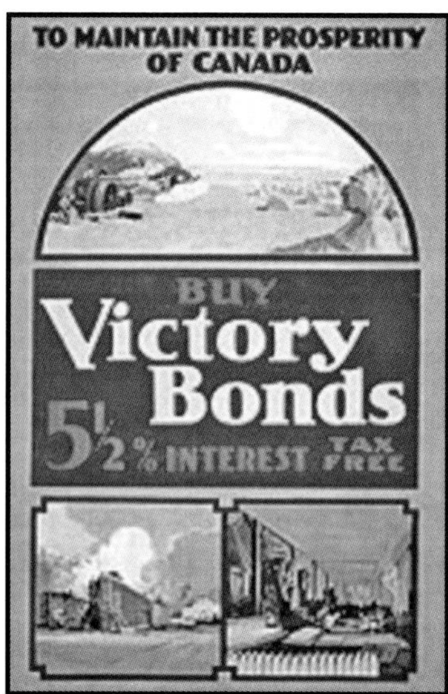

The Canadian government sold bonds to private individuals, companies and organisations to raise money to pay for their participation in the war. The bonds were loans that could be cashed with interest in 5, 10 or 15 years. They were issued in five different years between 1915 and 1919.

One hundred million dollars worth of Canadian Victory Bonds were sold during 1915. As we read, John was among those who bought them.

And its very wistful I feel when I think that its nearly Christmas. I'd give very much to have one with just you and Honor and Betsy.

To-day I had a very kind parcel from Winnie Carson, containing cake & congratulations & toffee. She's a very nice person, isn't she?

I'm getting quite a commercial man. I bought 200,000 bricks yesterday at 27fr a thousand. I thought the price excessive so I requisitioned them instead of buying them.

I also bought 700 francs worth of Emprunt de la Victoire for myself. Its issued below par so I only paid 612fr.50. In 15 years it will be paid back at par, so I shall get back 700 francs and in the meantime I get 35 francs a year interest so that for 612.50 I get back 700 principal and 525 francs interest which comes to 1225 francs or exactly double 612.50. Another point is that I'm buying when a pound equals about 28 francs and with any luck in another fifteen years I shall be paid with the old pre-war rate of about 25.50 so that I ought to make money there too.

> *Here John has written figures in the margin*
> *350*
> *175*
> *525*
> *700*
> *1225*

I'm afraid I'm sitting up late & to-morrow I shall have the uncommon experience of finding it hard to get out of bed.

I'm very sorry for you over in Ireland and as Honor tells me that you haven't a nurse I'm afraid you're having a very hard time. I wish we could both be back in the Flat again for a few hours together.

Your very loving,
J.S.

1.1.16

Dearest Mother,

A very happy new year to you & Honor. I'm writing this in bed for I've just got into a most attractive billet where there is electric light at the head of the bed.

I most awfully sorry for the time I've been without writing. I've been meaning to do so for long enough, but, Mother dear, I've hardly a minute to myself. To-day I was in the office from breakfast till 7.30 & then went out on business & got back for dinner at 9. To-morrow will be just the same. You see I'm a sort of Harrods. I've got 20,000 customers who may ask for anything from a bag of nails to a snow-plough and I've got a Sergeant-Major and a clerk to help me to run the business. Then again I get little

Extract from: 'Work of RE in the European War 1914–19, Supply of Engineer Stores and Equipment'

Sandbags.

Trench warfare legitimately involved the use of such enormous numbers of sandbags that it became necessary to buy up all available supplies in this country suitable for the purpose, and to obtain supplies of some millions of bags from America and Canada, pending arrangements being made for manufacture in India, and even then doubts were raised as to whether the available jute crop would suffice.

However, through the agency of Messrs. A.J.Henry and Co, one of the principal firms in the trade, who took up this agency on a fixed percentage basis, contract were entered into with the mills in Calcutta, and regular monthly shipments followed. The estimated requirements at the time were about 10 millions a month, but as the British armies in France increased in strength and became responsible for longer lines, so requirements of bags increased, and the issues to France alone for one month rose to over 40 millions, the total for one year being 313 millions.

The control exercised under the arrangements made with the India mills of only one farthing per bag on the one year's supply to France mentioned above would amount to over £326,000. The bags supplied were made of fairly low quality cloth, but it sufficed, and the price delivered in this country, was at one time about 2 ½ d. per bag, and at no time more than 3d.

The arrangement for supplies from India, however, involved storage of large quantities in this country to meet emergencies, and difficulties in regard to storage frequently arose. To meet the difficulties partially it was arranged with Messrs. Henry & Co to build a store at the wharf at Greenwich, the store to be sufficient for 20 million bags, the site to be granted free of rent, and half the cost of the store to be paid by them on condition that the building was to become their property 6 months after the war. As one of the conditions, they agreed to unload stock, and reload as required on payment of actual cost of labour. As the usual wharfage charges for bags going in and out amounted to about 4s. 6d. per ton each way, and the usual charges for bags in buildings to 6d. per ton per week, the arrangement with Messrs. Henry resulted in a considerable saving.

The need for sandbags enabled a considerable number of orders to be placed with the prisons and detention barracks, as the making up of these bags was found to be a useful means of utilizing unskilled labour.

The provision of sandbags during the war totalled up to about 1,300 millions – about 338,000 tons shipping weight, and at a cost of about £15,000,000.

side jobs to look after – at the present moment I'm building a convalescent hospital and a laundry, both to be lit by electricity, apart from having to arrange for the building of numberless stables and recreation rooms. Then there is the probability that some of my lorries won't turn up – to-morrow I asked for 8 and I'm getting 4. That means cutting down work by one half … & then perhaps one of them will go 8 or 19 miles to a place & find that what they're fetching won't be there till to-morrow or else they'll take them to the wrong place. Whatever happens at any rate it will all be blamed on the Adjutant R.E. who will reply that whoever is grousing is jolly lucky to have what he's got and that to-morrow he can go without. Its not the Staff who are so hard to deal with. If they don't do what I want I just say "Well I'm afraid no material can go to the trenches" and then they behave. Its the people in the trenches who ask for ten times what I'll give them and the other people who give me a tenth of what I ask for. However, "c'est la guerre", which is the invariable French reply to any grouse.

Apart from all that is the fighting side. Practically everything in trench-warfare is or should be discussed with the C.R.E. and the Adjutant R.E. opens the correspondence, asks the C.R.E.'s opinion and answers it. And there's more of that work than is shown in official communiqués because it wouldn't be very exciting reading for the British Public (tho' excellent for the Bosche Staff) to know that such & such a place had a machine-gun or observation post. Altogether then I have a pretty long but quite an interesting day.

I've run across several fellows I knew at the Shop and I find that Thorburn is quite close. I scribbled him a note & told him to come & see me. I hope he'll be able to. I can't get to him at present.

Graham Reid is being married on the 4th of this month and I'm awfully glad. He had a very bad time once when his girl was thought to be dieing. She's a Canadian & so of course he couldn't go to her. They've been engaged for 4 or 5 years and he's an absolutely splendid fellow & so they'll be very happy. He's in England with some sort of paralysis which I believe & hope is only temporary. He's such a fine athlete that it would be too cruel if he got anything serious. He'ld have skippered the Shop at Rugger our last term if we'd had one.

The wiring was a great success both by day & night and I wrote a little brochure called "Notes on Wiring" which was distributed to the Division. I'm beginning to get evil returned for good because now the Infantry are worrying me for wire & pickets to practise with.

(2015 Estate Barbara Bruce Littlejohn)

A taxi and a bus in central London 1914

Thanks very much for forwarding Geoffrey's letter I'll try & write him sometime when I've a little less to do though I'm not quite sure when that'll be.

I'm so sorry to hear about Honor's cold & I hope it's not going to be a nasty one. She should come to Sunny France to cure it. You should hear some of the Tommies' remarks about Sunny France, even last year which we're now told was a dry year. I think it was – though I didn't then.

There's just a chance of my getting leave in another month, but it's doubtful. I'm not really due till the end of February but having been out before, the 3 month rule needn't necessarily apply, I find. That'll only be, however, if I can make myself look sufficiently ill and in need of a rest.

With much love to Honor & mind she strafes her cold.

Your loving

J.S.

14.1.16

Mother Dearest,

I'm getting leave from Jan 29th to Feb. 5th. I shall get into Leeds at 9:30 p.m. (King's Cross & GNR) on the 29th. I shall get into Victoria about 3 p.m. and I've asked Betsy to meet me and come up with me by the 5.45, but it'll mean rather a long day for her I'm afraid. Could you and Honor meet me with a taxi at the station and then we'ld all go up together. Have you got my mufti at Leeds? I'ld like to get into it if I could.

I oughtn't really to get it yet but they don't keep too much to the 3 months if you've been out before. I asked the Colonel last night if I should have any chance of getting it at the end of the month. He grunted and said he didn't suppose we'ld either of us get any at all. Then to-day apparently he asked the Staff and they said Yes without any demurring.

I believe it was my School of Cookery got it for me. Q is the Administrative side of the Staff. They manage leaves & anything that isn't actively killing or frustrating Huns. The Corps said our Division must have a School of Cookery by the 15th. This was on the 9th. The AA & QMG (You won't understand that, but he's a Colonel and head of Q) came round & asked if I could do him one. I said it couldn't be done in the time but I'd see. The next day I went with him in a car to choose the site and we decided to put up a lean-to roof and build a brick oven in a certain place. In the meantime I had arranged to get the bricks and timber sent down, and work

Schools of cookery

The Army Service Corps ran Schools of Cookery, set up specifically to teach the art of field cooking, which was inevitably very different to anything a chef might have been doing before he enlisted. Each company of soldiers had two cooks – one went with the company to the trenches and the second stayed behind the lines preparing food which would then be taken to the front in 'hayboxes' (for solid food) or 'dixies' (for stews and soups). Movement of any sort to and from the trenches could only take place at night, which was when resupply of rations and water took place, Sappers went in to do maintenance work and wiring, and units changed over.

Rations and Supplies

The Army Service Corps was responsible for supplying everything that was needed at the front line – food, equipment and ammunition for the troops as well as horses and their forage. It was their job to work out the logistics of getting huge quantities of rations and supplies from Britain by boat across the channel, by train to advanced supply depots, by motor transport to divisional refilling points, and finally by horse to forward dumps where units could collect what they required.

Size of forces on Western Front			**Monthly issue in millions of lbs or gallons**			
	Men	**Horses**	**Meat**	**Bread**	**Forage**	**Petrol**
1914	20,000	53,000	3.60	4.50	5.90	0.85
1918	3,000,000	500,000	67.50	90.00	32.25	13.00

(Long long trail. *www.1914-1918.net)*

(IWM Q850)

Drawing rations at an ASC dump.

(IWM Q5307)

Filling water carts at a water depot.

begun as soon as possible. So when he rang up on the 12th and asked how the thing was getting on I was able to say that the thing had been finished that morning. The AA and QMG is an awfully nice fellow (a Major and temporary Lt-Col and quite young) which was why I troubled to get the thing done for him. In return he's got me my leave.

I had been getting a little stale but now I'm ready to work like a Trojan till the 29th and then I'm going to have an A.1. slack. I'm not going to bother about anything.

One thing I shall do that night will be to have a lovely long bath. I can get a wash-tub full of water here but not a proper bath.

With love to Honor.

Till tomorrow fortnight

Your loving

J.S.

14.2.16

Honor Dear,

I'm awful. I got stopped in the middle of this and it's three days till I've started again. All I can say is that I've written no others in the meantime. I wrote one to Betsy a few days ago and otherwise this is the only one I've written since I've got back. Even now I ought really to be in bed.

It isn't entirely hard work though mostly so. I never get off before dinner and most nights we've had someone to dinner & that

The Bablet is a naughty boy - he loves arguing till 3AM. Please take the matter in hand. I am sure - Kathleen - you will agree! signed ???

There! You see what I'm worried with. I told Garforth I was trying to write a letter which I'd begun on the 11th and he said he'ld add something to it . He spotted your name quite wrong and I'm sure I don't know why he calls me the Bablet. I'm a mis-used fellow.

John and Elisabeth at the time of their marriage

What I was going to say was that people come to dinner and then it's impossible to write and to get to bed early too. We had two rubbers of bridge to-night and I won 3f 85 at 5d a 100. It's a splendid game, isn't it? What I always think is that if I went to a theatre or had any other sort of enjoyment for a whole evening it wd. cost me quite a lot. Therefore even if I lose (at the stakes we play for) I'm still to the good. If I win its so much the better. We never play high. I don't want my friends' money & I don't want to lose mine. One simply wants something to check one so that one isn't making one's partner lose money through foolishness. As a fact, if you play for long you find that your gains and losses just about equal each other. There's no game in the world like it.

The new pipe I bought when I was at home is going splendidly. It was horrible extravagance spending 11/- on it but it is lovely. I'm getting such a shine on it that I'll soon be able to shave at it.

I'm awfully pleased with my signet ring. I can't find the sealing wax and it's after 12 so I'm not going to bother my clerk; otherwise I'ld shew you on the outside of the envelope how nice it is.

Now I'm going to stop. I only wish I cd get the chance of writing more letters. There are many I want to write. Cheer oh! I'ld have sent you a valentine if I could have finished this letter sooner, but now it's Feb 15th.

Your loving brother,
John X.

John must have taken further leave at this time, because he married Elisabeth Wicksteed in Leeds on 18th April 1916.

Trench Raids

Trench raiding was the practice of making small scale surprise attacks on enemy positions. Raids were made by both sides in the conflict and invariably took place at night for reasons of stealth. Any attempt to raid a trench during daylight hours would have been pointless because it would have been quickly spotted: enemy machine gunners and snipers had a clear view of no man's land and could easily shoot anyone who showed their head above the trench parapet.

Typically, raids were carried out by small teams of men who would black up their faces with burnt cork before crossing the barbed wire and other debris of no man's land to infiltrate enemy trench systems. The distance between friendly and enemy front lines varied, but was generally several hundred metres.

Trench raiding was very similar to medieval warfare insofar as it was fought face-to-face with crude weaponry. The raiding parties were lightly equipped for stealthy, unimpeded movement. They would be armed with a selection of weapons including home made trench raiding clubs, bayonets, entrenching tools, trench knives, hatchets, pickaxe handles and brass knuckles. The intention was to kill or capture people quietly, without drawing attention to their activities. Clearly, this would have been impossible if they had routinely used firearms during raids.

Standard practice was to creep slowly up on the sentries guarding a small sector of an enemy front line trench (looking for the glow of cigarettes in the dark or listening for conversations) then kill them as quietly as possible. Having secured the trench the raiders would complete their mission objectives as quickly as possible, ideally within several minutes. Raiders were aware that the longer they stayed in the trench, the greater the likelihood of enemy reinforcements arriving. Grenades would be thrown into dugouts where enemy troops were sleeping before the raiders left the enemy lines to return to their own.

Trench raiding had multiple objectives, including:

- to capture, wound or kill enemy troops.
- to destroy, disable or capture high value equipment e.g. machine guns.
- to gather intelligence by seizing important documents (e.g. maps) or enemy officers for interrogation.
- as a reconnaissance for a future massed attack during daylight hours.
- to keep the enemy feeling under threat during the hours of darkness, thereby reducing their efficiency and morale.
- to maintain aggressiveness and fighting spirit in the troops by sending them on such missions.

5 Jul 16

My Dearest Honor,
I don't feel in the mood when I can write a good letter but now at least I have the time for it and so first I can apologise for the way I've neglected you. I've never thanked you for the parcel you and Mother sent me nor for the picture, but it doesn't mean that I'm ungrateful. It's quite possible that soon I may be able to thank you properly in person.

They said that I've got to have a rest. I don't know where or for how long but it's possible I might get a month in England.

I've had nothing to do for two days and it's rather nice. I haven't really got the energy to revel in the fact of doing nothing as one ought to, but it's quietly comforting. I've no desire to dash about to theatres & things but I shall be very happy sitting down under a tree with my Elisabeth and doing nothing.

It will be interesting to see how long I take arriving at wherever I go. I suppose I might get away from here to-morrow I don't know at all.

Did I tell you that I went over the lines in an aeroplane one day. It was simply topping except when he did a channel steamer motion coming down.

Otherwise I haven't had many excitements though plenty have been going on – raids every night nearly and remarkably successful ones by this division.

Au revoir

Your loving brother,

J.S. X

This is the last letter written from France.
John went home on leave and then spent four months training, in Aldershot and Conway, before being posted to a very different theatre of war in Salonika.

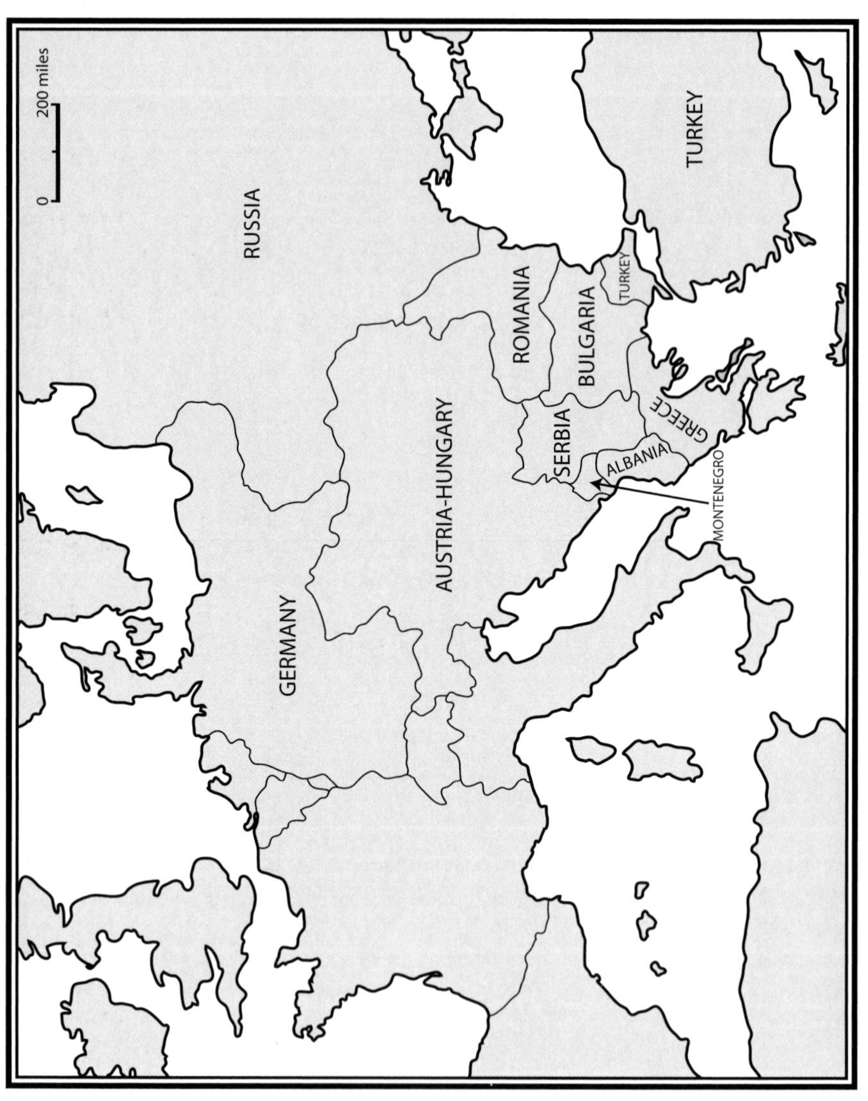

New Balkan States and Central Europe 1914

BACKGROUND TO THE SALONIKA CAMPAIGN

On learning of his posting to Salonika, John would certainly have made it his business to get fully up to date with that theatre of the war. He might have asked the following questions – and no doubt would have shared the answers with Dearest Mother and Honor

Where is Salonika?

- Salonika (or Salonica, formerly Thessalonica) is the second largest city in Greece, at the north west corner of the Aegean Sea.
- It is one of the largest deep-water harbours in the Aegean, with easy access to the Mediterranean, and therefore has always been of strategic importance.
- The southern borders of Serbia and Bulgaria are about forty miles north of the city. That whole area, including parts of southern Serbia and Bulgaria, has always been known as Macedonia.

Why is the British Army there?

- In late September 1915 two divisions, one British and one French, were rushed to Salonika from Gallipoli in an attempt to support Serbia against imminent invasion.
- On 6th October 1915 the Austro-Hungarians, supported by German forces, invaded Serbia from the north. On 14th October the Bulgars advanced into Serbia from the east, linking up with their German allies in defeating Serbia in November.
- The Allied support was too late, despite fierce fighting by the French and British against the Bulgars continuing into December, after the arrival of a fresh British division.
- Despite the British wish to evacuate Salonika, for political reasons the Allies have remained there. The failure in the Dardanelles had convinced Bulgaria to enter the war on Germany's side, and Greece to break her treaty with Serbia.
- A strong Allied presence in Salonika and Macedonia would check the German influence over Greece, protect the strategic port, and also maintain a base from which to aid Romania if she entered the war on the Allied side.
- In the event, Romania declared war on Austria-Hungary on 17th August 1916, but was beaten in a four month campaign against forces from Germany, Austria-Hungary, Turkey and Bulgaria.

So who is on our side in the Salonika Campaign?

- France, Serbia, Italy and Russia

How did the Serbian Army recover after the 1915 invasion?

- It was driven into Albania and then evacuated to Corfu. After a year of regrouping, reequipping and retraining with the help of the Allies, it arrived in Salonika in the summer of late 1916 (120,000 strong) to join the Allied Salonika forces.

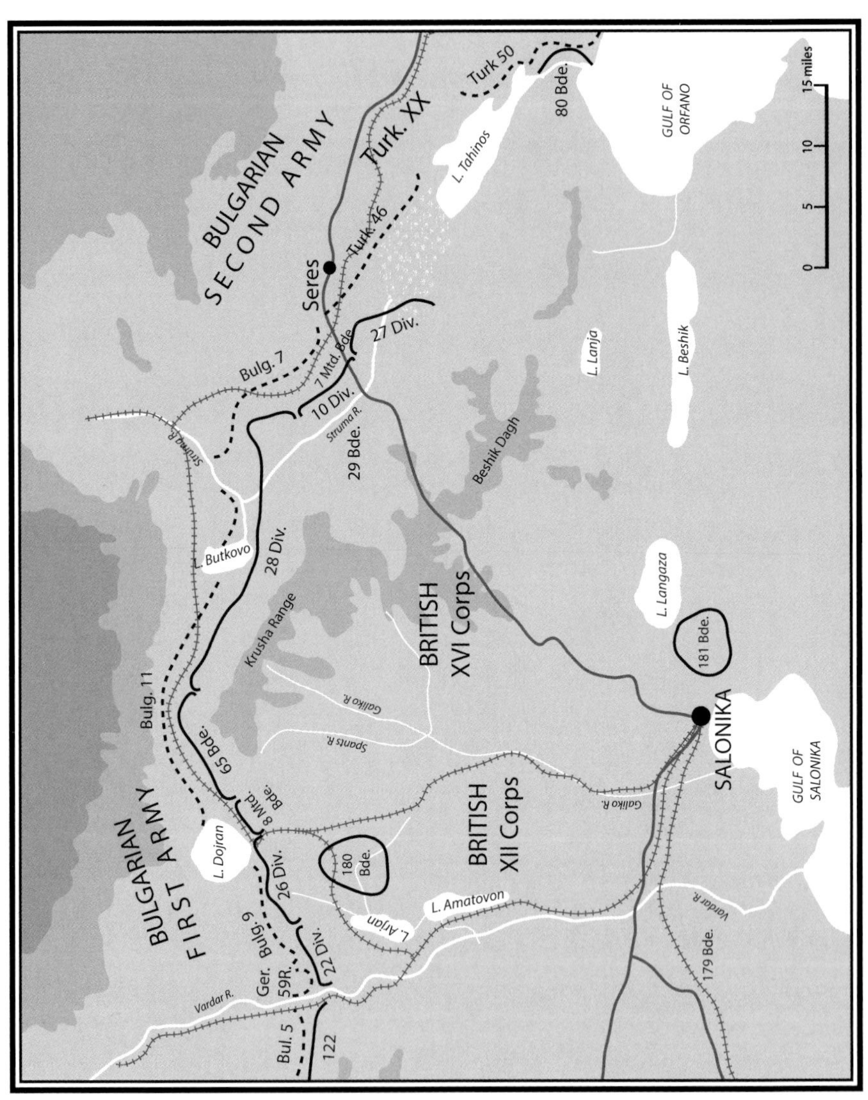

British Salonika Army deployment on 1st January 1917

And who are we up against?

- Germany, Austria-Hungary and Bulgaria

What about the Greek Army?

- In 1914 Greece was divided in its allegiance. King Constantine was pro-Germany; however, his prime minister was pro-Allies. Officially the country was neutral, a situation that caused great problems for the Allied forces as they deployed to Salonika.
- After much discussion and hostility, in late December 1915 the British-French military commanders took over complete control of Salonika city from the Greeks.
- In October 1916, the prime minster set up a Provisional Greek Government in Salonika, bringing the Greek Army into the war on the Allies' side. A neutral secure zone five miles deep was then set up to the south west of Salonika, policed by a British brigade, to prevent any retaliation by Royalist troops.

What's happened since we arrived in Salonika?

- The Allies' immediate strategic decision was to reinforce the Salonika force. During 1916 that included four British divisions (22nd, 26th, 27th and 28th) arriving from France.
- On the ground, immediate plans were made in December 1915 to defend the city from potential attack by the Bulgars or Austro-Germans from the north.
- Over the next months, a defensive line of trenches and wiring was constructed some 7–10 miles north of Salonika, linking the Gulfs of Salonika (to the west) and Rendina (to the east) along a line of hills and lakes. The British contingent was responsible for about 15 miles of this front defensive line.
- The whole line, which came to be known as the Birdcage, was completed and occupied by early summer 1916.
- From the summer of 1916 onwards French and British brigades and divisions started to redeploy north from the Birdcage up to the southern borders of Serbia and Bulgaria.
- The British zone of operations extended from the mouth of the River Struma (in the east), to Lake Butkovo then west towards the River Vardar. A new front was progressively developed.
- Fierce engagements against the Bulgars took place throughout the summer and autumn of 1916, particularly in the area of Doiran, including artillery shelling by both sides and brigade-level attacks to gain ground from the enemy.
- These British offensives were in conjunction with a notable success by our Serb and French allies to capture Monastir to the west.

What challenges am I likely to be faced with?

- More front line work and road building.
- Malaria (rife in Salonika in 1916).
- Very unlikely to get any leave because of enemy attacks on our shipping.

J M Cordy RE must have travelled out to Salonika at much the same time as John and describes the journey in his memoirs.

Two days later I was on my way, crossing the Channel and then by train to Marseilles to board the boat which got loaded and lay at anchor waiting for the convoy to be made up with two other boats and two French destroyers. Jerry's submarines were sinking a lot of our boats at that time. The weather was very good and we would stand on the side of the boat and watch four or five year old boys dive from a rowing boat to retrieve coins which we threw down for them. The water was perfectly clear, and the boys would grab the coins almost as soon as they hit the water.

Our boat got into a line with a destroyer each side. The first day we sailed, we had a boat drill, and the next day action stations. At the sound of the alarm we would have to be at the side of the ship with loaded rifles. Our boat was a captured Austrian boat, converted to a troop ship, very narrow, and it rolled about like a cork. Several on board were seasick. We were about three days out when the alarm sounded and we all took up our stations. It was amazing how the destroyers cut through the waves, and sped up and down the convoy hoping to cut a submarine through if it shew its conning tower. After a short time, the all clear sounded and we sped on our way. One wonderful sight was to see Vesuvius in eruption, the colours of the phosphorus and the lava pouring down was magnificent.

We arrived at Salonika harbour and marched to Summer Hill Camp, a camp of bell tents. The weather now was far from good. If tea was left in the mess tin at night, it was a block of ice by morning, and yet by mid-day we would be wearing shorts.

(IWM Document 2623)

LETTERS FROM SALONIKA

24/1/17

Dearest Honor,

I find I've played a practical joke on myself & you. I got you some beads in Salonika & packed them in a tobacco tin. I wrapped the tin up & addressed it & sent it off by registered post. All was right until I came to want some tobacco from a similar tin and found the beads – which are no more good for my pipe than the baccy is for your neck. I'm very sorry, but I'll send them along soon.

I can't write more than a scrawl, because I was travelling last night & only got two hours sleep, but I'll try and write again soon. I've just joined my company and my address is 131st Field Coy R.E., Salonika Army.

With lots of love to you both.

Your loving brother

John

Feb 16th 1917

My dearest Mother,

For days I've been meaning to write but I waited for another letter from Betsy which would confirm the one I got before when she wasn't quite sure. I wanted to be able to talk about her great news when I wrote to you for that's the thing thats uppermost in my mind these days and its no good writing a letter when you can't put down the one thing of all that you're thinking of.

Isn't it splendid, Mother? All those last weeks at Conway and before that at Aldershot I used to pray that "before I went out to Salonika I might have begotten a son". In some ways perhaps its as well that we didn't know when I came away for it would have made it harder to go but I would give much to be able to put my arms round her now and tell her how glad I am.

She tells me you are still in Leeds (on Jan 28th) and I'm awfully pleased that she'll have been able to tell you herself.

British Salonika Force (BSF) in early 1917

At the start of 1917 the BSF had six divisions forward, holding a front line of approximately 90 miles, running from the River Struma in the east to the River Vardar in the west.

Typically each division was made up of three brigades, each of four battalions, with three or four artillery brigades and three Royal Engineer field companies.

131st Field Company RE, John's new unit, supported 26th Division. Thus on arrival in Salonika, he was immediately pitched into the intensity of supporting the division's front line units.

The Bulgars' Defensive Position

The key to even a passing understanding of the Salonika Campaign is an appreciation of the Bulgar defensive position along their southern national border with Greece. The History of the Corps of Royal Engineers Vol VI contains the following excellent brief description:

> 'The line taken up by the Bulgars in front of the British sector was immensely strong and, whether viewed from in front or studied in detail after the war, disclosed not one weak point. The main enemy defences ran along a line of steep and almost trackless mountains rising like a wall in places to more than 4,000 feet above the plain. This barrier was broken very occasionally by narrow and easily defended passes. On our right the hills descended steeply to the sea leaving but a sandy track along the shore. Next came the Angista valley leading to Drama, its entrance protected by the broad and swampy Tahinos Lake.
>
> Then came the famous Rupel Pass, by which the Struma enters the broad Seres plain curving through the malarial swamps east of Lake Butkovo. The pass itself presented an almost impregnable gateway. To the west runs the Belasica Planina range, unclimable for forty miles except by a few precipitous tracks. At its western end is the Kosturino Pass. This was little more than a track and its entrance was protected by Lake Doiran and the very difficult country to the west of the lake. Finally there was the Vardar valley, in places almost a gorge with high mountains on either side'.

Throughout 1916 the German and Bulgarian engineers had constructed a formidable defensive position in the area to the west of Lake Doiran – broken country, with numerous hills and ravines, overlooked by a dominating ridge line of high hills. Three lines of trenches, with a depth of up to two miles, included many concrete observation posts, bunkers and gun positions.

What a lucky little beggar it'll be with you for a Grannie. You must send me an official report giving me all points good and bad of your grandchild, when you've made your inspection.

Don't you think that Betsy and I are the happiest pair of rascals you've ever come across! I've known it ever since we were married but we go on so splendidly that now our love and happiness have grown so big that it takes three of us to share them.

I only hope that she won't be anxious and worry too much about my being at the war. That's one reason I'm very glad I'm here this year and not on the Somme. There's no need for her to be anxious about me here. There might of course be a little fighting here someday but it won't be like France because neither side has much in the way of heavy artillery and what there is is ours.

I'm enjoying myself very much. A day or two after I had joined the Company I came up the line on detachment, living in a dug-out just behind the line and responsible for the work on a certain sector. Just before I came down I got instructions to prepare accommodation for a second section. I had Infantry for the digging & so thought it an excellent opportunity for beginning a nice mess for the two of us. I liked being up very much and was sorry to go back but I had quite an interesting job for the next week, rebuilding a French bridge which being only designed to take a 2-ton load got tired eventually of lorries going over it instead of through the ford. Now I'm up the line again living in one of the new dug-outs. It was very bare when I came, having no table, no shelves, no anything except a wire-netting bed. That was the most important thing to have and now I've got a table with a shelf below it and a sandbag curtain coming over in front, so that I can keep my washing clean. I've got shelves up and the wall tapestried in sand-bags, a couple of trench-boards make a nicer floor than ordinary earth and they've a sand-bag carpet on and I've got a boot jack made out of an old bit of board.

We've just got into the mess today. I found the roof just going on when I came up again. But I couldn't stand up in it quite so I raised the wall one layer of sand-bags and deepened the floor six inches so that now it's all right. It's about 7 foot by 9 foot and has a door and a window, each with a sand-bag curtain at night. There's a table and shelf or two and a seat along one wall, upholstered in sand-bags. The walls at present are only partly tapestried and we need some more shelves but anyway we've a charcoal brazier and a little parafine lamp and we're both writing away hard.

Engineer support to 26th Division

It is clear from the 131st Field Company RE war diaries covering the period January-October 1917 that the company was extremely busy supporting its division – not only across the full width of its front line trenches, but also in many other tasks further back. The range of work, with much similarity to the Western Front, included:

At the Front:

- Supporting infantry raids and assaults with wire cutting parties using Bangalore torpedoes.
- Erecting wire obstacles in front of forward trenches.
- Planning and supervising the digging of new fire and communication trenches, with the help of explosives in rocky ground.
- Maintaining and improving trenches by sandbagging, revetting and draining.
- Constructing reinforced dug-outs for operation rooms and accommodation, often with anti-mosquito doors.
- Constructing artillery observation posts and ammunition pits.

Behind the Front:

- Constructing and fitting gas-proof doors to medical dressing stations.
- Constructing battalion rest camps, including water supply.
- Carrying out anti-malarial precautions, including cutting or burning grass and undergrowth round camps, and draining ponds.
- Constructing prisoner cages.
- Road and bridge repairs on essential supply routes close to the front line.

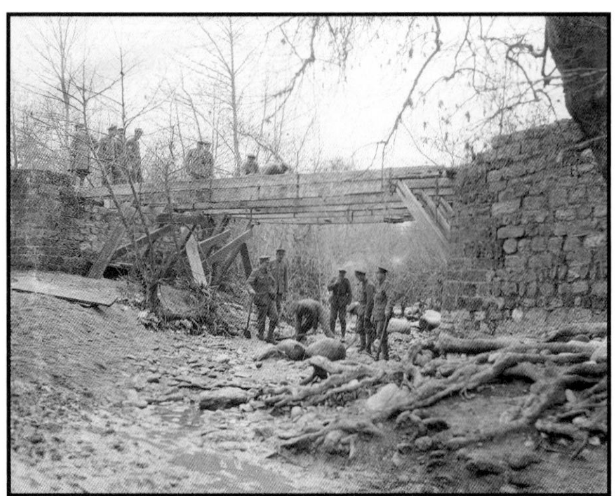

Sappers reconstructing a bridge Jan 1917.

(IWM Q32673)

I've got an old Yorkshire man called Johnson as a batman. He used to be a driver in the 12th Company. He likes me for that as I'm a link with the Company and I think he also respects me for coming from Leeds. He works in peace in a colliery halfway between Leeds & Wakefield & Leeds is therefore one of his alternative "Saturday nights". He will talk for hours if you give him the chance. He's told me all about the only time he got caught poaching & the magistrate (whose rabbits they were) paid his fine.

I'm finishing this in bed in clean pyjamas. I don't think I've ever have such well-aired ones in my life. After washing them Johnson absolutely refused to let me have them till he'd had them out in the sun for two days and they are just lovely. This dug-out is getting nice and tidy now. Johnson stole me a brazier from someone and I've had it in here a couple of nights now.

Johnson isn't the batman they gave me at first. I had a fellow called Hammond before I knew Johnson was here. He has got a septic arm and wasn't allowed to come up the line so I asked for Johnson & I shall stick to him. I ran across him at Aldershot and he told me he was on draft for Salonika. He went some time before me but the morning after I arrived at the Company he came up to my dug-out to call on me.

I dined with Colin Smithells last night. He's commanding a company and his mess is about 200 yards from ours. It was great coming across him. My sector is a little way off from here (the other Section have this one) and I pass Colin's place two or three times a day. That generally means wasting half an hour bucking to him instead of going off to look after my work. He took a snap of me this afternoon. I must try to get one of the prints when it's developed in years to come.

I'm going to try to write to Honor tomorrow and the letter will probably go by the same boat as this. She'll make a very attractive Aunt, I think, don't you.

We start life rather early in the morning these days and it's getting on for eleven so I'll say good-night.

Your very loving son,
JS (X)

Honor 1917 – 21 years old

Feb 17th 1917

My dearest Honor,

I'm more annoyed with myself than I can say for not having written for your 21st birthday. I suddenly remembered on the 10th and then on the sheep as a lamb principle I waited longer. But anyway it's never too late to wish you very many happy returns of Feb 11th and all the other 365 days too.

I'm writing this in our new mess. Our little oil-lamp doesn't give a very excellent light and you might think the place looked rather dingy, but then we haven't got all our wall-paper up yet – only round the "settee" where we lean against the wall. But it's not at all bad as messes go up in the line. We're building a new officers cook-house just below us and we've got an old length of water-pipe we're going to rig up as a speaking tube to it. We'll have a bell in any case, hanging up an 18-pounder brass cartridge case in the kitchen with a wire from it to the mess.

If ever I get a chance of picking up something nice I'll collar it for you for a birthday present, but just now I have nothing much except timber and wire and a few nails and those are so awfully heavy in the post. I've still got those unlucky beads which I really will send off one day but they aren't a birthday present just an un-birthday present. They aren't worth tuppence but I like the colour rather. I don't know that they will suit you but I hope they will. At any rate I hope the tobacco arrived safely. You needn't keep it for me for it was rotten tobacco. The only reason I regretted it was that just then I had great difficulty in getting any at all. I thought I'd be clever and buy lots on the boat, so as to get it cheaper and then the beastly boat had been so long away from England that it had run out and had nothing but some very very black black plug. At first I could never smoke more than a quarter of a pipe of it but in the end I quite liked it.

Betsy's Great News will be quite an old story to you by now. I'm so bucked I don't know what to do. What fun you'll have being an aunt. Aunt Honor sounds rather nice, I think.

Colin Smithells is coming to dine here to-morrow. I dined with him a couple of days ago. We don't live more than two or three hundred yards apart this week and I pass his place every day on my way to work. If you see Mary you must tell her that he's looking remarkably fit. He lends me 6 men each day. They finished off the digging of the Mess and are on the new cook-house now. I'm going to get them to make one or two paths after

(IWM Q31589)

Hundreds of Greek boys were paid one franc per day to pick up stones for road making under supervision of the Royal Engineers in Salonika.

(IWM Q31589)

that is finished as we're on a fairly steep hill-side and one always falls over stones and things in the dark

How's all the art getting along? You'ld love to come here and sketch. We get some of the loveliest views you could get anywhere. It's very like the Lakes here, hills about the same height and lakes here and there but there are lovely great snow ranges in directions, some quite fairly close. When the weather is nice as it has been to-day its like an English summer and when you get onto some of the hills and look across the sky-blue lake onto great snow-peaks beyond you could get nothing better. When I think that I might still be in Flander's mud-flats I shudder (not that the mud here is anything to sneer at; but looking over the hills you forget it and in France you can see nothing else.)

I've run across Gibbins once or twice. He's commanding great gangs of Greeks on a road near here. My week behind I was on the same road further up, making it with Infantry. Our junction was a broken French bridge which I was repairing and his camp was quite close to it. I spent most of my time on the bridge rather than the road and used sometimes to eat my sandwiches with him.

I met Tony Scattergood in Salonika and Phil Fox came out on the same boat. Yesterday I came across an RE sergeant of another Company who used to be a Corporal in the 12th Company. My O.C. has a brother who was in my batch at Chatham and is now married so that makes three of us in the batch who are sensible fellows.

I've been finishing writing this in bed, where I do most of my correspondence when I do do any. I don't think I've written to anyone from here except to you Mother and Elisabeth.

You'll forgive me, won't you, for being so late.

With all love and good wishes –

Your loving brother,

JS

PS I wrote to Mother yesterday but sent it to Grange Court *[Leeds]*. Its just occurred to me that Glebe Place *[London]* will be better.

Blackwood's

Blackwood's was a British monthly magazine founded in 1817 by publisher William Blackwood and originally called the Edinburgh Monthly Magazine. With a mixture of thoughtful reviews, criticism and satire it reached its maximum circulation in about 1850 but continued to be published until 1980. It also printed fictional horror stories. Many of the regular articles told of things that were happening throughout the British Empire along with political comment (the magazine was ostensibly a Tory work). It had a great readership amongst those in Colonial Service or stationed abroad.

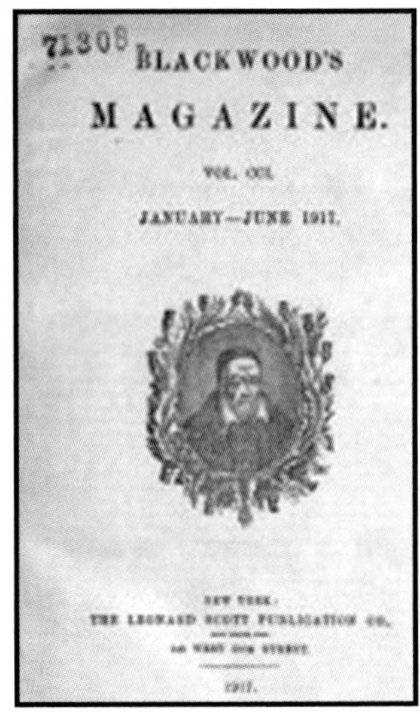

The Fall of Baghdad

For some years before 1914 Germany had developed Turkey as an ally, so when war was declared the Ottoman Empire became an enemy of the British Empire. On the coast in the oil-rich south of the region of Mesopotamia lay the port of Basra, an important refuelling point for the British Navy. On the outbreak of war Britain decided to protect its oil interests here. Troops drawn mainly from India, seized Basra and then moved north towards Baghdad. For the next two years this Middle East theatre of war was finely balanced, but on 11 March 1917 Baghdad fell to British Empire troops and the Baghdad-Berlin railway was captured. As a result Germany conceded an end to its alliance with Turkey.

March 12th 1917

My dearest Mother,
I'm up the line again now but there's nothing very exciting going on. They've reduced the Sappers in the line temporarily so I have two sectors to look after with less men than I had last time on one, so that I'm not able to get so much done. Its quite good fun however and one gets to know lots of Infantry fellows.

While I was back with the Company I spent most of my time finishing off the bridge. I had been going on quite nicely, expecting to take ten days over it when suddenly someone said it must be ready in 36 hours. It was quite unnecessary of them but I did it. At least I had it ready for traffic, which was all they wanted, and then I went on quietly finishing it properly. I got rather stumped over one place where I wanted to put an extra support but couldn't see how to quite because the rock below water level ran in an awkward way. I remembered however the story of a young Engineer who, having passed his written exams, got stumped in his viva by a bridging question about a river and a rock. But he got full marks because being so sick of being stumped he exclaimed "Oh damn the river and blast the rock", and the examiner said the method was excellent. So I did the same thing in a modified way. I couldn't dam the river but I cut it off from the bit I wanted to get at. I had to come up here just at the critical time so I don't know whether my way worked properly or not. The moral of that is that one should always remember improper stories as they may come in useful!

I've just got the Jan. & Feb. Blackwoods, and am enjoying them. I found someone who takes the National and I had a great time reading Maxse on President Wilson in the Jan. & Feb. numbers. Leo has no use for the Yanks. I don't know if he'll have changed at all now. If you can get hold of the Jan. and Feb. numbers you'll find them awfully good reading. Asquwith gets a farewell kick and there's a flesh- creeping article on the Hidden Hand.

We've heard to-day that Baghdad has fallen which is excellent news if true. I'm just going to turn in now so I'll say good-night with lots of love to you both.

Your very loving
JS X

I do hope the furniture has rolled up all right.

(IWM Q32578)

British troops attending an open air service on the Struma Front.

Easter Day
8.4.17

My dearest Mother,
I'm having quite a good time these days. My section is back having a rest. I have to improve the shining hour by giving them a little training at the same time, so we do little bits of Infantry Drill and digging, or put up wire & blow it away, all of which just keeps them sufficiently occupied to keep them fit, while they get lots of time off. We're in a nice little camp and the weather is glorious. I wear a coat for the 8.30 parade and after that it comes off till just before dinner.

I was able to get to an early service this morning. I suppose there were about 20 or 25 there and we formed a half-circle in front of the altar which, probably consisting of a packing-case, was covered with the Union Jack and stood under a very green small tree in the middle of a valley. We started off with "O God our help in ages past" and had the hymn for absent friends just before the three or four minute sermon. I love that hymn but it always makes me want to weep. I enjoyed the service immensely.

Easter is a kind of halting point where one can stop and look back on the past twelve months. Exactly a year ago I was still a bachelor in Bethune: now I'm a married man in Salonika and the months between have included the most wonderful times of my life – our hurried wedding and the first short honeymoon. Then my sick leave and our longer second one, when we just wandered from place to place utterly happy and bothering about nothing. We had our third and fourth at Aldershot and Conway. Before us all the time we had the motto carpe diem: so we carpied each diem in turn till the last morning, when I steamed out of Llandudno Junction at 3.30 a.m. leaving a wonderfully brave little Betsy on the platform. Then came the wonderful news about our child.

Mother darling you must go up to Leeds and see your grandchild when It arrives, and tell me all about It. Its length, breadth, depth, width and height and what kind of parade voice Its likely to have.

I wish very much that Honor could get a chance of running up to see Elisabeth for a day or two, but I suppose her Pensions will keep her. I'ld stand the fare all right. I'm sorry that, after all, none of her sisters are coming home, because she's very much alone in that big house with no one at all her own age there. She's wonderfully cheerful in her letters but I'm afraid later on she may get depressed sometimes.

Colonel Gadke was a German army officer, considered a high authority on army efficiency who, in 1910, wrote a critical article about British forces in *Berliner Vorwarts*, a Socialist publication. He continued to write a column throughout the war, changing his views a bit and becoming more realistic than most other German journalists about Germany's precarious situation – which did not endear him to the German Government. It would seem that John had met him some time before the war and respected his views.

The following article was published in The New York Times on 20th October 1915

GERMAN WAR CRITIC WARNS COUNTRYMEN

Colonel Gadke Belittles Advance in Serbia and Admits Loss in West.

Special Cable to THE NEW YORK TIMES.

LONDON, Wednesday, Oct. 20.—A dispatch to The Daily Chronicle says that in his weekly war review in the Berlin Vorwärts, the Socialist organ, Colonel Gadke thinks the war has now reached its highest point.

His observations do not make very encouraging reading for those of his countrymen who believe the German arms are advancing from victory to victory and that the enemies of the Fatherland are in their last gasps.

Speaking of the Serbian campaign, he warns his readers to beware of overestimating the initial success obtained by von Mackensen, as it is only, he points out, a beginning. From the first, he says, it was, of course, apparent that the Serbians would not be able to withstand the German-Austrian drives across the rivers. Here it was a matter of superior artillery and higher technical skill, but it will be well to remember that Belgrade was once before in Austrian hands, and that an Austrian army came to grief on the Save. Gadke points out that the nature of the interior will certainly have a serious effect in reducing the preliminary speed of the advance, and that the further the German-Austrian armies penetrate, the more they will suffer from the inhospitable nature of the country, the pathless forests, the abrupt mountains, and the lack of roads and railways.

With regard to the war on the western front, Gadke is in opposition to all the military writers on the other German papers. He thinks it is wrong to say the recent attacks by the Allies had no success. To say so, he insists, is not to describe truthfully the situation. Both the German official statements and the reports of General Joffre clearly indicate the progress made by the Allies. It is clear, says Gadke, that progress has been made and that the German counterattacks have not yet succeeded in regaining all that has been lost. He does not believe the German lines have been cut through, but is certain attempts to do so will be made again and again, and that the situation is not without danger.

In the east he admits the Russians have gained ground in certain areas and that a sort of equilibrium has been established. His conclusion is that the Germans must prepare themselves for a long duration of the war and must make no speedy decision.

I'm sorry you find London trying. I expect the geyser has a lot to do with it. It may be the "useful, quick method" you expect me to think it, but its not nearly as useful & quick as turning on a plain tap. We had one at Aldershot and it meant that one always thought twice about having a bath. What was so jolly about the flat was that you never bothered to think about having one. You probably meant not to have one and then having got inside the bath-room you just did. I know that most days in The Winter I had about three. One before a dance, one when I came in from it and one when I got up late the next morning. That was a great winter with its gas strike and its dances. I used to dance five with Elisabeth at each dance, no more no less, except the last one when we had eight. I used to come back and think about her and wonder whether she really liked my asking for so many or whether she just didn't like to hurt me by refusing. They were wonderful days – but I mustn't start reminiscing again or I'll never stop.

I wonder if you have any more news about the second cottage. You must let me know at once what rent they ask. I'ld give a great deal to be able to come and help to arrange it with you this summer.

I wonder how much America will be able to help us. Financially of course we're now safe. Soon they ought to be able to send a couple of divisions across to us and later on quite a lot.

Financially of course this old war helps me quite a lot – but I shan't be too sorry when its all over.

Best of love to you both.

Your very loving,

JS (X)

May 24th 1917

Dearest Mother,

Thank you very much for the Times with Col Gädke's thing and for your letter which I got a couple of days ago. It had taken nearly a month to come. My address by the way is as above. You put 131st Div R.E. on those two. It wasn't that which delayed them, but it might do.

Old Gädke is always awfully sound. I'ld love to see him again someday but I don't suppose I ever shall. Neither of us is very likely to be in the other's country for some years after this show is over.

We are back resting just now. We had rather a strenuous time for a bit but the Company was very lucky. We did a good deal of night work, which got rather tiring after a bit but on the whole we had quite an interesting time.

The First Battle of Doiran (22 April – 8 May 1917)

As part of an Allied plan across the whole front, the BSF launched two major offensives, ten days apart, against the Bulgarian defensive positions west of Lake Doiran. 26th Division was involved in both operations assaulting over frontages of around 3,000 yards, with the objective of capturing and holding the Bulgarian forward defensive line. On each occasion, following an initial heavy artillery barrage, the leading infantry battalions advanced after cutting their way through the enemy wire obstacles. Twice, after sustained and fierce fighting over a number of days, in almost impossible terrain, the BSF was forced to withdraw with very heavy causalities. By any standards this represented a serious defeat, despite the bravery displayed at every level.

Extract from 131st Field Company RE War Diary – 22 April 1917

'Lt Baines with 1 NCO and 3 sappers went out with wire cutting patrol. 6 Bangalore torpedoes (8 foot lengths) carried. Lt Baines with officer of 7th Royal Berkshire Regt went forward and examined wire which was to be cut. The wire was found to be about 15 foot thick and very dense. Lt Baines and L/Cpl Meyrick crept forward and placed two Bangalore torpedoes on the ground beneath the wire. The torpedoes were placed about 25 yards apart. Two clean gaps were cut right through the wire, one gap 15 foot wide and the other about 12 foot wide.'

(National Archive WO 95/4866)

Bangalore Torpedoes

The problem of clearing a path for infantry through dense barbed wire obstacles was first encountered during the siege of Port Arthur in the Russo-Japanese War in 1904–05. A relatively simple solution to the problem was invented and developed by Indian Army Engineers at Bangalore between 1907–12. Although still in its infancy, the Bangalore torpedo was widely used by combat engineers in the First World War, particularly during the Salonika campaign.

The device consisted of one, or more, rigid metal tubes filled with explosive. As we learn from the war diary above, each tube was 8 foot long. The whole torpedo could be made of any length by coupling tubes together. A smooth nose cone was screwed to the front of the leading tube, to allow the whole torpedo to be pushed through wire entanglements without becoming snagged. At the other end a firing device, with a fuse and safety pin, was attached. This would activate the explosive in the first tube, which in turn would immediately cause all other forward tubes to explode.

The Bangalore torpedo was technically simple in design and operation. However, positioning it accurately under enemy barbed wire and detonating it without being observed, required good training and resolute courage.

I did one or two fairly interesting reconnaissances, on one of which I blew up some wire with Bangalore torpedoes. They're lovely things. They make a beautiful gap in the wire. You just push them through, pull the lever & run like a stag and then up she goes. The old Bulgar thought they were shells, I think, of some enormous size and probably sat at the bottom of his trench thanking his stars the shells were short and wondering when the next would come. Anyway he didn't shoot at us which was all we required.

I saw Gibbins the day before yesterday – he dined with us on Christmas Day if you remember. I went over to look at an aerial cable railway his company had. I brought it back and spent yesterday erecting and experimenting with it. We call it the Heath Robinson – Hindenberg Line.

I ran across Colin Smithells several times on my night work. I brought him back with me one night to hear the gramophone and he took notes of ones to send to Mary for hers. His object was to pick out ones which would amuse Mary and scandalize Mrs Cohen. I was awfully surprised that Mary had been allowed to have one. In fact only a day before I had written to her just to let her know that Colin was very flourishing and I had mentioned that I intended getting a gramophone to scandalize Coniston.

I'm awfully glad that you've now got the Cottage definitely. I've invited Gibbins to stay there after the war for our bust and he says he will.

I forgot to say in mentioning the Heath Robinson – Hindenberg Line that we broke it – just as well as the people in France broke theirs.

Its quite good fun being back for a day or two. We've had a jump put up and went and took our horses over it last night and also tried a little tent-pegging. On Sunday we're having some sports, partly mounted & partly dismounted and they might be quite good fun. I'm afraid my section is a bit weak in runners, but we ought to do fairly well in the tug-of-war and things like that.

We manage to make up a bridge four, too, most evenings. Two of us are pretty keen. The other two haven't played quite so much, but we have some quite good games and they're learning quickly. I wish old Gibbins had come to this company because he's extraordinarily good. However, its more expensive playing with really good players even if it is more fun.

This old war looks like lasting quite a long time more, I'm afraid. I often wish I could be up in Coniston with you again, but we're really having a fairly good time just now. The weather is hot but hasn't yet come beastly.

Lots of love to you both.

Your loving

JS

Submarines in the Mediterranean Sea

The war in the Mediterranean Sea was primarily aimed at commerce; enemy U-boats attacked and sank many merchant ships trading with France and Italy, and also some of those bringing imports to Britain. Initially, with Italy a neutral power until May 1916, the Austro-Hungarian Empire used their naval bases on the Adriatic Sea quite undisturbed. The Germans sent parts of U-boats overland to Turkey and re-assembled them in Constantinople (Istanbul), but they ran into difficulties getting their ships through the Dardanelles and soon decided to use Austrian bases on the Adriatic instead. The Allies attempted to cut off the Adriatic Sea at the Straits of Otranto, but that was only a partial success. Manning such a wide stretch of water was difficult and it tied up many patrol vessels.

Then the Central Powers made two mistakes that caused international outrage. In November 1915 an Austrian boat sank an Italian passenger liner, SS *Ancona*, off the coast of Tunisia with the loss of over 200 lives (including 9 Americans); the following month a passenger liner, SS *Persia*, was sunk with a loss of 343 lives. Then in March 1916, Italy discovered that Germany, technically their ally, was mining their naval bases. In May 1916 Italy declared war on Germany.

Despite the inclusion of Italy as an ally, merchant shipping continued to suffer huge losses throughout 1916, which reached a peak in early 1917 when 94 ships were lost in one month. At about this time the Italians and British started convoy operations, and in April 1917 Japan, an ally of Great Britain, sent 14 destroyers to the Mediterranean to escort and guard the convoys. This joint action managed to greatly reduce the number of enemy U-boats and curtail their activities, though ships were still being sunk right up until October 1918 when the Germans elected to abandon the Mediterranean.

(IWM Q32717)

Sorting the mail in Salonika.

Aug 14th 1917

Dearest Mother,
It's a long time since I heard from you and I'm afraid it must be that the submarines have robbed me. They seem to get 3 or 4 days' mail each month, both ways.

That's almost the only real grouse we have here as compared with France. The mails come at any time – in any order, and some of them don't come at all. And it all makes one seem so far away and so cut off from everything and everybody.

Yet really we've got an awful lot to be thankful for. We've got lovely scenery and lovely weather and though we mayn't have the luxuries of France yet we're spared lots of their hardships.

We aren't being shelled day and night as they are and we don't get many casualties except in actual fights. Things were pretty lively in April and May but they're very quiet now. Of course we have more sickness, but its been very much less this year. There's been practically nothing except malaria – no dysentery, typhoid or sunstroke – and the total malaria cases are much less including men who had it last year, who are the majority.

I've been keeping wonderfully fit. As long as one can keep under cover from about 12 to 3 or 4 the heat is not so bad, and it'll begin to get cooler soon. Even now one feels it in the morning with the day getting shorter, though its just as bad in the middle of the day.

I'm on detachment now with two sections. I was alone for a time but now I've got a fellow called Miscambell who comes from Antrim. He's a T.C.D. man and he's got quite a dry wit.

I mentioned something about Count Plunkett being in goal. He said "Oh he's out now. They had a great night the night they let him out. They killed a policeman".

Another time he was talking of a certain Bulgar attack on the Struma when our artillery caught them between two barrages and we actually buried 5000 of them without their getting to our line. He was talking of seeing it all from a certain hill and said "You could see our shrapnel bursting right into them and they were falling in heaps. It was a wonderful sight – if you like that sort of thing". The last phase was sort of jerked on. It doesn't sound very funny written down, but it was.

Malaria

During the very hot summers, from April till the end of August, they (the British Army) met a foe more fierce than any Bulgar and at whose hands they suffered far greater casualties. This was the anopheles mosquito, active everywhere but particularly so in the swampy valleys, the Struma valley itself being probably the worst malarial district in Europe, and its malaria the most malignant. In May 1916 when the 10th and 28th Divisions entered the valley, they found that the Bulgars had withdrawn some distance from the river, leaving the mosquito to do its work, which it did with dreadful efficiency. One battalion of the 28th Division, when they left the plain, could find just enough officers and men to drive out their transport wagons.

(History of the Corps of Royal Engineers Vol VI)

And 1916 was by no means the end of our troubles from malaria. It was only the insignificant beginning. The problem was tackled most energetically and the medical authorities initiated preventive measures on a very large scale in the way of oiling and draining stagnant waters, cutting down and burning great tracts of brushwood, making sluggish streams flow swiftly. The healthy men were protected in every way possible – mosquito-proof huts, gloves, head nest and nasty ointments; and the men already infected treated with all the medical skill which a close acquaintance with the disease on a large scale had given us. But the chief difficulty about dealing with malaria on such a scale is that the patient is subject to frequent relapses.

And this explains why, despite of our experience and improved methods, the total admissions for malaria rose with each summer; why the thirty thousand of 1916 had become sixty three thousand in 1917 and sixty seven thousand (in a much depleted Army) in 1918. By the summer of the latter year the Salonika Army was full of listless, anaemic, unhappy, sallow men whose lives were a physical burden to them and a material burden to the Army. Practically everybody in the Army had malaria.

(Salonika & After, *H. Collinson Owen, 1919)*

British Army statistics: Total admissions to hospital in Salonika from malaria 162,517 of which 787 died.

(Official History of the War: Macedonia Vol 2, *1935)*

George Noble Plunkett (1851–1948) was an Irish nationalist whose three sons took part in the Easter Rising in 1916, which aimed to end British rule in Ireland. One son, Joseph, was executed for his part in the insurrection. Count Plunkett was deported and imprisoned in Reading Gaol for several months. He became the Member of Parliament for North-Roscommon in 1917 but continually abstained from Westminster. As a member of the Sinn Féin party, he was vociferously against any Anglo-Irish treaty and in 1938 was a member of the Second Dáil that assigned a sovereign power to the IRA.

Life has been pretty strenuous for the last month or two. I think we had just begun some training when I last wrote. That was quite good fun – rather like the old Shop days, running about making maps and pretending to blow up bridges. Now we're up in the line and though there's nothing much as regards the Bulgar yet we're dashing about so much fighting the mosquito that really one begins to think him the worst of the two – which he is, except that I hope he's impartial. We killed millions of him by setting light to the whole country. A good grass fire is a splendid sight, especially running before a good wind at night. I wondered whether it was grass fires which gave the old Greeks the idea of the Furies.

One great thing too about having the country all burnt is that you're not continually worrying about whether the fire-belt round your camp is big enough to stop a fire, for once you've been burnt round you're safe from fires.

By the time you get this, Mother, our little brat will have arrived I expect. Its rather hard being so far away and so cut off from news but I'm trying not to worry, for it does no good. Its opened my eyes to one thing and that is what it must mean to a woman to have her man on service. At the most man has only nine months in which to worry about his wife – and it's a feeling which gets less and more acute at different times and is only about the danger of one battle. But a woman never knows when the battles will be and she has only the end of the war to look forward to for security. I don't know how they stand it, Mother mine.

I don't know what I should do if anything happened to my Betsy. I suppose while the war lasted I should just carry on – there'ld be nothing else to do. After that I don't know. But anyhow its too awful to think of and only makes one morbid. So I'm going to keep my mind on the joyous side of it all.

It's so awkward not knowing whether it will be a boy or a girl. It wouldn't matter so much if I were closer, but it means that I, writing, don't know, while you on getting the letter already do know. It's not that I mind really which it is, it's just that one can't build castles in the air for an infant without one piece of solid fact to go on – its sex. That has to be the foundation of the castle. If its a girl I should be able to take her on my knee and play with her hair and if its a boy I shall be able to beat him. The joys would be about equal from my point of view but the che-ild's appreciation would again depend on the question of sex.

(IWM Q71868)

Lake Doiran, Salonika 1917.

Coniston Lake and the mountain Old Man, on the breast of which is situated the village of Coniston. The view is taken from near Brantwood, Ruskin's home.

Its the 14th now, I ought to get a cable in less than three weeks at any rate – perhaps little more than a fortnight.

You'll let me know all about the number of yells to the minute and their degree of intensity, won't you, when you've seen the small person.

With all love,

Your own dear boy,

JS (X)

I'm afraid I been harping mostly on one subject, but I'm also longing to hear how the new part of the cottage is looking.

Sunday, Aug 19th

Dearest Mother,

I've just got the letter you wrote on July 10th, so it took almost six weeks to come. The lavender in it is topping, but you forgot the pansy.

Sunday is a topping day. Last night we went down to the Company and had dinner there and kept the Gramophone going till about 12 and now we've just got up for lunch. I've just had a wire telling me to go and see an Infantry Company commander sometime to-day, but I'm going to wait till to-morrow. I don't mind working all day in the week but while things are quiet in the line I'm going to be firm about Sundays. I'm sure a thorough slack once a week helps to keep you fit, and hitherto I've kept remarkably fit.

Its topping to hear about Coniston, I often think of it for this is a lovely country and reminds one often of the Lakes. The actual lakes here are duller, having at least one side all marsh as a rule so that you can't get to the water, but the hills are lovely. They're on every horizon and away to the north they seem to stretch on for ever – as they do really, more or less.

I forgot if I mentioned Adolf's death when I wrote the other day. I was awfully sorry to hear about it. Its awful to think of his little wife. If anything happened to either of us now we could at any rate look back on six months of a happiness that can come to very very few – but with them, they only had a few weeks didn't they? I think, too, from what I've heard that Adolf had begun to find his soul, in the war.

(IWM PST 10286)

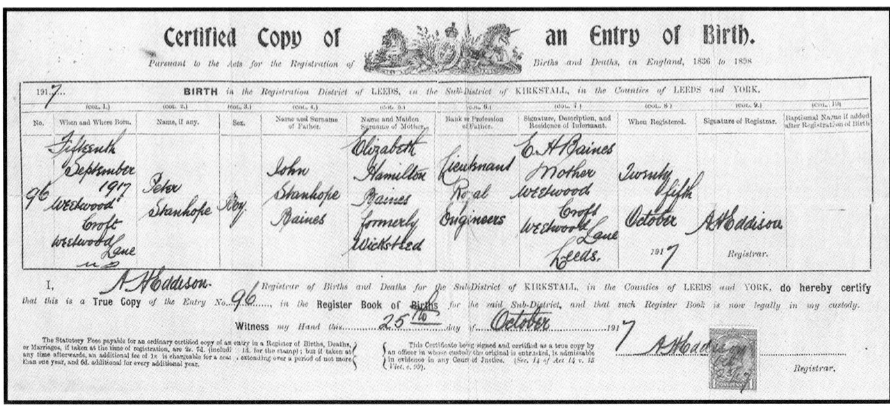

Certified Copy of an Entry of Birth.

Pursuant to the Acts for the Registration of Births and Deaths, in England, 1836 to 1898

1917 BIRTH in the Registration District of LEEDS, in the Sub-District of KIRKSTALL, in the Counties of LEEDS and YORK.

No.	When and Where Born.	Name, if any.	Sex.	Name and Surname of Father.	Name and Maiden Surname of Mother.	Rank or Profession of Father.	Signature, Description, and Residence of Informant.	When Registered.	Signature of Registrar.	Baptismal Name if added after Registration of Birth
96	Fifteenth September 1917 Weetwood Croft Weetwood Lane	Peter Stanhope	Boy	John Stanhope Baines	Elizabeth Hamilton Baines formerly Wickstead	Lieutenant Royal Engineers	E. H. Baines Mother Weetwood Croft Weetwood Lane Leeds.	Twenty fifth October 1917	A H Eddison Registrar.	

I, A H Eddison Registrar of Births and Deaths for the Sub-District of KIRKSTALL, in the Counties of LEEDS and YORK, do hereby certify that this is a True Copy of the Entry No. 96, in the Register Book of Births for the said Sub-District, and that such Register Book is now legally in my custody.

Witness my Hand this 25th day of October 1917

A H Eddison Registrar.

The Statutory Fees payable for an ordinary certified copy of an entry in a Register of Births, Deaths, or Marriages, if taken at the time of registration, are 2s. 7d. (including 1d. for the stamp); but if taken at any time afterwards, an additional fee of 1s. is chargeable for a search extending over a period of not more than one year, and 6d. additional for every additional year.

This Certificate being signed and certified as a true copy by an officer in whose custody the original is entrusted, is admissible in evidence in any Court of Justice. (Sec. 14 of Act 14 v. 15 Vict. c. 99).

Peter's birth certificate

Do you remember Gibbins, the Canadian who used to dine with us sometimes at Conway. He came on Christmas Day and it was he who came on my draft and I'd seen him several times out here. One of our trench mortars blew up as he was going into the emplacement and it killed him. On the boat and at the base I suppose I was with him about 20 hours out of 24 for 3 weeks, sharing a cabin or a tent or a railway carriage and I don't think I've ever known a finer fellow. He was a fellow I loved more than a little. I wonder where it'll all stop. Out of 16 of us who were the same year in College there are 8 left and its the same with most other rolls. I suppose it might finish next year – but its just as likely not to. I doubt certainly if we can really beat them by the end of next year. However, it'll stop one day and won't that be a day just. I shudder to think of that night. There are 20 million men under arms or thereabouts. Think of 20 million men stuck all over Europe on the same night and not one of them sober. But it's a lovely thought.

Honor will be up with you now. If only I could be there too.

Lots of love,

Your loving

JS (X)

Peter Stanhope Baines was born on 15th September 1917. All we have of the letter dated below is the PS.

5 Oct 17

PS

I nearly forgot to mention the cottage. I'm awfully glad they've really got under way with it. The new windows in the Nursery ought to make it a lovely room. I'm enclosing a cheque for £4, just over half of my bridge winnings. I like doing things with the mammon of unrighteousness – bridge winnings are certainly that. 35/- have got to start Peter's Savings Bank. I had one wonderful morning when nothing could go wrong. I won 35 drachmae & during the last hand came my cable, so of course Peter had to have the money. That's really better than giving Betsy a hat, because she just keeps the money & won't buy the hat till I can see it.

131st Field Company RE War Diary

8 Sep 17 Lieut Baines went to Hospital with fever.

22 Sep 17 Lieut Baines struck off the strength of the Company today having been in hospital for 14 days.

(National Archives WO95/4866)

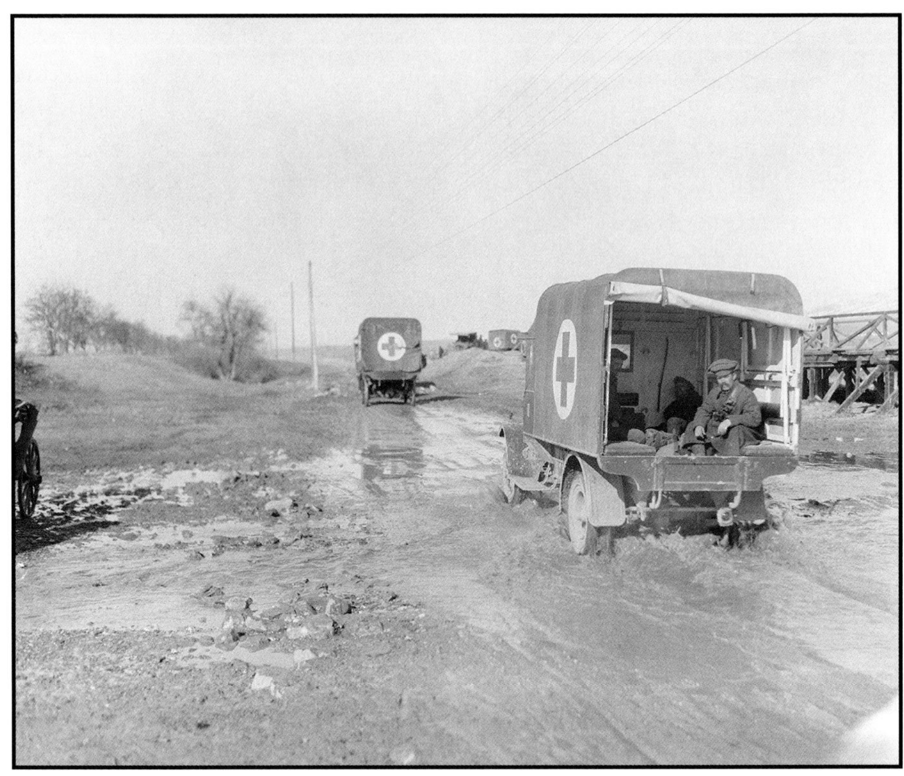

(IWM Q31652)

420th West Lancs Field Company RE War Diary

14 Oct 17 Lieut J.S.Baines, 2Lieut R.D.Keane, 2Lieut L.Worth and 49 ORs arrived at Mirova from GBD temporarily attached for special work.

(National Archives WO95/4803)

15.10.17

My dearest Honor,
I've been a most poisonous time without writing to you and I really am awfully sorry. Somehow in the hot weather one didn't want to write much and also the main fact in life was that Peter was on his way, so that till he came there wasn't much to write about. Now that he's here safely I'm feeling much freer.

I feel an awful brute Honor, for I've been sometime in even thanking you for your telegram. It was topping of you to send it and coming a day after the one from Weetwood it continued me in my treading on air. It's still my latest message from England for Peter hadn't quite arrived when the last letter I've had was written. In fact I don't know exactly his birthday. I think the 15th but he may have come late on the 14th.

I've been wonderfully bucked with life ever since I got the cable and am planning triumphant careers for him. I haven't decided quite whether he's to be Prime Minister or Engineer-in-Chief.

I've had about a month's holiday. I got a very slight go of sandfly fever, had ten days in hospital (not in bed at all as my temperature had gone by the time I got there) about 12 days in the Officers' Convalescent Home and a few days at the Base afterwards, waiting for orders. I had a particularly jolly time at the Con Camp where I went for several picnics. I played an awful lot of bridge and was 18,000 points up on the whole which at a drachma a hundred comes to about £7. Thats better than paying a mess-bill isn't it.

I've not got back to my old Coy, but am at the moment attached to the 420th West Lancs Field Coy R.E. As I've just been telling Elisabeth we're miles from the front, miles from the back and miles from both sides. I'm more than two hours ride from the Company itself even & they are by a long way the nearest Englishmen to me. I've a little camp with 17 Sappers and I've about 60 Turks working for me. Do you remember I had some Turkish books at Conway and never looked at them. I sent them home about six months ago very foolishly but I'm learning Turkish hard. I have a booklet with a few dozen words in which doesn't help much but is something. I talk to the Foreman and write down words in a note-book & learn them up afterwards. He doesn't speak English but speaks Greek. I only remember a very little old Greek & know no modern but it's sometimes a help when signs break down. It's easy enough to learn nouns & certain adjectives but verbs are rather hard. Next time you meet someone with

420th West Lancs Field Company RE

John served with his new company for almost exactly a year (14 Oct 17 – 6 Oct 18). Unlike the divisional field companies, 420th West Lancs Field Company was part of the Salonika Army Works force. Its role, therefore, was not engineer support to the front line, but was to carry out engineer tasks, of a wide variety, further back.

Throughout this time the unit was based at Mirova, at almost the centre of the British sector, mid-way between Salonika and the front line on the Bulgarian border. As we know from his letters, John and his work force spent long periods away from the company base, working on their own.

The scenario of an advance south by the Bulgars, over-running our own front lines and threatening Salonika, was a threat that was taken seriously throughout 1917 and 1918. As a strategic contingency measure, much effort was put into constructing the framework of a new defensive line some 15–20 miles back, including trenches, dug outs and wiring in pre-selected defensive positions.

Another vital component of this strategic work was the construction of a network of lateral roads across the whole area, linking the road and railway to Doiran in the west with the Seres road in the east. These would allow the essential movement of infantry and artillery in the event of a fighting withdrawal to their reserve positions, and also for resupply from Salonika. 420th Company played an active role in this high priority road construction throughout the year John was with the unit.

Ethnic Groups in Macedonia

The treaty of Bucharest in 1913, which ended the Balkan War of 1912–13, created new boundaries between Greece, Serbia and Bulgaria in the southern Balkans' region. As a result, Macedonia, which had always been defined as a geographical region rather than a political one, came under control of those three countries.

Throughout the war local Macedonians provided valuable labour for the British Salonika Force, particularly for the Royal Engineers, enabling their local economies to survive. Regarding themselves proudly as Macedonians first and foremost, their ethnic mix included Greeks, Serbs and Turks – all co-existing peacefully in their own separate rural communities.

Later in the campaign Bulgarian, Turkish and German prisoners of war were also used as labourers.

whom you have no language in common try & get him to tell the word in his language for "speak" or "talk". He may get as far as giving you the word for "teeth" or even "beer" but that's about as near as he'll get. You will eventually have mutually to say "No compree" & pass on to the next word.

The work we're doing is defence-work – trenches, wire etc. It's an interesting scheme but all the sighting is finished so I'll probably get rather bored soon. That's why its nice to have a chance to amuse myself by learning Turkish. The Turkish also has a better chance than if I could, say, play bridge. The only fault I found with hospital life by the way was that I wasn't awake early enough to play bridge before breakfast and that we had to go to bed at a certain hour at night, so that the bridge was curtailed both ends of the day as well as at meals.

Let me know, won't you, when you see the brat & what you think of him. I wish I had a chance of seeing him some time before he reaches military age.

By the way there's one thing I've been meaning to crow about ever since I landed in January. The Greek pronunciation of Salonika is Sa-lonn-ika and not Salon-ee/eye-ka. If you want anything else you can be French and call it Salonique. The Macedonian Turk calls it Salonia pronounced Sa-lonn-ia.

I dine at 5.30 or so here & it's now about 8, so I think I'll turn in.

Lots of love to yourself & Mother

Your loving brother

JS (X)

A house in a Greek village.

(IWM Q32542)

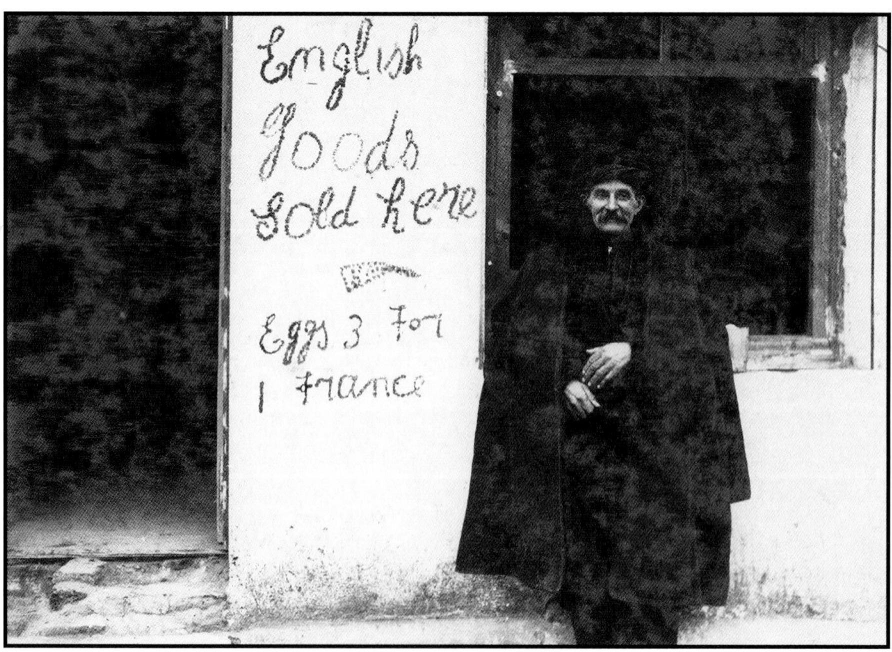

(IWM Q32687)

An enterprising egg seller in a Greek village.

Oct 29th 1917

Dearest Mother,
I got your letter of Sept 24th yesterday and hope in a day or two to get your second report. I expect its some where in the country but my last few letters have come in extraordinary order. A week ago I got E's letters of Sept 20th and 29th. Two or three days later came hers from 15th to 21st and Oct 2nd & Aunt Hilda's letter and one or two others. Yesterday I got E's of Sept 9th, Oct 6th and three about 25th Sept. Also yours & ones from Mrs Webb and the Bishop. Mrs Webb's being of Oct 7th.

One of Betsy's letters told me you liked him quite a lot on your second visit. He seems to be putting on weight well & giving great satisfaction all round. I'm glad you thought him strong & vigorous.

Its topping to be hearing such lots about him. After the first effects of the cable had died down it was hard to realise that I really had a son, but now I'm beginning to feel that he does belong to me and that I know something about him. I've got a lock of his hair. Its a great treasure and is about this size: *(here there is a shaded rectangle 1cm long)*

It would have been nice if I had been home to have asked the Bishop if he would christen him but as things are perhaps it would make Mr Wicksteed feel rather awkward as it would be from his house. He would feel differently about Mr Draper & as it was old Draper who married us I think it would be rather nice if we got him to do the christening. Elisabeth wrote to me about it and I think perhaps that will be the easiest way.

I'm having quite a jolly time here and not minding being alone. One feels nearer home alone as one can think about it more. I'm getting lots of fresh eggs & milk from the village. The latter is rather dear, I pay a franc daily for a pint & a half about, but it's worth it. The eggs are 2½d each, but the Turks are trying to raise the price to 3d.

The work here is quite good fun. I'm fortifying a hill with trenches & wire. At first I thought it was going to be dull because everything seemed to have been sited but I find I have a fairly free hand in making additions to the scheme.

I'm really working under the Engineer-in-Chief. He is rather a canny old Scot & scared me a bit at first the day he came round, but when more or less accidentally I started laying down the law about something he got quite interested & seemed keen for me to work out various schemes. He told the Major that I seemed to be taking an "intelligent interest" in the work. It was just by chance that I started talking of the probable way the enemy

(IWM Q32631)

A village wedding in Macedonia.

would attack if ever he came, but as he seems to like it I've got lots to tell him next time he comes. (He might be worth keeping in with).

I'm getting on fairly well with my Turkish. I wish I hadn't sent back the books I brought out with me. Its not a bad language I think and it isn't hard to get hold of a smattering of it, enough to get on with but rather pidgin, but I expect I'll find plenty of worries when my books come out again. I don't know if I shall have the necessary energy for tackling it in written form as well.

I'd like to get a job in the Levant later on. It's nearer home than India & a much nicer climate. If I could get enough Turkish now to be able one day to get a second-class interpretership it might help me lots later. If in three or four months I'm still using native labour I may have a shot at Greek but I want to get on a bit more with Turkish first as its muddling trying to learn two languages at once. I'm always trying to put German words into the middle of my Turkish. I suppose because it's another language of which I know a little but very little.

There is an interpreter who comes up here about twice a week. His primary drawback is that he speaks remarkably little English & his other one that he speaks no Turkish. My head foreman however knows a little Greek.

I wanted to talk to the Headman the other day about something so I took the Interpreter & Chawoosh (foreman) down to the field where the headman or muktar was engaged in ploughing. I declaimed to the Interpreter in English to put it into Greek for the Chawoosh to put it into Turkish for the Muktar. As I say, the Chawoosh doesn't speak much Greek & the Interpreter not much English, so things were a little vague, but I'd brought a full case of cigarettes & we were all very friendly.

A young Sapper called Parker has just come to this company, not having left the Shop very long. When you had tea in my chamber in College my last half, he was one of the juniors who polished off the fragments that remained.

I've come across about half a dozen Wykehamists out here; Selby-Bigge I saw the other day and another College man called Snow, a roll senior to Parker, was in the Con. Camp with me.

I've sent Peter's announcement of his arrival to the Wykehamist. I must write & tell Monty he's to be got into College.

Selby-Bigge I found enlisting & training Macedonian muleteers speaking Greek & Bulgar fluently & a little Turkish. Humphrey Dakin was also in

Elisabeth and Peter 1917

Peter in College at Winchester 1930
He did make it!

Greek word

πολυφλοισβος (pronounced poluphloisbos) is a deliberately exaggerated version of a word that means "loud roaring" In this exaggerated version it implies "one hell of a din!". It is the sort of word that might have been used as an 'in family' expression or joke.

the Con. Camp with me and I ran across Colin Smithells at the Base just before I came up here.

I got a letter from Mrs Cohen in answer to one I wrote & also one from Mary about Peter.

I suppose you saw that little Osmaston had been killed. It's rotten luck. And poor old Gibbins as well. You remember them both at Conway. I got very fond of Osmaston & had a kind of hero-worship for Gibbins. I'm very glad that I knew them both well.

I was just wondering the other day if we'd ever get those bricks back from the Mathisons. Peter will be quite happy without them for a year or two but he'ld like them after that, when he starts his elementary construction courses. I'ld give anything to see him now, but it will be lovely when we can start building brick towers together. Do you remember the dug-outs I used to make behind a bush in the Mount Preston garden. They were only 191K pattern but quite solidly roofed, with a continuous layer of chips. I shall certainly start early on Peter's education in military engineering. I'm afraid that besides that I can only give him Civil Engineering. He'll have to go to his grandfather for the mechanical side. But bricks and a stream to dam are quite good fun in the civil line.

His mother too can give him some of the practical part. I think her finest effort was when her father left his one remaining pipe at the works and she made a hookah for him out of a doll's bucket and a length of flexible gas-piping. If that's not R.E. work I don't know what is.

Have you tried him with πολυφλοισβος yet? I suppose it's a little beyond his imagination for the moment as he isn't living by the sea. I hope he won't suddenly announce something dreadful such as that when he grows up he's going to be a German.

I suppose you'll be back in London now. I hope the planes aren't bothering you much. Raiding squadrons are about the most unpleasant things I know if you're out of doors and near a crowd or anything else you think might be an attractive target but you can feel fairly safe if you get indoors. I'm glad you're on the Western side of London. A special reason for getting indoors is that even if there are no planes above you, you may quite easily get nasty bits of Arcline flying about. They mayn't do very much harm unless they hit exposed flesh but they make a beastly noise as they come & fall with a rather nasty thud.

With lots of love to Aunt Honor and Great-aunt Letty!

You're very loving,

JS (X)

John makes the comment that he is glad Dearest Mother is on the western side of London. By the end of 1917 Londoners had probably come to realise that, in 1915, the Kaiser had specifically forbidden any air raids to take place on royal palaces or residential areas of London.

Bombs on Britain

Germany made the decision to bomb mainland Britain in May 1915. It had a fleet of airships at the ready. Zeppelins, as they came to be commonly known in Britain, quietly and stealthily floated at over 10,000ft. There was little defence against them initially. Their targets were military bases, barracks, fuel and ammunition dumps, and particularly London docklands. But difficulty in navigation meant that it was the east coast of England that bore the first brunt of attacks.

Black-out legislation came into force but, as far as London was concerned, the river Thames was always a good navigation aid to the enemy – so thousands of Londoners took to sheltering in the Underground at night. In September 1916 the City of London was damaged and on 3rd October there were 189 bombs dropped on London with 71 civilians killed. In November the same year and in January 1917 air raids took place over the Midlands and even as far north as the Leith dockyard, near Edinburgh.

The British had by now developed several ways of countering the Zepellins – with barrage balloons, anti-aircraft artillery and eventually fighter aircraft – and by 1917 most of the air ships had been withdrawn and their place taken by heavy bomber aircraft.

These aircraft did more damage than air ships had done, and they could fly daytime raids, which caused great concern to the civilian population. After a particularly heavy raid on London, in which 162 people were killed, a great number of children were evacuated to the countryside for the first time.

Although the overall number of deaths in Britain from air raids was not huge (around 1,500), the shock and fear they created (and the worry they gave to troops overseas about the wellbeing of their loved ones) had a big psychological impact on the civilian population.

5.11.17

Dearest Mother,
I sent you the other day a handle which I found in digging a trench and now enclose a small copper coin. They're neither of them of any value, dating only from the coming of the Turks between 1450 & 1500.

The hill which is the Keep of my trenches had evidently once a Monastery on top of it. We get lots of roof-tiles and some floor tiles in our trenches & bits of broken pots, of which I sent you one (I had to break it further to get it into the tin I'm afraid, but it can be stuck together). We've also got that one coin.

I chatter away with my Turkish foreman in a mixture of signs, pictures & pidgin Turkish. He pointed out some old foundations to me some time ago, since when we've hit a good many others. It was he who first said there had been a church here & I cursed myself for not having realised it sooner. I had thought the village might have extended up there once but had emptied through lack of water. Naturally a church is the only thing you'ld build on top of a hill when all your wells were at the bottom. But it covers a fair area so I suggested that it wasn't all church but that there was a big wall round & that we'd cut through priests' houses probably. To-day however, we both had the idea of a monastery, so I went to the highest bit & examined the ground & found signs of a rectangle of walls with the longest sides running due east & west. Later I got a pick and shovel & messed about from the inside of the rectangle. I've got the inner face of the north-east corner laid open & will do some more to-morrow. I'm almost certain that this is the church itself. Just before I left off I came across a handful of bones. I have them here in a tobacco tin at the moment, but I'll put them all back eventually. I'll probably find some more of the gentleman tomorrow & hope that in the meantime he won't come looking for his shin or whatever it is in my tent to-night. If he does I'll threaten to give his beastly bone to the first dog I meet unless he goes back to bed at once & I'll comfort him by telling him its a ration baccy tin they're in and that anything proceeding from the English Government is the holiest thing you can get that isn't actually consecrated.

A Macedonian Treasure Trove

John would have known very well, as a classical scholar, that there was a strong likelihood of finding interesting old coins in Macedonia. One senses that the trouble he takes to describe the coin in such detail in his letter, as he does with later finds also, is not just to show off his knowledge; he knew that Dearest Mother would also be interested, with their shared classical educations.

The history of Macedonia is complex, with endless sub divisions, invasions and occupations. As early as 6th century BC it was under Persian rule; then it became a colony of Greece; for a while it was then an autonomous kingdom in its own right until it was fully annexed by the Romans in 146 BC.

After around eight centuries of Roman occupation, it was invaded by the Slavs, Avars, Bulgarians and Magyars in the 7th century AD. In 1014 it came under Byzantine control once again. In the 13th century it was part of the Bulgarian Empire, and in the 14th century part of the Serbian Empire. Thereafter it was part of the Ottoman Empire, a situation which continued for five centuries until the Treaty of Bucharest in 1913

So – no pressure in identifying any coins found during sapper excavations – Persian? Greek? Roman? Slav? Avar? Bulgarian? Magyar? Byzantine? Serb? Ottoman? Take your pick.

The coin is very worn & as the green has only come off in one or two places its more easily examined in artificial light, held quite close to a candle. On one side you can make out fairly easily the head of a man with a beard. The copper shews brightly on his hair, dully on his cheek and the green covers his nose, beard and shoulder. There's been lettering on the left of him but I can make nothing of it. The reverse is more interesting.

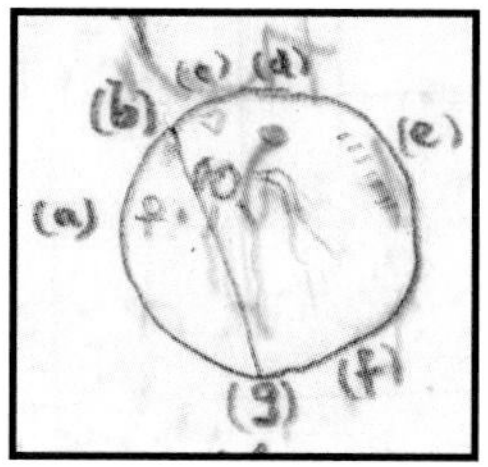

There's a figure which I thought first was a womans till I made out the monogram against it at (a) which I presume stands for Xpioros. There's a big scratch right across it from (b) to (g). Just between this & the head is what may be a halo. The three smudges at (b), (c) and (d) may possibly be the remains of cherubs. Above (f) is a figure I can make nothing at all of. It looks at first sight like a colossal goose. There have been letters once at (e] but they're too far gone.

I don't suppose anyone would know anything about such a coin. Research in mediaeval Byzantine things has probably not been much gone in for, since round the Aegean if you find the Venus of Milo you say she's modern & decadent so what'll you say about things of the year 1500. I hope we may run across something of which more can be made, but here's the coin for you anyway & perhaps you can interpret the goose. I did think of the Holy Spirit but gave that up as unlikely.

I've not had any more letters since I last wrote & things go on as usual. My works are beginning to take form a little & I'm prepared to hold them against the Prussian Guard. In a month or two they'll be the strongest thing I've ever dreamt of unless very heavily bombarded with H.E. from big howitzers. Even then I'd rather defend than attack them, provided I had plenty of trench mortar bombs & rifle ammunition. There's nothing I'ld enjoy more than the battle of the __________ and since it's never likely to come off I've a good mind to write the account of it now, allowing the Bosch to get further than he ever would do just so as to make it interesting & bring in a successful counter-attack.

I'm much looking forward to your next letter on the subject of Peter. He's seven weeks & two days to-day. That's a great age, isn't it.

I got a letter from Tangles two days ago congratulating me. He's just back from leave where he got engaged to Monica Whitcombe, a daughter of that doctor you mentioned who minded Mrs Lupton. She's a cousin of Phil Whitcombe's, but a very much finer specimen. I've danced with her once or twice and Elisabeth came down to the Sandhurst match with her,

Chaperones

In the Edwardian era, and up until the first World War, it was generally recognised that marriage was a woman's main aim in life. At the age of eighteen a girl would put up her hair and lengthen her skirts – two ways of indicating to the world that she was in the marriage market. To guard her reputation, her parents would make sure that she never went unaccompanied to a place where she was likely to come into close contact with men. She would always have a chaperone keeping an eagle eye on her.

Chaperones were often a girl's mother, or other relation, and one chaperone could have two or more girls in her charge at a time. As well as watching her charge and noting who she was speaking to and how many dances she had (and with whom), a chaperone would often be expected to introduce a young girl to men considered to be eligible for marriage.

There was not much dating fun in those days. A man was not expected to flirt or show any feeling for a woman until he was sure that he wished her to be his wife. After two or three outings with a chaperone, and maybe a visit to her in her home, a man would most likely talk to her father about his feelings before he ever declared them to the girl.

my last term at the Shop, as E. had no chaperone & Tangles had raised one for Monica. She's absolutely sterling and they should be very happy together. They're thinking of getting married next time he gets leave, which from this country might be in another three years. My having been in hospital may put back mine but I shan't get it for another year or two, in any case. In two years the war ought to be drawing to a close I should think, unless this Italian show lengthens it again.

With lots of love to yourself, Honor and Aunt Letty

Your loving

JS X

PS Is it hard and fast that Mary S.is engaged to that fellow whose name I've never remembered and never wish to. Elisabeth told me something about it but nothing very much. I refuse to write & congratulate her. If there's any chance of it breaking I might perhaps write & "hope she'll be happy" but I expect she'll not catch my meaning. I shall be very sorry if it does come off for I've always been rather fond of Mary

6.11.17

Dearest Honor,

I've just got to-day your letter of 17.9.17. You addressed it 121st instead of 131st and they sent it to the 127th which is about the nearest thing to 121st out here. It puzzled them there so they wrote on it "Unknown with 127th Field Coy R.E." & sent it away from the base, however, it got to the 131st Coy and thence back via the base here.

Thanks so much for all your congratulations about Peter. I hope you'll be able to get up to Leeds sometime or other to see him. He'll be awfully bucked if you do. He's getting more a man of the world now I believe though the last letter I've had was written a month ago. He's seven weeks and three days now but I suppose his knowledge of the English language is still rudimentary.

(IWM Q62966)

The line of reserve trenches being dug by John's unit (see Page 160) were likely to have been similar to this used in 1915 on The Kosturino Ridge, rather than the traditional full depth trenches used at the front line.

(IWM Q31667)

Three generations of a Macedonian village family with a passing officer of the Argyll & Sutherland Highlanders

I've been realising to my joy that if Peter is as sensible as his father I shall be a grandfather at 46 and a great grandfather before I'm 70. Dick only just missed getting beaten by the next generation didn't he. It seems to me awfully sound to marry young. You see it's obvious that as the world progresses each generation ought to be rather better than the one before. So if your family can run through six generations while some other is getting through four you're two generations more up-to-date than they are. That's sound logic isn't it?

The Major of this Company came & lunched with me to-day and afterwards I walked a couple of miles over what will be the extension of my line. When I got back I found that the Commander in Chief had been here to look at my work. I'm awfully disappointed at not having been here to point out its main beauties to him. He might have made me a General on the spot. He'ld also perhaps have altered a lot of it, so that it's maybe as well I wasn't here. If there's one thing I loathe its having any scheme altered, once its started.

I'm afraid I've not yet got the parcel you so kindly sent from Leeds but I expect its wandering about & will turn up in the end. I shall be glad then not to have had it sooner. Not getting back to my old company has made all my mails take longer to reach me & parcels, of course, are always much slower than letters.

I've got a lot of ladies working for me now. They all seem about 60 but they seem able to manage a pick & shovel all right. My people are all races, mostly Turks with a few Bulgars & Greeks thrown in. The Turks are much the nicest and I'm great friends with my Chawoosh or foreman. We have long conversations on all sorts of subjects in Turkish. A literal translation of any of my Turkish sentences would be rather amusing but we get on quite well. There's a lot of drawing of pictures and lots of signs & gestures & whenever I get hold of a new word down it goes in my notebook.

It's nearly 5 now when I have my dinner. So I'll close down.

Lots of love to you both

Your loving brother

J.S.

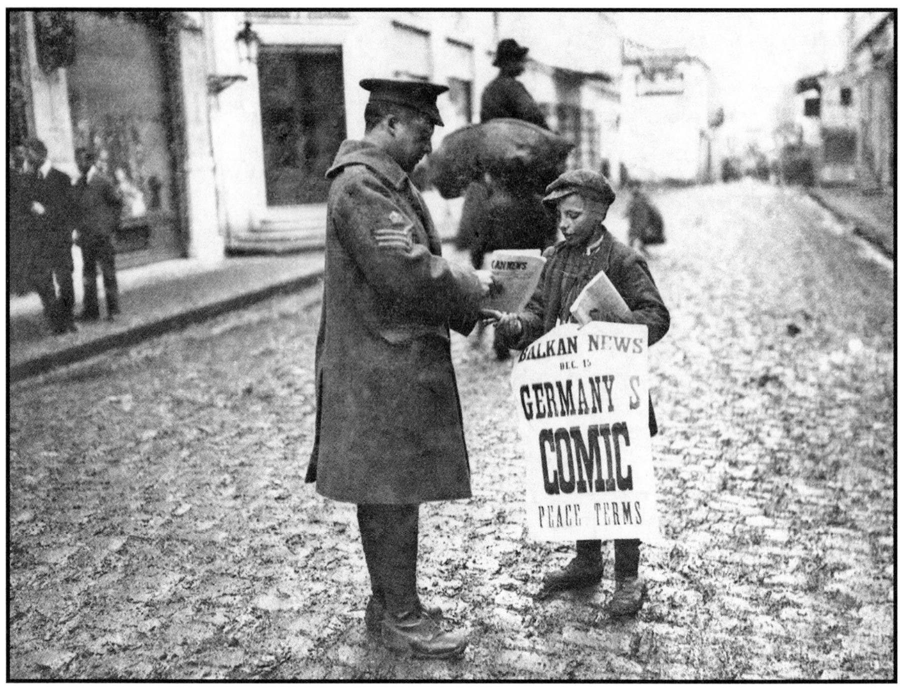

(IWM Q32643)

A soldier buys a copy of the British Salonika Forces newspaper, *The Balkan Times* from a vendor in central Salonika Nov 1916.

The Salonika Fire

On the afternoon of 18 August 1917, a fire broke out in the old Turkish quarter of the city. A combination of tinder dry wooden housing, a Vardar wind and totally inadequate fire fighting services led to a very rapid spread of the blaze. Soon, the streets were filled with refugees clutching their belongings and trying to load carts with furniture and other goods. Chaos reigned as a teeming mass of humanity tried to save themselves and their property. Troops of all nationalities intervened to try to stem the flames. The multi-national make-up of the relief effort led to some confusion, as did the mass of refugees.

Once the fire was under control the Allied military commands had to focus quickly on provision of disaster relief for an estimated 80,000 people rendered homeless by the blaze. British relief camps were opened at Karaissi, Dudular and Kalmaria by 20 August, a full day before the fire had burnt itself out.

From: 'Under the Devil's Eye' Alan Wakefield & Simon Moody 2004

18.11.17

My Dear Mother,
Here's another coin, in rather a better state of preservation. The rather vacant-looking gentleman in the fillet seems to have part of his name round him still, but I'm afraid I'm not up in the Byzantine people & so can't make any sort of a guess. There used to be lots of semi-independent kings towards the end of the Empire & it's just as likely to be one of those as an emperor. The reverse is still harder to make out but it looks rather like a masterful matron with a fierce stick in one hand and a small boy in the other.

I also enclose a sprig of honesty which I found here. It's the only honesty I've ever heard of in the Balkans and even that is not very largely developed!

I've been reminded the last day or two of a letter I censored last year in which one of my Sappers told his mother or aunt or someone "It is for a good cause for which we are fighting for, but it is bloody cold here just now". There's certainly no better summing up of the situation. It was the night before last that it was particularly true but last night I was fairly comfortable. I get a pint & a half of milk every day & last night I had it heated. I normally have a wooly sleeping vest under my pyjamas but last night I wrapped a scarf round my middle as well and then put on a cardigan. I strapped in a mac in my valise on the top of my two blankets & my double sleeping bag and had a tunic on the top of that. I also wore a pair of long stockings. So I was able to be reasonably comfy.

This morning, it being Sunday, I had my breakfast in bed and then had a hot bath. I've been fairly regular with my cold ones but this was my first hot one for a long time. A collapsible canvas bath is not, of course, quite like one which you can lie in full length & wallow in, but its nothing to sneeze at.

I read Blackwood, XIXth Century and Land & Water after that. I take in those and also Punch & the Weekly Times. They make a lot of difference to one's powers of keeping up to date. Away here I hardly ever get even a Balkan News and since the fire that has only been a one sheet affair & has little in it except the official communiqués.

I think perhaps, you'ld like seeing Blackwood and so I've written to ask Betsy to tell the publishers to send it to you during 1918 as a Christmas present from us both to you and Honor. Old Blackwoods too are just as nice to have as old Punches so will you have them bound each six months and ship the bill along to Betsy who'll pay it for me. She pays all my bills for me these days and so not only saves me from financial worries but also

***Parkin**, which originated in northern England, is a moist, soft, slightly sticky cake made with oatmeal and black treacle. It is particularly associated with the Leeds area of Yorkshire, which is where John's family lived. Parkin would have been especially suitable to send to John, even as far as Salonika, as it can be kept for a long time in a sealed container and connoisseurs often prefer to eat it a bit aged.*

Traditional Yorkshire Parkin Recipe

Preparation time: 20 minutes Cooking time: 90 minutes

Ingredients

8oz/220g soft butter
4oz/110g soft, dark brown sugar
2oz/55g black treacle/molasses
7oz/200g golden syrup/corn syrup
5oz/120g medium oatmeal
7oz/200g self raising flour
1 tsp baking powder
4 tsp ground ginger
2 tsp nutmeg
1 tsp mixed spice
2 large eggs, beaten
2 tbsp milk

Preparation

1. Heat the oven to 275OF/140OC/gas 1.
2. Grease an 8" × 8"/20cm × 20cm square cake tin.
3. In a large heavy-based saucepan melt together the butter, sugar, treacle, golden syrup over a gentle heat. Do not allow the mixture to boil, you simply need to melt these together.
4. In a large, spacious, mixing bowl stir together all the dry ingredients. Gradually add the melted butter mixture stirring to coat all the dry ingredients and mix thoroughly.
5. Gradually beat in the eggs, a few tablespoons at a time. Finally add the milk and again stir well.
6. Pour the mixture into the prepared tin and cook for 1½ hours until firm and set and a dark golden brown.
7. Remove the parkin from the oven and leave to cool in the tin. Once cool store the parkin in an airtight tin for a minimum of 3 days. If you can resist eating it, you can even leave it up to a week before eating and the flavours really develop and the mixture softens even further and becomes moist and sticky.

Recipe and photograph by kind permission of Elaine Lemm

helps the trades people. Life's not long enough to pay bills on active service though I always square up everything I can before leaving England.

Since beginning this letter another officer has arrived here. He's a sort of mixed blessing. I shall not, on the one hand be so inclined to turn into a kind of Robinson Crusoe but I shall not, on the other, have so much room in my tent. My furniture was constructed so as just to leave me room to get in and out. With another bed in I've had to scrap one table. My armchair too, really takes up too much room but its too much a friend for me to let it go.

Please thank Honor much for her parcel which arrived two days ago. I've just finished the parkin. It was too good to last long. I'm afraid that in the course of its travels some postal gentleman coveted the chocolates. Powolony ought to have sewn it up instead of just tying up a cardboard box. But this parkin was so good that I can forgive him for not being a Yorkshireman & leaving it to me.

It's only just past the middle of November but one never knows how long letters will take and so I'll make this my Christmas letter. It'll not be such a happy one as we had last year at Conway but anyway it's one more Christmas nearer the end of the war. It should, I think, be the last war one but one. Last years was a very happy one and I don't so much feel sad about Gibbins and Osmaston as glad that we were able to know them. A very very happy Christmas to you both and may we soon have another all together

Your very loving boy

J. S. X

I'm hoping soon for your second report on Peter. He's been learning to smile but I suppose he'll be a few more months before he can explain what the joke is.

Autumn in northern Greece

Dec 2nd 1917

My Dearest Honor,
At last I am really sending you your beads though I'm afraid the old thread they were strung on broke long ago. They are in a separate envelope from this letter and I hope they'll arrive safely. They're very trumpery things but I liked the colour of them. I told you at the time that they weren't a birthday present. That's still to come but you can think of them as a Christmas one if you like.

Are you still pensioning on 27/6 a week. You people ought to raise a strike you know. The Government ought to give you far more than that. I'ld have a shot at learning shorthand & typing if I were you and then you might get Lloyd George or someone to take you on as a private secretary. Ernest Gowers would probably fix it up for you. Then you could tell Ll-G what a fine fellow I was & he'ld make me Minister of Reprisals or whatever the next Ministry they'll form will be – not that I insist on a new one. If Fisher gets tired of Education or Balfour gets fed up with his job I'm quite ready to take on either of those. A private secretaryship would be more interesting wouldn't it and have a better screw.

I hear there's something in the air about revising the pay & allowances of Subalterns & Captains. I hope it'll come off & that it won't turn out to be an increase of 2/– in something else. That was what Sapper Captains got in the last "Increase of Pay".

There's really no news here and such scraps as there are I have given to Mother. I'm beginning to get a trifle fed up with being here. It's much worse just now when the Italians seem to have scored off our mails completely.

Your Parkin turned up quite safely and was very good. Thank you ever so much for it. I'm afraid that someone had liked the chocolates you mentioned but they can't be helped. I like to think that it was still fairly hot when they started and that perhaps they'ld have melted.

We've been having lovely weather. There was a pretty sharp snap a fortnight ago but since then it's been like an English summer, a little colder perhaps at night but warm enough to make you walk about in shirt-sleeves at mid-day. The trees have almost all turned colour now and are beginning to think of shedding their leaves (it's Dec 2nd). There are more trees about here than where I was before and the tints are wonderful.

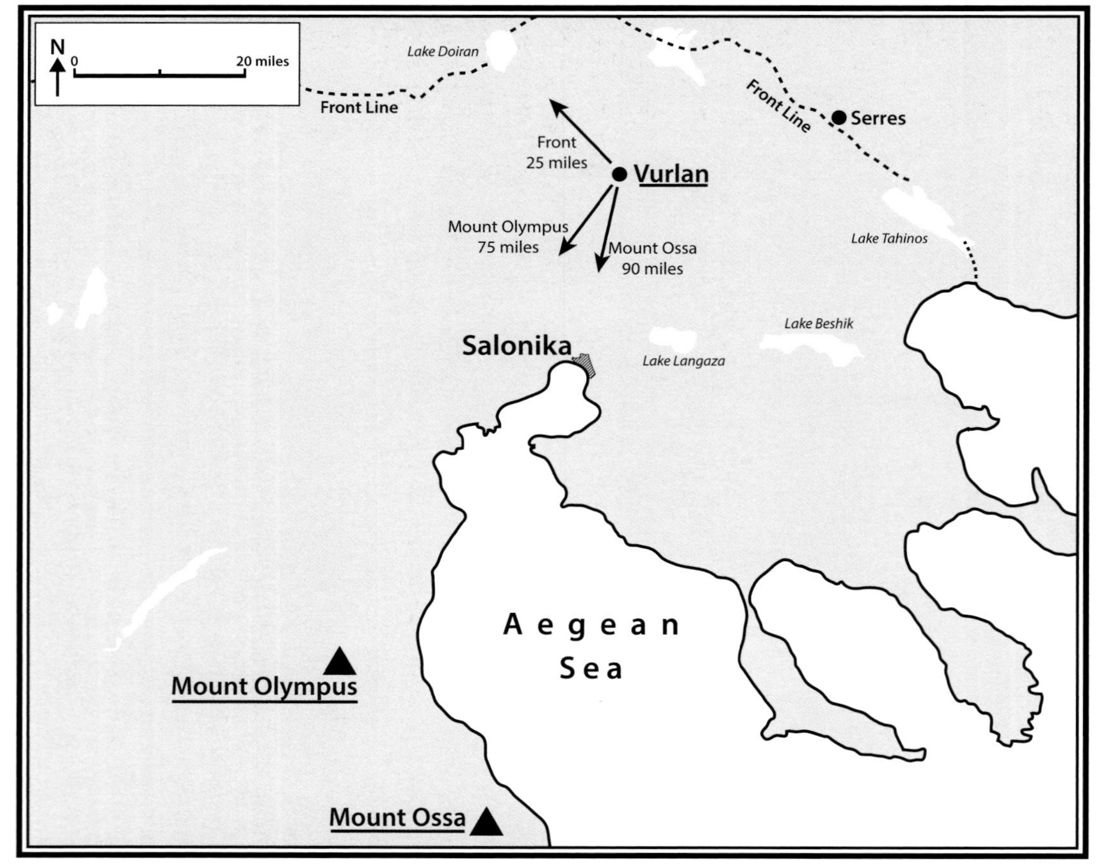

Views from Vurlan

I can get splendid views on three sides, good almost always for about 30 miles while on a clear day its far more. Olympus we can see most days. He's just 100 miles off and Ossa, another 50 miles off, stands out well at sunset & dawn usually even if you can't see him at mid-day.

With glasses I can see shells bursting 25 miles away in places I used to know only too well, and I admire the effect which distance lends to the scene!

I find this is my last sheet of note-paper so I'll send my love & Christmas wishes and hope that we'll get the next one together.

Your loving brother

JS X

Dec 10th 1917

My Dearest Honor,

I was positively snappy on Thursday when after 20 letterless days there was at last a mail. There were a lot of papers & magazines & two letters one from you of Nov 8th & one from Elisabeth of Nov 3rd & got an awful shock seeing the way most of them were addressed Now what have I written, I asked myself, that's made Betsy think I've got an acting Captaincy. Now letters will be coming like this for six weeks before I've been able to stop them and I'll look no end of a fool. (My temper had been getting worse every day that we were without letters). On opening Betsy's letter, however, I found a cutting from the Nov 3rd gazette which soothed me, though it took me about 48 hours to get over the shock.

I spent many hours that night wrecking the sleeve of one coat and on the other turning two stars & one band into three stars & two. There's more work in that than you'ld think for you have to unpick lots of things to get at the end of the braid.

It's an immense relief. I'm not feeling now that through being in this country & through belonging for the time to no particular unit I was missing the chance of an acting Captaincy, which most of my batch were getting. My rank now is fixed and I can enjoy any job given me without worrying about anything.

I'm still in the land of the Turks. There are times when things pall a bit but its not a bad job on the whole. I don't know whether my exalted rank will make me be sent anywhere else but I don't expect it will for a bit.

British Army Rates of Pay 1914

War Office Instruction 166 (1914) gives the following daily rates for officers, in shillings (s) and pence (d):

	2nd Lt	Capt	Lt Col
Cavalry	8s 6d	13s 6d	29s 6d
Royal Garrison Artillery	8s 6d	13s 6d	24s 6d
+ armament pay	1s 0d	2s 0d	5s 0d
Royal Field Artillery	8s 6d	13s 6d	28s 0d
Royal Horse Artillery	9s 6d	15s 0d	29s 9d
Royal Engineers	8s 6d	13s 6d	21s 0d
+ engineer pay	1s 0d	4s 0d	14s 0d
Infantry	7s 6d	12s 6d	28s 0d
Army Service Corps	7s 6d	12s 6d	21s.0d
+Corps pay	3s 0d	3s 0d	6s 0d
Royal Army Medical Corps	14s 0d	15s 6d	30s 0d
Army Veterinary Corps	13s 8d	15s 6d	30s 0d

War Pay

Rates of pay rose each year. Additional War Pay was added, for the combat arms only, from 29 September 1917 for the rest of the war. The rate was 1d per day for each complete year served since the start of the war.

I should think you'll find propaganda much more fun than pensions. Will they give you better pay at all? I don't suppose you'll have much of the deciding just yet of what to propagand, but let me know if you do 'cause I want to propagate lots of Doctrines. I'm madly keen on the necessity for breaking up Austria & so spoiling the Mittel-Europa scheme. If we don't do that we'll have let Germany win the war even though she should have to give up Alsace-Lorraine. If you want to know all about it read the X1Xth Century. Any month will do. You get the same article twice over every month but the title is different each time & sometimes the signatures. They're all worth reading, however.

By the way I'm a bloated plutocrat now. While the war lasts & I get the various extra allowances, I now get 25/- a day instead of 17/6 i.e.about £460 a year instead of £320. As Betsy is living at home and I'm about 40 miles from a shop I can't spend a respectable amount of money however much I try. So I am going to play the high & mighty Sapper Captain giving a tip to his little sister. I'm enclosing a cheque for a fiver for you and also one for £20 for Mother which she may find useful after having had the move & the doing up of the cottage.

These aren't Christmas or birthday presents. They're just so that you can wet my third star for me next time you feel you want to drink!

While I was in the low Camp I sent Mother £4 out of my bridge winnings which I hope she got but the mails seem to be in an awfully bad way just now.

Let me know if you get this letter safely.

You make me very jealous by being able to go and visit your nephew. I wish I had a chance of seeing him & his mother some time before he gets his commission.

With all love to you both.

Your loving brother

J.S.

Aeroplane in the Balkans watched by a group of Serbs

(IWM HU081081)

General Sarrail, commander of the Allied forces in Macedonia (16 January 1916 – 22 December 1917) with Gen Sir George Milne, commander of the British Salonika Force from 9 May 1916.

12.12.17

My dearest Mother,

I've just got your letter of Nov 6th. It was about a week later in arriving than Honor's which was written two or three days after it.

Thanks awfully for your congratulations on the Captaincy. It came as a great surprise but a very welcome one, for I'd been feeling cut off, here, from any chance of an acting Captaincy and now I haven't to bother about that at all.

I think I must have missed a letter from you for you said from Whitby that you would write again about your second glimpse of Peter and I've not had anything until this last letter.

I hadn't thought about Dick and Peter being at Winchester together. That must certainly be arranged mustn't it. I should think they ought both to be able to get into College. I don't know whether Dick would inherit very many brains from his mother but I think Peter should be all right in view of all his grandparents.

I love your saying you don't mind The Huns & miss them when they don't come. I must say however, that I don't care for bombing raids. Its not so bad when you're indoors but when I'm out in the open with any troops under me I must say that I prefer bullets, shells & trench-mortar bombs.

One day last March I was just moving camp. It was about an hour before dark. I had all my pack-mules there, about 15 or 20 and the Sappers were just finishing loading them up. Suddenly the Bukharest Troupe came along & flew straight over the top of the camp. I sent the Sappers off into bombardment slits but the drivers of course could only stand by their mules. I wanted to go up to the Mess (equally unsafe but more comfortable) but I felt it was more or less up to me to stay with the drivers.

The Hun did not, I was glad of, drop anything onto us and as it happened we saw a very good fight. There were about 20 Huns most of whom were bombers not fighters and they were attacked by six of our scouts. Two Huns were brought down & the remainder let fall their bombs anywhere to lighten themselves and went home as fast as ever they could go.

What really annoyed me more than anything was that it was almost dark by the time I was able to start on my three mile walk & I'd only once before been over the ground. We arrived eventually, however.

I've had four Times from you – Nov 2nd, 3rd, 11th, 15th, for which many thanks. In the latest of these is an extract from a Salonika Despatch

THE TIMES 15th November 1917

A YEAR'S WORK AT SALONIKA
STORY OF POSTPONED OFFENSIVES

A dispatch from Lieutenant-General GF Milne, Commanding-in-Chief the British Salonika Force, was published last night as a supplement to the *London Gazette.* The dispatch covers the period October 9, 1916, to October 1, 1917. General Milne acted under the supreme direction of General Sarrail, Commander-in-Chief of the Allied Forces in Macedonia.

Since November 29, 1916, the British troops have held that part of the front covering Salonika and extending from the mouth of the Struma by Lake Dorian to the Vardar — a distance of approximately 90 miles. On the Strurna sector the line was gradually pushed forward, the Dublin Fusiliers capturing practically the whole garrison of three villages. But at the beginning of last summer, in view of the unhealthy character of the low-lying area, the British troops were withdrawn to the foothills on the right bank of the river all the bridgeheads being retained and the evacuated area daily patrolled. This arduous duty was successfully carried out by the Derbyshire and Surrey Yeomanry.

On the Dorian-Vardar sector minor operations were undertaken last winter with the purpose of harassing the enemy who was strongly entrenched in mountainous country. Battalions of the Cheshire Regiment, the Suffolk Regiment, the Northumberland Fusiliers, the Welsh Fusiliers, and the Devonshire Regiment showed conspicuous skill and gallantry in these operations.

Towards the end of February, 1917, General Milne received instructions from General Sarrail to be ready to begin offensive operations in the first week of April, and in preparation a corps was pushed forward in March on the high ridge between Lake Dorian and the Vardar. By April 6 General Milne's preparations were complete, but General Sarrail found it necessary to postpone the offensive until the 24, when the British infantry entered the hostile trenches along the whole front attacked. The fighting was of a most stubborn character, the Devonshire, Berkshire, and Manchester Regiments and the Shropshire Light Infantry being specially named for their dash, tenacity, and determination.

Preparations had begun to take advantage of the commanding positions gained on the ridge when General Milne learned that "owing to climatic and other reasons" the operations by the Allied troops on the right bank of the Vardar and near Monastir had had to be postponed. General Milne was next told that May 8th had been fixed for the re-commencement of the Allied advance. Accordingly an assault was made by the British troops on the enemy positions between Lake Dorian and the "Petit Couronne" Hill. In the face of great opposition the troops,

(*continued on next page*)

in which Milne manages to shift most of the blame onto Sarrail – and quite justly I expect.

Milne was up here on my job a day or two ago and was extremely gushing about everything. He's rather a strafer by reputation so I was quite glad he was in a good temper.

I wrote to Honor the day before yesterday and in honour of my Captaincy enclosed cheques for £20 and £5, the latter for her and the former for you. I hope you will be able to find it useful for some little extra. I was sorry only to send you £4 the time before but I wasn't quite sure how I stood at the time because of Peters arrival. I'm now however in quite a sound position and am beginning to collect Peter's school fees.

If I can collect & invest £45 a year and always reinvest the interest I calculate that after 12 years I can stop saving and draw out £100 a year for 8 years. An extra investment now is of course worth twice its value nearly in 12 or 13 years time so I'm quite glad to be able to start straight off with a £100 which came from Grannie's money.

I've had quite a good mail today with lots of news about Peter. He seems to be getting along very well, though apparently the Old Man made quite a good fight for survival at his christening. When Garforth and Thorburn, however, really have time to set properly to work, I don't suppose the Old Man will have much chance.

With lots of love to you and Honor

Your loving son

J. S. X

Boxing Day. 1917

Dearest Mother,

I'm writing this from Coy H.Q. where I came yesterday & stayed the night. I'm waiting till after tea before going back so as to catch any mail there may be.

I came over here just after 2.30 at which hour my detachment had their Christmas dinner. They had a certain amount of stuff sent up from the canteen and there was half a plum pudding per man – tinned ones & quite a good size. (In the mess here I think two of us got through about one & a half). I had also got them a sheep which was roasted whole. I was very glad I had done as the ration meat was bully. The fly in the ointment was that

(*from previous page*)

among whom the Argyll and Sutherland Highlanders, the Oxfordshire and Bucks Light Infantry and the Berkshire Regiment are specially noted, made progress, though against repeated counter-attacks all the points gained could not be held. By May 20 the new line was consolidated. A further advance was in progress when, on May 24, General Milne received definite instructions from General Sarrail that offensive operations were to cease all along the front. Since that date there has been, apparently, no essential change in the situation on the Dorian-Vardar sector. In minor engagements and raids the Royal Scots, the Scottish Horse, and Lancashire Fusiliers are named for good work done.

General Milne draws attention to the great improvements effected in means of communication, in spite of an exceptionally wet winter, and states that the supply of the troops has proceeded satisfactorily. The wastage among animals has been exceptionally low.

As to the health of the troops, Gen Milne states that it has been "on the whole satisfactory", and he calls attention to the work not only of the R.A.M.C. but of the British Red Cross Society and the Order of St John.

"With the advent of the cold weather (writes General Milne) malaria abated rapidly, and the sick rate remained low during the winter. Preparations for the next summer in the form of anti-malaria work were, however, steadily pursued, drainage of swamps and canalization of streams were extended, and the personnel for technical work strengthened; but what proved of almost greater importance was the instruction of all ranks in the value of field sanitation and the prevention of disease in the field. The results have been most satisfactory, and, while giving the full credit to the various ranks of the medical services and to the devoted band of nursing sisters, I consider that the greatest diminution in disease in this army, as compared with last summer, is due chiefly to the fact that the value of preventive measures is fully realised by all ranks, and that the whole Army has profited by the experience of last year."

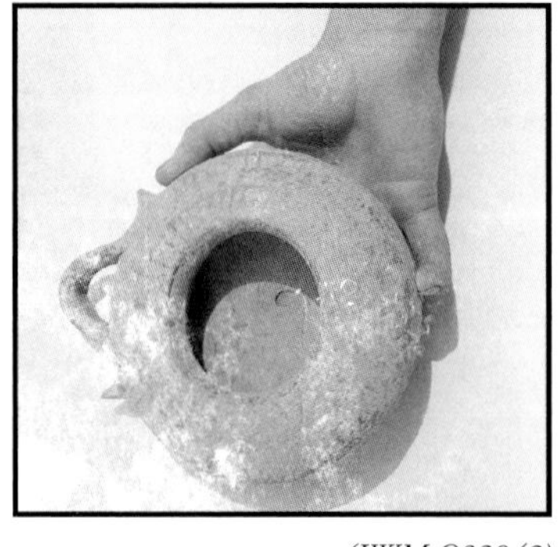

(IWM Q32842)

Could this be one of John's finds?

An earthenware vessel probably a lamp, date 8th Century, dug up in Salonika by the Allies in 1917.

the beer didn't turn up, but they had a rum ration & 3 bottles of port & 2 of sherry, which wouldn't go very far between 35 of them. However they'll be having the beer to-night.

I solemnly went in & wished them the usual things as one does on Christmas Day and in the conventional way they very solemnly sang the jolly good fellow and drank my health.

After that I rode over here and had quite a jolly evening. We played poker between tea & dinner. I'd never played before though I've often wished I knew the game. I had beginner's luck & raked in 13 drachmae which was quite a lot at the low stakes we played. It's not as good a game as bridge of course but it's quite a good game to know how to play, for jolly evenings when you have too many for bridge or don't feel serious enough for it.

We've been finding lots of pots and coins lately. We've got trenches through an old graveyard and the graves generally have a jug & plate & often a lamp & often coins. The latter are mostly Roman but some are Greek. One may have been Alexander the Great. I didn't ask the Sapper who found them to let me have that one but I've got some rather poor rubbings of it. Its certainly some Alexander for it has a ΑΛΕΞΑΝΔΡ on it quite clearly except just the end of the name. One of the Roman Johnnies is called Antoninus Pius. I seem to remember his name. Weren't there two Antoninuses about 100 or 150 A.D. who were rather more respectable than most of the others.

There's a brass one which the Greek Foreman gave me which has an oar-rowed ship. Its wicked, however, the way these people clean them by rubbing them on stones. The ship might have been three times as interesting if it had been given a chance.

I don't think I'll be able to get the larger bits of pottery home but some of the smaller bits & two very nice little earthenware lamps I'll certainly manage somehow or other. One lamp is really lovely. It's very simple but has a slight pattern indented.

The most pleasing thing of all perhaps is a little earthenware whistle. Its about two inches long and gives as good a blast as it did 1500 years ago, or whenever it was buried. I'll let you have it and some times when Peter comes to stay with you he'll be able to blow it as a great treat. If he always were in the same house as it, he would certainly lose or smash it in the end & it would be a pity to lose it.

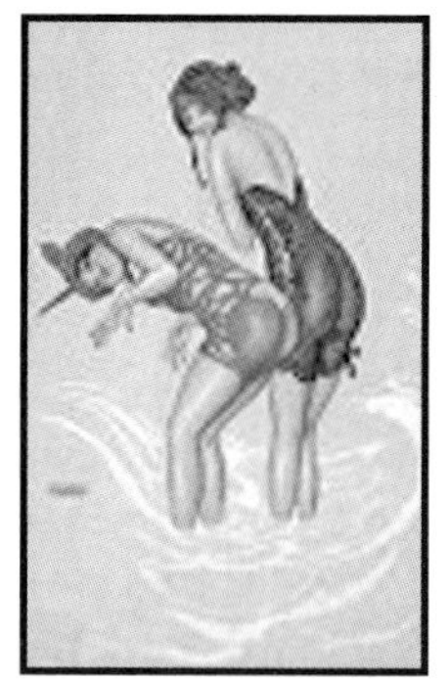

Ernst Ludwig Kirchner 1880–1938 was born in Germany of Prussian parents. He initially studied architecture, but later committed himself completely to art. He was an expressionist painter and a founder member of the artists group Die Brűcke (the Bridge) which sought to create art that 'bridged' the traditional and avant-garde movements and was a major influence on modern art in the 20th century. Kirchner wrote of Die Brűcke that "anyone who directly and honestly reproduces that force which impels him to create belongs to us". In his youth he led a bohemian life style which overthrew many social conventions, and his paintings and drawings from this time are focused on nude females in nature.

In 1914 Kirchner voluntarily joined up for military service, but at the end of 1915 he suffered a nervous breakdown and spent the next two years in sanatoriums in Switzerland recovering from a dependence on morphine and alcohol, with occasional visits to Berlin to paint. In 1918 he moved to live in Switzerland permanently and his health gradually improved. His paintings from this time are mainly mountain scenes.

In 1931 Kirchner was made a member of the Prussian Academy of Arts, but as the Nazi party took power it was increasingly difficult for him to sell his paintings in Germany. In 1937 the Nazis declared his work to be "degenerate" and confiscated all his paintings that were hanging in museums. After Germany annexed Austria, Kirchner feared that Switzerland might also be invaded and in July 1938 he committed suicide.

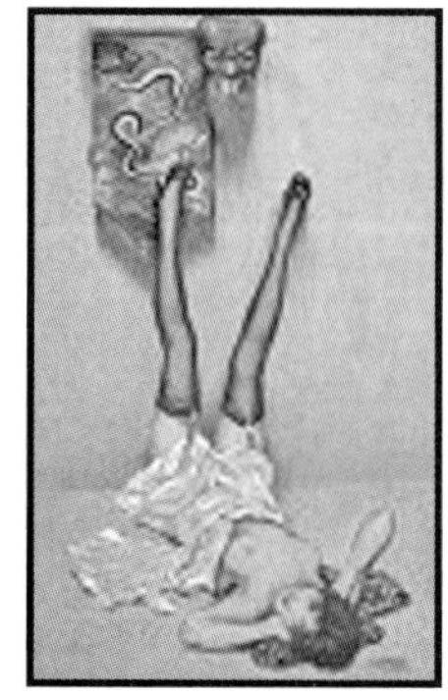

This was only just a note while I was alone in the mess for a moment. Now that the others are beginning to come back I'll wind up & will write again soon from my own camp.

With love to you both.

Your loving

JS X

Jan 6th 1918

Dearest Mother,

The days continue, one just like the other & there's nothing really to tell.

We've had a fairly heavy fall of snow and I'm very glad to be in a dug-out instead of a tent. It really is a very cosy little room. I can't quite remember whether I described it in my last letter or not. Its 12ft by 7ft with two bunks at one end. There are heaps of shelves and hanging pegs and the furniture consists of two rustic armchairs & a small table. There's a third chair which can be brought in when needed. The ornaments are bottles of the English period and pots, plates, lamps etc of the Roman period. The Bosch metereological paper balloon being a bright red makes quite a nice splash of colour pinned flat to the wall in one corner and the sandbags & oat sacks with which the walls are hung make really quite a nice background for about a dozen Kirchner pictures of ladies of varied charm and in various stages of dress or undress! Some of them are really quite nice.

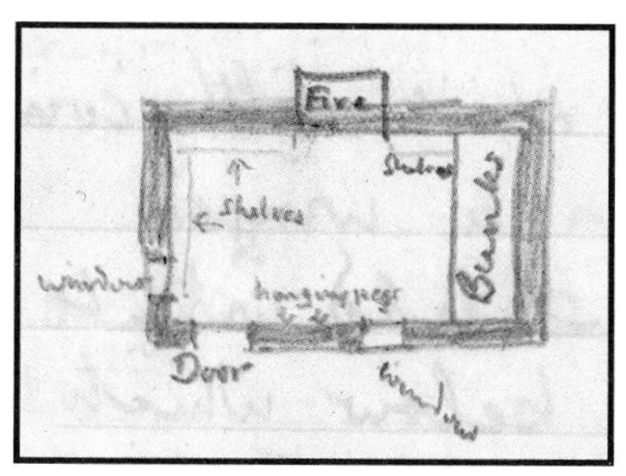

We've had a good many coins lately of one kind or another but I'm rather afraid to trust them to the post. I've only taken about a dozen as it wasn't really I found them.

I enclose several rubbings of the Alexander one and another bit of paper with attempts on three other coins. The brass one with the boat with EU?IVOS on it has a head on the other side but unfortunately that one has been cleaned by being rubbed on a stone & very much worn. The Greek foreman gave it to me. Old somebody Decius is typical of about half the coins we get i.e. Roman with that funny crown. But Antoninus Pius has a laurel wreath not the crown. And an extremely pretty little girl

Coin rubbings enclosed with letter of Jan 6th 1918

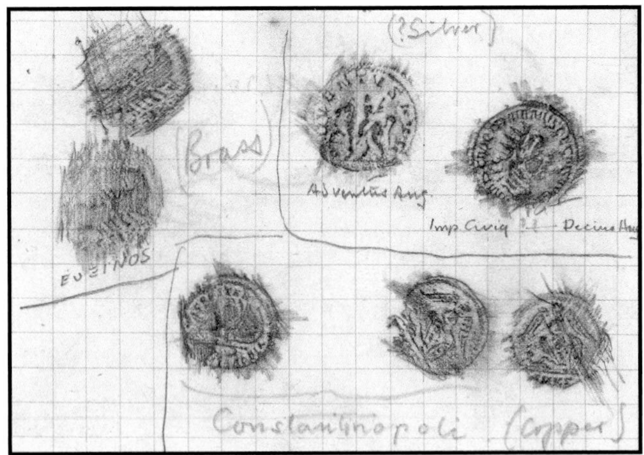

Without being able to see the actual coins, the only additional information about them to add to that given by John, must be purely speculative.

The **brass coin** possibly reads EUXINOS and Pontus Euxinos was the name given to what we now call the Black Sea, when its shores were colonised by Greeks 8th-6th Century BC.

The **copper coin** (Constantinopoli) – Greek letters below might well read NIKE who was the Goddess of Victory – always depicted with wings.

The **Alexander copper coin** – several rubbings of the same coin – appears to be Macedonian, with the head of Alexander the Great on one side and an infinitely debatable depiction on the reverse.

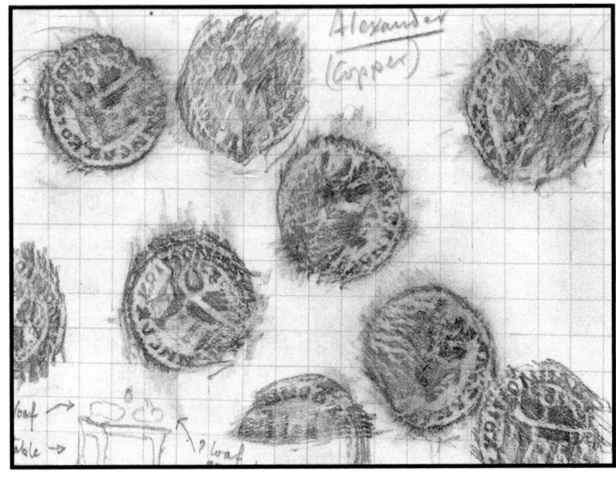

called Salonina Aug: (I think that's her name) who has Juno Regina on the reverse of her coins, hasn't a crown – but has very nice hair. We've had two of her coins. She's about 18 in one and rather older in the other but I'm wildly in love with her. The one with Constantinopoli on is a very neat little coin. The reverse is a winged lady with a shield with 4 Greek letters below which I can't make much of. The first I can't read & the others appeared to be MKΓ. I can't make it into NIKH any how. The Roman ones all have something similar to "Adventus Aug" on the reverse. The Pius Anthony has "Victoria Aug"; someone who seems to call himself "Divo August" (though I may be wrong) has an altar and "Consecratio" on the back of him; & another fellow who starts off "Imp Cordianus ......" has what I thought was "Romana Eternae" on his back. But it didn't seem quite right & I find that the first N might just as well be an E which gives Romae Aeternae which would probably lose him fewer marks.

I'll try & get someone going on leave to take things back to England as it would be a pity to lose them. I'm afraid the larger jugs would be rather hard to manage but the little pots, the plates and the lamps should be all right. I told you, I think, about the little earthenware whistle. Peter can blow it when he comes to stay with you and it really makes a very fine noise.

Kennedy has gone away & so has Marshall who was up here for a short time, but I was only one night alone for yesterday a fellow called Blair rolled up. He's very quiet but isn't a bad fellow.

By the way I believe I forgot to mention Sonia. I think you said something about sending it & Elisabeth said she was sending it & a copy came by the same mail as her letter. I hope that was hers so that you won't both have sent it. It's one of the best books, anyway, that I've ever read and I'm awfully glad to have got it. It's a historical essay. I shall read it again in a couple of months I expect

Wd. you ask Mr Collingwood whether that spiky crown is any particular set of Emperors and if so could I have a list of them with their dates. The two coins I sent you were from the "Monastery" itself but our pots and all these other coins are from the graveyard.

I hope Honor won't get either 3 or 7 years.

Lots of love to you both

Your loving

JS X

Page from *The Wykehamist* showing a list of attendees at Old Wykehamist Dinner 23rd February 1918 – Salonika

226 THE WYKEHAMIST. [No. 572—Mar. 23rd, 1918.

The dark clouds, Sisters to the solemn hour,
Wait on thy passing, and the heavy air
Bears, as we bear our sorrows silently,
The leaden burden, and there is no voice—
Mute, with bent heads, before the open grave,
We stand, and each one feels his pulses ache,
And his throat parches, and the unspoken grief
Closes an iron hand upon his heart.
Three times the volley strikes the solemn vault
Of that imprisoning arch, and piercing clear
The bugles cry upon the dead, "Arise!"

And thou shalt rise, yet we turn sadly away;
The scarlet and blue pennants droop; the night
Draws darkly on, and dawn, when dawn shall come,
Throws a drear light upon the Eastern sky,
And Dome and Minaret wake ghostly grey,
And in the trees a little wind goes sighing.
Hail and farewell; the laurels with the dust
Are levelled, but thou hast thy surer crown,
Peace, and immortal calm, the victory won.
Somewhere serene thy watchful power inspires;
Thou art a living purpose, being dead,
Fruitful of nobleness in lesser lives,
A guardian and a guide; Hail and farewell!

J. G. Fairfax, Lieut., A.S.C.

Baghdad, Nov. 18th, 1917. (D 00-05).

Obituary.

Cecil Henry Offer came to the Science School as an Assistant in 1908, and worked there until the outbreak of the war. He was a member of Mrs. Beloe's Club, and of the College Servants' Cricket and Football Clubs. In 1911 he joined the 1/4th Hants (T.), and in October, 1914, he sailed for India with the Battalion, later proceeding with it to Mesopotamia. After the battle of Hannah he was reported missing. He was seen to fall, wounded or killed; and is now officially presumed killed.

To those who knew and valued his character and work, his rapid promotion to the rank of full sergeant at the age of twenty-two was no surprise.

An officer of his Company writes:—"I always looked up to him as quite the smartest sergeant in the Company. Up to a certain time he had the distinction of having been *the only man in the Battalion* who had not reported sick while in Mesopotamia. We all felt his loss very deeply."

To the Editor of the Wykehamist.

G. H. Q., British Salonika Force,
February 23rd, 1918.

Dear Sir,—The attached list of those who attended an Old Wykehamist Dinner in Salonika on February 5th may perhaps be of interest to some of your readers:—

Lieut. M. E. Antrobus.
Captain P. Ashton.
Captain J. S. Baines.
Captain J. B. Bettington.
Lieut. J. A. Selby-Bigge.
Lieut.-Colonel D. Burges.
Major W. S. Cowland.
Lieut.-Colonel B. Cruddas, D.S.O.
Captain P. Stormouth-Darling.
Brig.-General G. W. Dowell, C.M.G.
Rev. T. V. Garnier.
Lieut. C. L. Godson.
Lieut.-Colonel Sir E. I. B. Grogan, Bart., D.S.O.
Major R. Macfarlane.
Lieut.-Colonel H. G. G. Mackenzie.
Lieut.-Colonel B. J. Majendie, D.S.O.
Lieut. C. C. Wykeham-Martin.
Lieut. Ian McL. A. Matheson.
Captain D. J. Mitchell, M.C.
Lieut. E. Ç. Nepean.
Lieut.-Colonel E. H. Nicholson, D.S.O.
2nd Lieut. L. McC. Parker.
Captain B. M. Patton.
Major R. Peel.
Captain R. A. Powell.
Major C. E. F. Rich, D.S.O.
Major the Hon. H. Ritchie, D.S.O.
Captain J. W. Rooke.
Lieut. A. G. I. Schwabe.
Captain E. G. Sebastian, D.S.O.
Lieut. G. H. G. Smith.
Captain A. G. Thompson.
Major W. A. Trasenster.
Brig.-General E. J. F. Vaughan, D.S.O.
Lieut. S. B. White.
Brig.-General B. F. Widdrington, D.S.O.
Lieut. F. G. M. Williams.

Yours faithfully, Robert Peel.

To the Editor of the Wykehamist.

Sir,—I think that a register should be kept of College and Commoner Editors of the *Wykehamist*; on consulting both the Sen. Co. Prac.'s annals and the Prefect of Moberly Library's book, I can find no sign of their names being perpetuated. The *Wykehamist* plays such an important part in the expression of Winchester opinion and in being the official chronicler of our life, that surely the names, at least, of its Editors should be preserved, and steps should be taken to secure the necessary information.

Yours, "Generis Monumenta Prisci."

To the Editor of the Wykehamist.

Sir,—I write to bring to your notice a very obvious reform. The only justification for Wrench Card's continued existence in these days of economy is that it should be issued by the end of the first week of the Half; recently it has come out so late that its only use is for juniors to tick off the last ten days of the Half upon it. The reform which I suggest is that Wrench Card should make its appearance at the proper season, or—failing this unlooked for triumph—that it and the person responsible for its delayed production shall be forthwith abolished.

I am, sir, yours, etc., J. D'E. Firth.

To the Editor of the Wykehamist.

Dear Sir,—May I avail myself of your columns to apologise for the non-appearance of Wrench Card this Half, and to make some defence against the storm of criticism which I feel sure will be levelled against me on the subject. Under present conditions there appear to be two courses open with regard to this production; either it may be published at the beginning of the Half, in which case it will contain nothing at all; or one may wait till after Short Roll has come out, in which case it will be a compendium of accurate information about past events, but unfortunately no one will buy it. This being so, I have followed the advice of "R. G. L." in one of your issues of last Half, and not produced it at all, thus saving at once the country's paper and my own time.

Yours, etc., J. Pennycuick, *Aul. Prae.*

Printed and Published by
P. & G. Wells, Booksellers to the College.

February 4th 1918

Dearest Mother,
Many thanks for your letter. I'm afraid I've been bad again lately at writing – only once I think in January and I'm very sorry. Until yesterday I'd only written one letter to Elisabeth too since the middle of January for I've been horribly busy. My numbers have gradually increased from the 40 to 50 Turks I first had to over 400 and the centre was done first so that while at first I had a handful working near me I've now 400 getting more and more scattered to right and left. And we've been "getting a move on" lately which may or may not mean more work done by the men but certainly means more for the officer. I've decided now however that knocking about from 7.30 till 5 (except for lunch) is well enough but that continuing on paper from after dinner till midnight is a luxury. So I've appointed a clerk. He has an easy day & a beastly evening, and I just signed the things when he's through with them.

I've been meaning to tell you that the coin I gave you a rubbing of with what looked like "IMP CIVIQ THAIDEUS DECIUS AUG" is "IMP?? Q.TRAJANUS DECLUS AUG". The only thing I don't know is what "CIVI" or "CM" is. It looks of course short for CIVIS. I found it was Trajan by making out the name on another Trajan coin. The latter has "Dacia" on the reverse which is rather nice. "Adventus Aug" is rather dull. We've found nothing else lately I'm afraid. I hope you've been able to find out who Salonina Augusta was. I like her.

The Wykehamist dinner is tomorrow. I'm riding over to HQ early tomorrow morning and the Colonel is lending his car to Parker & me to go down in from there. Parker is one of the juniors who sat very sedately in their toys when you had tea in Fifth with us. It'll be great fun to stand on a chair once more singing Domum.

I've got rather a nice little Tabby kitten now. She's perched on my knee at the present moment. She wears a green ribbon. The first day she came she tried to escape up the chimney and fell back into the fire, which was silly, but she soon developed a purr like a motor-byke & has lots more self-confidence now. She's rather sedate for her age and is most persistent at night. I can hurl her out of my sleeping bag 20 times but I've always fallen asleep by her 21st entrance so that she wins in the end.

I've got two officers with me now, but I'm letting one do survey & the other mostly roadwork.

Organisation of Local Labour

As we learn from his letters, John frequently controlled large numbers of local civilians on his work projects, particularly on road construction and stone-breaking in quarries. What were his responsibilities towards them, apart from supervising their work?

'The administration and payment of the very large numbers of civilians employed caused at first considerable trouble. The system adopted by most units was for each man, woman and child to be given at the end of a day's work a piece of paper showing the day's earnings, and signed perhaps merely by the sapper in charge of the gang. These "pay slips" were honoured by the unit on the next pay day, or even by the base paymaster, having passed through the hands of Jewish discount firms in Salonika. The "pay slips" had to be backed by rolls giving often unpronounceable names and the earnings of the workmen'

In the second half of 1916 this system was replaced by the creation of a Directorate of Civil Labour, responsible for the recruitment, administration and pay of all civilians.

(History of the Corps of Royal Engineers Vol VI)

And how did the British sappers treat their local labourers?

'It never occurs to the British soldier that because he is in uniform, occupying someone else's country, he has the right to do things which he would not dare to do in his own. He is just as good-humoured to the Balkan peasant woman as he would be to one of the "lydies" who sell flowers on the fountain of Piccadilly Circus. He doesn't think that because he, a foreign soldier, sees a Balkan chicken he has a mandate to "pinch" it. It simply doesn't occur to him to play the conquering warrior game. He has a phrase of his own which shows this. He speaks of himself as "the brutal and licentious soldiery", and we all know that once Tommy has made a joke of a thing he has absolutely robbed it of its sting. The same British Colonel told me that in several years experience with his Division he had not known a single case of assault on women, and had any such occurred the case must have come through his hands. And yet we employed a great deal of female labour in road-making, with men of ours constantly in charge of them. Tommy was a great civilising force in Macedonia. Even the most mulish of the peasants – and they can be very mulish – began to realise that something new was abroad: that soldiers could be up and down roads and on the side tracks everywhere and that nobody's head was broken, no woman was carried off, and no chickens or eggs were looted.'

(Salonica & After, *H.Collinson Owen, 1919)*

One is a Devonshire person who's had 20 years in Ireland. He's 45. He uses Irish ways of saying things, quite unmeaningly, with a cockney accent & never stops talking. But he's very keen on any job he's given & that's a great thing in these days of hurry. He's talking hard now.

I got Honor's letter too yesterday. Please give her my love.

I'm glad the cheques arrived safely.

Your loving

JS X

Feb 18th 1918

Dearest Mother,

After six weeks of what in England would be good weather for July the weather has broken. So we've had a first-class blizzard which cut off our rations the first day and made work impossible for two days. Today it didn't snow particularly hard so we routed out what Turks we could – about 70 men & 20 women instead of 400 altogether – and in a foot of snow they tried to do a certain amount of work. The wind has got up again now so we'll probably wake up to another blizzard tomorrow.

The great comfort during the blizzard has been your parcels – posted in November – which arrived four days ago. Sherlock Holmes and Chesterton and Harrod's sweets have made a lot of difference.

I've got a couple of Majors here now. One is just doing Survey and the other is in charge the Sector. I'm doing a sort of cross between Adjutant and Second-in-Command to him.

Between Belloc & Garvin & the XIXth Century I'm not expecting to be clear of this country for over a year and I don't think any but those who arrived here in 1915 have any chance of leave in that time – which is quite right really.

There's something to be said for being here. One is getting a very varied experience and one is certainly much safer than in France. I'm not now getting time to work at my Turkish as I should like to, but even so I've got a certain amount of it and it may easily be useful later on if I can get a job here or in Palestine after the war.

I'd like that afterwards. This is really a very jolly climate and the scenery is wonderful. We would have quite a nice house in peace-time if I had a Public Works Job and you and Honor would come out for the Spring.

(IWM Q32713)

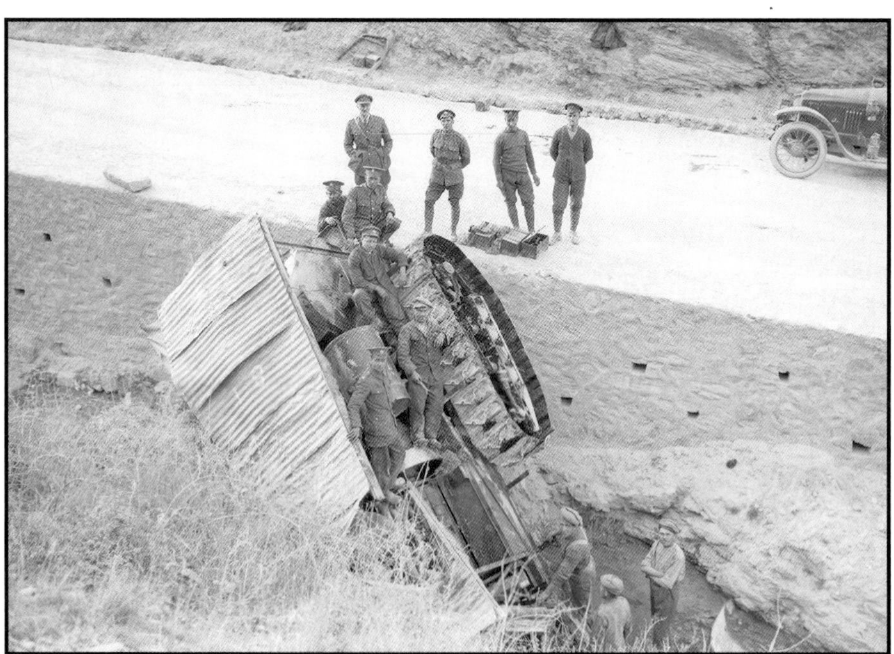

(IWM Q32806)

Holt tractors, imported from USA, were used in Salonika for hauling heavy guns and moving supplies, including artillery shells, from roadheads and railheads to dumps. They were also used by the Sappers for heavy tasks in road making, such as drawing tree stumps (top photograph, January 1917), and in quarries. Clearly they did not always manage to stay on the roads (lower photograph, March 1917).

That's the most lovely time of year, though the autumn & much of the winter is also lovely. I know now why Solomon said ______

"For lo! The winter is past:
The rains are over & gone:
The flowers appear upon the earth;
And the voice of the turtle is heard in the land."

(Turtle, by the way does not mean a turtle-dove, but a tortoise).

The flowers here in the spring are lovely. You get all the English flowers almost & most lovely peonies – about the beginning of June you finish up with myriads of poppies; after that everything is dried up.

There's an awful fellow here called North who talks more than any 10 people I've ever met & with less sense than the lot of them added together. He's from Devon and has lived 20 years in Ireland. I simply can't write another word through him.

Love to Honor & many thanks to her for Chesterton.

Your loving
J.S.

March 4th 1918

My dearest Honor,
It's the deuce of the time since I've written a letter at all, for I've been having quite a rushed time, but yesterday it was both Sunday and a thoroughly wet day and so I decided to be virtuous. I kept yours & one to Elisabeth till the last as I knew I should write none after them and in this way I managed to get off seven letters, so that I have now very few to answer of more than 18 months standing. In the end I didn't do either of the kept-back letters, so I'm making an attempt to-day.

Thanks awfully for the Chesterton. I enjoyed reading it greatly & have passed it onto the Major I have up with me now. He's reading it very carefully. I'm afraid I raced through it and am keeping the slow and careful reading for the next time – a few weeks hence. That's always the best way of reading a book.

Did you read it by the way? It's really jolly good. He doesn't so much take the History of England as pick out one thread which runs through it. He doesn't mind missing out the whole of the 18th Century for instance.

(IWM Q31797)

Tracks immediately behind the front line in Salonika were essential routes for evacuating casualties, either by stretcher bearers or mules, to the Field Ambulances. The construction and maintenance of these were therefore high priority tasks for the Sappers throughout the campaign.

(IWM Q47630)

Main roads running up to the front line were in constant use by infantry with pack mules and motor convoys with essential supplies. During 1917-18 the Sappers, including John's unit, also constructed a network of smaller, lateral roads behind the front line, for infantry and artillery to move rapidly back to reserve positions if the need arose (see Page 160).

I've just been reading "The rise of nationality in the Balkans". It sounds very stiff but is really awfully good reading. Still it probably excites me more than it would do you since the Balkans have always been rather a hobby of mine. It's another book which I rushed through and I'm going to read again carefully.

Your air-service propaganda photos are jolly good and have been much appreciated by all to whom I've passed them on. Will you let me know whether you're propaganding the dismemberment of Hungary. I see our Socialists haven't included that, nor has President Wilson though the Italian Socialists have. I think you'd better arrange for Northcliffe to do it through the Daily Mail. I can't think why it hasn't been done years ago. Just see about it will you, otherwise there'll be another war quite soon for us all, while if things are properly managed there should merely be a Serbo-Italian war in 1950. If your men don't agree tell them that I'm the future Professor of Modern European History at the University of Baines!

I'm afraid there's no news to give from here, except that Tangles has got a Field Company & so is now an acting Major. I'm very glad. He'll do it jolly well.

I heard from Geoffrey the other day. He's still in Trench Mortars.

We're all waiting to hear what the Bosch is going to do in France.

Lots of love to you both.

Your loving brother,

J.S

March 24th 1918

My Dearest Mother,

It's Sunday morning and after breakfast in bed followed by a bath I'm feeling quite at peace with the world. I have quite busy days now but there's enough interest to make them quite enjoyable. I shall be doing a good deal of roadwork shortly and several days lately the Major and I have been in the saddle all day choosing the routes we shall take our roads over. It's very pleasant going along these old tracks up & down nullahs feeding ourselves & the horses in some nice place & wondering who made the original tracks. We went along one yesterday which we call Alexander's Road. It was paved with large stones in bad places and followed a very fair gradient. After looking at lots of others we decided that as Alexander was undoubtedly a man of experience, his road would probably be the best for us. I know

420th West Lancs Field Company RE, John's unit, was part of the Army Works organisation and came under the command of Lt Col G S Pitcairn RE, the Assistant Director of Works L of C. – an officer with a formidable reputation:

I cannot leave the Seres Road without reference to a certain R.E. Colonel (wild mules could not drag his name from me), who did more, probably, than any other man to keep it in such excellent condition. In addition to the wonderful service he performed in his official capacity, he has earned our gratitude even more by his unconventional personality, from which a thousand anecdotes take their source of inspiration.

Colonel X was not a 'Regular' but a Civil Engineer, whose remarkable talent was quickly perceived and rewarded with rapid promotion. To the Regular Army point of view his methods appeared, to say the least, bizarre and such unconventional phrases such as "Passed to you, please," and "Through the usual channels" were unknown to him. He rode straight over every obstacle with a directness which was sometimes disconcerting to the 'Army mind'. All his considerable fund of energy he devoted to "getting on with the good work" and the individual suffered at the expense of the community, for he was no respecter of persons. But his chief claim to immortality was his remarkable gift of being able to swear in six or seven languages. At all hours of the day and night he would prowl up and down the Seres Road, on the look-out for slackers and 'lead swingers'. The average citizen of the Balkans takes not the slightest notice if you curse him in an alien tongue. He shrugs his shoulders with an air of good-humoured tolerance and the argument, as such, is terminated in his favour. But if you can express yourself fluently and devastatingly in his own language, his admiration and respect are at once aroused. So the Greek, the Bulgar, the Turk and the Macedonian respected Colonel X and if they were of an indolent disposition, lived in hourly dread of a visitation from this wise and terrible bogey-man.

(The Salonica Side-Show, *V.J.Seligman, 1919)*

Lieut Colonel G.S.Pitcairn … had had pre-war experience of road-making under similar conditions and was a good organiser, driving others almost as hard as he drove himself. His camp, known as "Pitcairn Island", was sited in the main quarry where he could ensure that the deafening noise of the stone-crushers continued unceasingly throughout the night.

(The History of the Corps of Royal Engineers Volume VI)

Greek words. John is talking about the conjugation of an irregular verb meaning "to come or go". He is correct with the present (βλώσκώ.) the future (μολουμαι)and the perfect (βεβλώκα) but the verb to come or go has no aorist (past) passive in any language. (You can never "be comed" or "be goned") so his word εβλώσθμυ does not exist!

lots of things now about the R.E. detachment which lived in that Roman Camp at Ambleside, why they put their road along the top of High Street and how they got their civil labour out of the villages.

We passed yesterday over what was a big battlefield in the second Balkan war where a large Greek army decisively routed a much smaller Bulgar one. Several villages had had rather a thin time of it evidently and you could see the Bulgar trenches on the one side and the rifle pits of the attacking Greeks on the other.

Since writing that paragraph the Major has had orders to go away at once. He being senior to O.C. 420th Field Company we've been very happy over here. Now I shall be running this detachment again and shall be under the 420th Coy which will be a nuisance as their Major is at times fussy. They may, however, be getting a new one shortly.

I'm awfully sorry that your knee has been so bad. I didn't realise when you first told me that it was a thing that was going to keep you in for any length of time. It must have been a horrible nuisance. I hope by now it will be all right again.

Elisabeth is greatly looking forward to taking Peter up to the cottage. She doesn't know if Janet Teale will come & so is thinking of Pleasance Napier if Janet fails. Pleasance is an amusing child who spent a weekend with us at Aldershot. She's full of life but at the same time thinks she takes it very seriously. She was going off, I think, to teach the Montefiore system to Sylvia Pankhurst when I saw her. I think she might amuse you quite a lot. She hails from Bedales.

I seem to have scored heavily through my parcels taking so long to arrive since you and Elisabeth are both sending me out a second lot. Thanks ever so much. I'm afraid the shamrock is rather late. I wished very much on S. Patrick's day that I had some.

I never gave you the parodigm (I think that's the word isn't it) of βλώσκώ. Blair was with me when I got the letter asking me. He agreed when I remembered μολουμαι for the future & favoured έμολον for the aorist but I was against that. I was pretty sure the perfect was βεβλώκα though it might have been μεμβλώκα or βεβλώμαι (the latter being unlikely) and I plumped for έβλώσθηυ for the aorist. How's that – βλώσκώ, μολουμαι, βεβλώκα, εβλώσθμυ. I'm not sure of the accents.

I've had a lot of Greeks here recently but haven't been trying to learn their lingo being content for the moment with Turkish. The other day I came across one gang during the luncheon hour & wanted the Sapper in charge to show him something. So I remembered που στρατιώτης; (*where*

G.O.C. "WELL, MY MAN, WHAT ARE YOU IN CIVILIAN LIFE?"
Dejected Private. "PROFESSOR OF GREEK HISTORY AT ONE OF THE UNIVERSITIES, SIR."

(Punch)

Fortunately John didn't need this Professor under his command.

is the soldier?) and asked "Poo stratiot". It worked all right for one went off to look for him. Presently however he came back & said "Finish soldier". That didn't mean he'd put him quietly away but just that he couldn't find him.

I've got a puppy now called Peck – short for "Kiöpek" which is the Turkish for "dog". He's a ball of black fluff with a few enormous paws projecting in places, two of which & his breast are white. He's probably got a bit of French retriever in him. He's a jolly little beast.

I've just been reading the Vicar of Wakefield, which Aunt Hilda sent out to me, and I've been wondering why I never read it before.

With lots of love to the propagandiste.

You're very loving,

J.S. (X)

Thursday 11–4–18

My Dearest Mother,

I've just got two delightful parcels marked "from I.W.A.London" so I expect they are the ones you told me you were sending through someone. It's far too good of you, Mother, for it is you, not us who need the parcels nowadays. We really get awfully good rations and you get such awfully small ones. So please don't send me such splendid ones any more. A little tobacco and a few sweets would be heaps for the likes of me.

Not that I'm not looking forward exceedingly to enjoying them, and I'm very glad to have something "in the house" just now because there's a wandering Padre who has decided to let loose a service on us on Sunday or Monday and I'll have to put him up for the night.

It's been quite hot today. The next month or six weeks will be hottish with cold snaps and then the fire will really get going in June.

I've been almost 6 months in this place now. The job has grown. I had a Lance Corporal & 6 men & about 50 male Turks in those days. Now I have another officer, about 60 NCOs and men, about 600 Macedonians of every age, nationality & sex, an ASC detachment of an officer, 100 men and 30 wagons and a doctor with his staff.

Can you imagine the OC 420th Coy on the top of Wetherlam, myself on the top of Hawkshead Hill, with detachments of my own at Ambleside and the Ferry. That's the sort of area and its through hills about the same

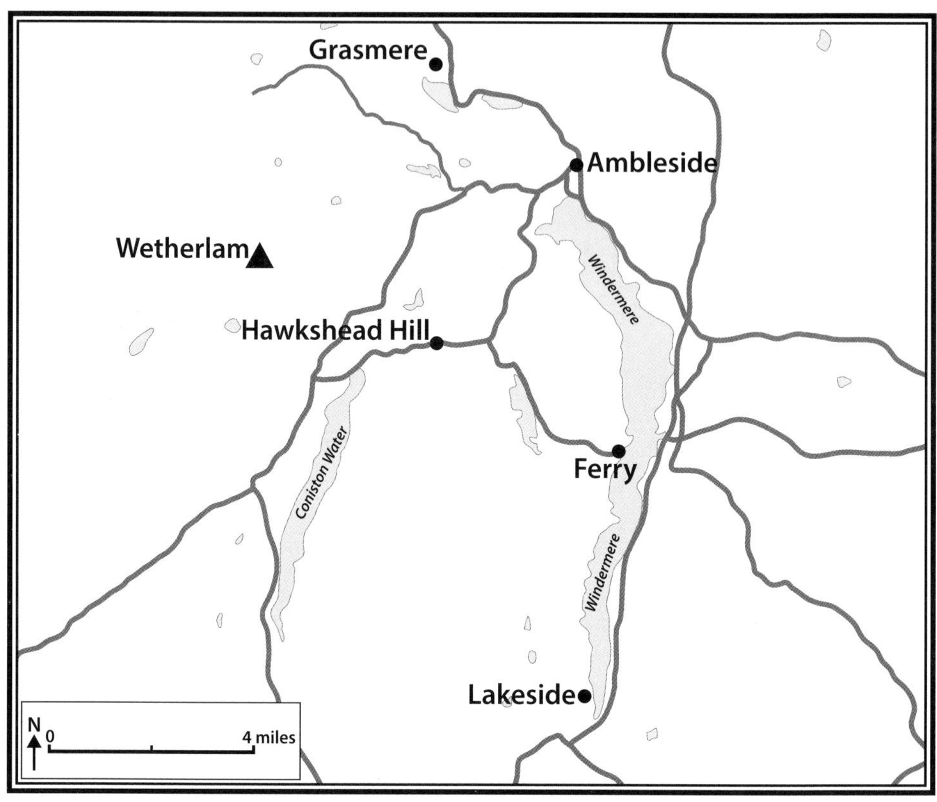

Comparison with the Lakes

height. The Ambleside detachment would be making a road to Grassmere, the Ferry people one to Lakeside and I one to Ambleside & one to the Ferry.

I'm on horseback most of the day. Last week I covered exactly 100 miles. That doesn't sound much but some days I was on foot near here and of course I was always having to stop and look at things and think about them.

Roads are really rather attractive things. Making one road and just working from one place would be awfully boring, but doing several is great fun. You go off along one of them one day and along another another day and give enough orders to last till your next visit.

Reconnoitring for a new road is the best fun. You smell about all over the place until you've made up your mind about the most likely route and then start pegging it out accurately. I don't really know anything about roads – or didn't a short time ago – but I don't tell anybody that. Presently I may get a little tired of them, but for the moment I'm quite enjoying myself. My roads are not like Watling Street or the Great North Road, but they've about as good a surface after a little as say the road past Atkinson Ground – and they're much more nicely graded. I wish they'ld give me a steam-roller. Then I would make them really nice, but it's wonderful what you get without one after a little traffic has been over.

I'm afraid this has been about nothing but roads but I'm not really doing much else now so it's what gets written about.

With the very best of love to you both.

Your dearly loving,

J.S.

Miss Fleming, whom I was with when wounded has been married. I got a letter asking me to subscribe to a wedding present. She should get a good one, shouldn't she.

Scottish Women's Hospital in Salonika

When war broke out in 1914, a group of women in Scotland wanted to contribute to the war effort and decided to raise money to provide medical assistance to anyone who might need it. Their motives had a secondary aim which was to promote the cause for women's rights and, by their involvement in the war, to help win those rights.

By the end of 1914 they had raised more than £5,000. Their initial idea of establishing a new hospital in Edinburgh was turned down by the Government. They were to 'go home women and sit still'. Undeterred they offered their services to Britain's allies. France and Belgium swiftly took up that offer and hospitals were raised, but it was Serbia which ultimately took up most of their resources. Throughout the war the Scottish Women's Hospital provided incredible help to Serbians, be they military or refugees, in every theatre of war on the eastern front.

In 1915 one of their earliest French hospitals in Troyes was ordered to pack up and move to Salonika. This redeployment suited them well as it was not far from their colleagues in Serbia. The major illness they had to face in Salonika was malaria, which was responsible for a huge number of deaths over the next 3 years.

Strengthened during 1916 and 1917 by contributions from an American Unit, the Scottish Women's Hospital in Salonika was able to fund an ambulance unit, which meant they could get out quickly to casualties rather than waiting for the casualties to be brought to them.

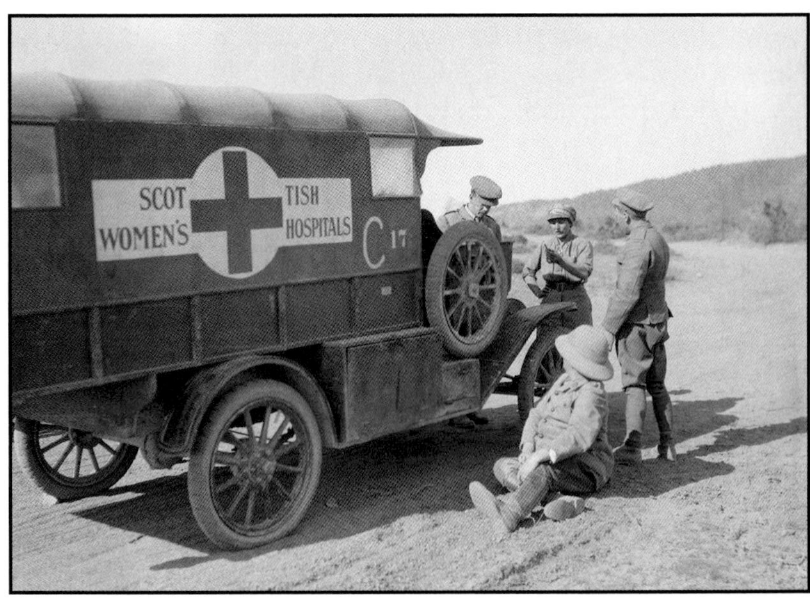

(IWM Q32487)

A motor ambulance of the Scottish Women's Hospitals broken down on a hill 1916.

April 21st 1918

My Dearest Mother,
There was some person or another – probably the great Anon-– who said that "Life is just one damned thing after another" and he was perfectly right on the whole except that he implies that there's a certain amount of variation.

I wish I could get leave but there's no earthly chance of that for another year or two at least. There's a chance of course that Germany will go absolutely the whole hog this year and that the Yanks will be strong enough for us to bring off big things next year – but I don't think it will be till the year after. When the war does stop they'll probably give leave from here fairly freely, though I suppose it will take a little time for us to get home finally.

There really isn't a single thing to talk about. Everything has gone a wonderful green & the flowers are beginning to be everywhere. I spend my days riding about from one place to another. I've been having annoying little goes of very mild fever for the last 10 days. Every other day my temperature goes up something rather less than a degree. It doesn't make one ill but just makes one slack.

Things don't seem to be going badly in France on the whole. I should be sorry if the Bosche took Bethune for I've quite a tender spot in my heart for it. I know all that Lys area pretty well.

The weather is lovely to-day. If only we could be all together in the cottage. It'll come one day.

I wish this were a better letter. The last month I don't seem able to write a decent one at all.

Best of love to Honor.

You're very loving,

J.S. (X)

I got a note the other day from Gladys Dodgshun. She's out here with the Skittish Widows Hospital. I don't suppose I'll run across her but I might be able to see her sometime if she's near Salonika & I could take her out to tea somewhere. I'm thinking of asking for three days in Salonika sometime next month.

Rationing in Britain

During the first two years of the war there was no great shortage of food in Britain as merchant ships travelled fairly safely across the Atlantic Ocean from America and Canada. By the end of 1916, however, there was concern that the store of wheat was diminishing and coal was in such short supply that it became one of the first items to be rationed – limited by the number of rooms a family had in the house.

The problem was greatly exacerbated when, in 1917, German submarines started attacking not only naval warships but merchant vessels as well, and a great many cargo ships were sunk. Initially the government hoped that a voluntary code of rationing would work, but that failed. People working in industrial or heavily built up areas with no gardens did not have enough food, while those with land to grow vegetables or keep chickens fared better and those with money could get what they wanted on the black market.

Under the Defence of the Realm Act (DORA) the government was empowered to take over any land required for war purposes; in 1917 around 2.5 million acres of land was requisitioned for farming. The land was worked by the Women's Land Army, conscientious objectors and, sometimes, prisoners of war. A large quantity of vegetables and grain was grown, but some things don't grow in Britain and supply of others can take years to increase, so in January 1918 rationing was finally brought in. Ration cards were issued for sugar, meat, butter, cheese and margarine. Everyone had to register with a butcher and grocer, who were then allotted the appropriate amount of each item. Fines were high for anyone trading on the black market. Although there was certainly widespread deprivation, rationing did work, malnutrition disappeared and no-one starved.

War bonds

May 13th 1918

My Dearest Mother,
I'm being rather unlucky with mails. I'm afraid I've been writing badly this year both to you and Elisabeth and its just those boats which do have letters of mine in which get sunk. She's had several gaps and you say it is very long since you heard from me.

It had seemed a long time since I had had a letter from you, though I'd been getting papers, but this last week I was lucky. I got your letter of April 12th and three more parcels, two of food & one of baccy. Mother darling, when food is so scarce in England you mustn't spend money on sending me stuff. I've told Elisabeth the same thing. We're far better off than you are and it ought to be me who should send parcels to you. The baccy was extraordinarily welcome though. The food parcels are topping too but I felt I oughtn't to have them, but the baccy came just when I was at my wits end to know where to get any from. I was down almost to my last pipefull.

Mother dear, Betsy sent me on the letter you wrote to her on April 14th, saying you couldn't go up to Coniston till August, and I'm very much pleased with her for sending you one of my cheques straight away. She does most of my money things for me while I'm here as it saves the risk of cheques getting sunk. I've arranged for Cox to count her signature as mine.

Mother, I don't want you to think of any cheques I may be able to send you as special presents to be put aside for getting particular things with, such as extra furniture for the cottage. I don't want them to be that. They're just to help you in your ordinary everyday needs. You shouldn't write that you've "no one to bring your troubles to". What else is a son for? And I'm living far below my income now.

I'm really rather ashamed sometimes at how little I'm spending. Betsy's own money goes to her clothes & most of Peter's and her father is giving us far more than he ought in the way of doctors bills and things. I'm really paying for practically nothing but my own Mess Bills. I've put about £200 into war bonds since I've been out here as well as Grannies money.

I'ld take a firmer line with old Mr Wicksteed but I'm very fond of him and I know he looks on me as a son and he'ld be hurt at my refusing. So Mother dear you must let me know when things are difficult. It was only because Alec told me that you would be all right that I agreed to take any of Grannies' money.

I was very, very sorry to hear of Arthur's death. It's only been in recent years that I've really begun to know him well of course but I'd come to

Stone Crushers

Crushing rocks mechanically was a relatively new technology in the early 1900s. The crushers were driven by a belt powered by a tractor. They were loaded by hand – labour intensive, but much less so than breaking up rocks with hammers. There is no record of the make of the machines used in the Salonika quarries, but they would have been similar to these:

A stone crusher powered by a Jelbart Tractor.

Earthmovers Magazine

A belt-driven stone crusher in operation.

A first-hand account of Salonika quarrying is given by J M Cordy RE in his memoirs:

'Work in the quarries and on the roads was very hard. We had an air compressor in a hut which worked some drills in the quarry as well as having hand drills. Some of the Greeks, big strong fellows, could swing a seven pound hammer, hitting the drill to make the hole for the explosives, for half an hour without stopping. I was in the engine hut one day when they set off the blasts in the quarry and a piece of rock came through the roof just missing me and the compressor.

Dagoes came from miles away. The men would ride on the donkey carrying the baby, and one to five or six wives would follow. The donkeys would be hobbled to stop them straying away and mating. One morning, one of our fellows undid the hobbles and the old boys had a job to round them up again, the males roaring and chasing the females.

The jaws of the stone crusher did very heavy work and eventually wore out and we could not get replacements. We tried in the blacksmiths shop to fit short pieces of small rail track in the place of the jaws, but it did not work, so hammering the granite to pieces was a big job for the old ladies.'

(IWM Documents 2623)

have a great love and respect for him. It's rather a strong thing to say, but I think he was the best judge of character I've known. It was only in man-to-man sort of talks that one discovered that. His creed was "I believe in the Baines family" & I felt that whatever happened, provided one didn't disgrace the family, he was behind one as a Baines who is ready to help a fellow Baines. He was like the Colonel of a good regiment, but with love and understanding for each member of it personally as well as for the whole. Somehow one didn't realise his age – though 70 is not very much – and I'd looked forward to getting more & more to know him well. I'm frightfully sorry for Florence. I know no-one who would be such a lovable husband.

There's no news to give from here. I'm making roads & tracks & have a stone crusher worked by a traction engine now which is a great help.

Garforth thinks he can get me to France. It would be lovely if I could get back nearer to you all.

With all love to you both.

You're very loving
J.S. (X)

Sunday May 26th 1918

Dearest Mother,

I was very glad to get your letter on Thursday evening. I'm not sure whether I get all your letters but I don't think I get all the Times. I've had three or perhaps four since the fighting began in France. The tobacco came from Harrods & I'm smoking it at the moment. I thanked you for that in my last letter but here's some more. I've not yet had "Deductions from the War" and I'm afraid you never got my letter with the rubbings of those coins. I'm glad I didn't send any of the coins themselves.

I'm still doing roads. My completely new one is now almost through – only as an un-metalled road of course. There's one part where I have still to improve the gradient but traffic can get past there by a steep way. I like doing work which I feel will last and will be an important thing in the development of the country if it is looked after at all.

Most of my other work is patching other roads which have been rushed through quickly as tracks and are being turned into nullahs by succeeding thunderstorms. It's those far more than the winter rain which do for the roads.

(IWM Q32693)

Local women breaking stones for road making 1917.

I got caught in one on Wednesday. There was no place to shelter & the hailstones were about the size of good big marbles. The biggest ones I measured were egg-shaped rather than round and were an inch and a half long. I had no coat, only a very thin shirt but fortunately I had my sun helmet which acted as a shrapnel helmet. I was less than a mile from home when it started and we hurried as fast as we could but my horse was already tired after a long day in hot sun. When I got in my fore-arms, shoulders and thighs were covered with bruises. One of my little Greek girls – a little thing about 10 or 12 was nearly drowned crossing what a few minutes before had been a dry nullah in order to get to a tree which would keep the hail off. She was washed off her feet & carried down. Fortunately the man in charge saw her & went off to her & got her out.

A lot of my women bring their babies to work with them and leave them under a hedge somewhere. The hail was rather rough on the babies & the Sappers put their own coats over them as far as possible. The women were awfully pleased and brought them eggs the next morning. Some of the Sappers are just like the head of a large family – say 20 wives & 20 daughters – & their family is very fond of them. They bring flowers for them and sometimes make them little bead purses or similar things to send home to their own "piccaninnies" – which is a Macadonian word just as much as any other.

The women get two drachmae a day and the children one. They also get their rations which is the important thing to them. Lots of them sell the English bread & eat their own rye bread. I believe they can get five or six drachmae a loaf. Everything is frightfully dear here.

I much looking forward to the Iliad. A Homeric dictionary would help but perhaps the translation will be close enough for me to be able to follow the meaning of individual words. I'm afraid I shan't remember a word at first, but if I begin on the books I've already read I may be able to pick it up again.

The kitten & puppy still lead a cat & dog existence. The puppy is very large now and I think the kitten is sorry she didn't respond to the advances he made through-out the first month or so that he was here.

I've moved my camp a mile or two so as to be in a more central spot. There's just the doctor and myself but we're close to the A.S.C. fellow who supplies me with transport so can get a certain amount of 3-handed bridge now and then.

The mess has canvas walls and a corrugated iron roof covered by oak-scrub thatch. The south wall is also thatched and there is a verandah on

Nearly 100 years later John's worst fear has come true – his poem has been examined by a French teacher of English. She comments:

This is an amusing little poem, in the best traditions of British 'nonsense'. However, the author is correct in recognising that it contains one or two errors of grammar and syntax. A correct and more authentic version would read as follows:

Il était une fois un brave chat venu d'Angleterre,
qui sortit pour aller se battre à la guerre.
Un dimanche il chassa
une petite souris
durant le temps consacré à la prière.
Le curé, abasourdi, s'écria :
"Ah! Mon Dieu! Mais c'est qu'il blasphème, ce chat! "
Il saisit la pauvre bête
par la queue et par la tête,
et de chaînes de fer l'entoura.'

We have no idea why John wrote this to Dearest Mother – perhaps a similar incident had happened during a service, but in any event it was to make her laugh. In the same vein, and to help any readers who are not French speakers, the editors have made a loose translation of the poem and added a moral:

An English cat, both brave and nice,
went off to war to fight the mice.
One Sunday during Morning Prayer
he chased a mouse, without a care.
The chaplain drew the line at that,
exclaiming 'Oh my God, that cat
has blasphemed – he'll pay the price
for skipping prayers to chase the mice.'
The mog was caught and tied up well.
What happened then … we cannot tell!

The moral of this little tale
is – toe the line, or go to gaol.
All combat roles must be ignored
when worshipping our peaceful Lord.

the north, east and west sides. Its very nice and cool. I'm writing this lying on a blanket in the east verandah. The mess itself is 10 foot by 8 and the verandahs are seven feet wide. Its proving quite a successful design.

The kitten felt very lost when we changed over quarters. She ran away at once, but in the middle of the night I felt something jump onto my bed and start purring. She was very restless for a day or two. She recognised lots of things but they weren't quite right. She's on the blanket with me now. She has remained an Officers' cat and really is more like a dog in some ways. She gives one a great welcome when one comes in at the end of the day. But I wish she'ld find some other place in my tent in which to deposit her half-eaten lizards.

Please give my love to Honor. I'm very glad she still enjoys her work.

You're very loving

J.S.

Waterloo Day 1918 — Envelope – **'examined by Base Censor'**

My Dearest Mother,

There's nothing like walking slowly on a tired horse for making one think of silly things. Can you translate this into English verse?

(1) Il y avait un bon chat d'Angleterre
Qui sortit pour se battre à la guerre
Le dimanche il chassit
Un petit souris
Pendant tous les heures de prière

(2) Le curé, étourdi, s'écria
"Ah! Mon Dieu! Qu'il blasphême que ce chat!"
Il saissit la pauvre bête
Par la queue et la tête
Et de chaines de fer la combla

Different uses of roads in Salonika

British transport in Macedonia – a typical road on a summer day

(IWM Q32013)

12th Bn A&SH leading 77th Brigade marching to the front line.

But you must not show it to anyone who is well up in French because I'm quite aware of most of the mistakes myself. The thing scans, only if the accent comes on the last syllable of each word – which is the French way of doing it.

It's still just roads I'm doing. My new one is getting on. It's through for traffic but in places the track is only temporary – the better grade which involves a good deal of cutting not being finished. In other places the track hasn't been cut but the natural ground is good enough for wagons to go over in this weather when the worst bumps have been cut off. Parts of it however are really very nice. It won't of course get metalled for some time but it's wonderful what a track will stand if it is decently cut out and then properly drained.

There aren't many diversions hereabouts. We can raise three for cards in the evening fairly often but very rarely four. We've had about three evenings of four handed bridge however in the last fortnight by various chances. One night a fellow called Coad camped here for a night on his way somewhere. He was in the same term & company as I was at the Shop and we had lots of gossip to exchange. Tonight there is another doctor coming over so that we'll be able to have a game.

I don't seem much forrader about getting to France but I still have hopes.

It's just getting quite hot now. We had a delightful winter barring a few blizzards and after it had begun to get hottish we had a very cold snap at the end of May and beginning of June. That's broken now however and each day we decide is the hottest we've had so far this year. There are a good many hotter ones to come however. My winter camp was snugly sheltered behind the shoulder of the hill but now I'm bang on the top of the hill where we get every breath of wind. In fact – as the design of the mess is rather summery we get rather more than we want at times.

I've had no more fever for some time. I've not had any since I was in hospital that was worth calling fever really. Just now I'm remarkably fit as I was all last summer. I think the hot weather suits me. One doesn't look forward to it but once it comes it's really not bad.

I do hope you'll be going to Coniston. I'm sure it would be good for you and I want Peter to get to know you. The accounts I hear of him are hardly impartial but he does seem rather attractive in his way. He seems an independent little divil and quite prepared to stand on his own feet. He seems always on them as far as I can make out in spite of all opposition.

This is the only letter to Dearest Mother, throughout the war, in which John appears to be tired and disenchanted. As he says himself, he has not had any leave from Salonika (for a year and a half) and is unlikely to get any in the foreseeable future. He is understandably concerned about what the outcome of the campaigns in Salonika and France will be, and what the future will hold for Europe. In time honoured fashion, he vents his frustration on the government.

We would love to have had some of Dearest Mother's replies to John. In response to this, we wonder if she might have sent a poem to help him get back to his favourite place – the peace and beauty of the Lakes?

William Wordsworth (1770–1830) was a Lakeland poet, so John would have known his works and very likely have had many of the same sentiments as those expressed in them. This is an extract from The Prelude, Book IV:

When first I made
Once more the circuit of our little Lake
If ever happiness hath lodg'd with man,
That day consummate happiness was mine.
The sun was set, or setting, when I left
Our cottage door, and evening soon brought on
A sober hour, not winning or serene,
For cold and raw the air was, and untun'd;
But, as a face we love is sweetest then
When sorrow damps it, or, whatever look
It chance to wear is sweetest if the heart
Have fullness in itself, even so with me
It fared that evening. Gently did my soul
Put off her veil, and, self-transmuted, stood
Naked as in the presence of her God.
As on I walked, a comfort seem'd to touch
A heart that had not been disconsolate,
Strength came where weakness was not known to be,
At least not felt; and restoration came,
Like an intruder, knocking at the door
Of unacknowledg'd weariness.

I dare say the journey will be a bit slow but I'm sure Coniston will be worth it.

I haven't had any answer to the note I wrote Gladys Dodgshun. I shouldn't be likely to come across her anyway.

I hope Ned manages to scrape into the Navy. As you say it would be the making of him. I think every Baines male ought to go in for public service of some kind. It'ld be a great thing to have him definitely settled in something decent.

Have you written to his parents warning them of all the retired Admirals you've seen at Brighton or somewhere trying to live on their pensions? That's the orthodox procedure isn't it?

Things will probably be pretty critical all this year in France. What we do next year will depend largely on how we hold in the last few campaigning months this year. We've had three months and there are four more. Its in September that strain may be greatest and if we were unlucky then in any way it might be the year after next before we're able to attack on the same scale as the Bosch is doing now.

If only we stick it we're all right in the end but if we make a peace giving the allies Alsace-Lorraine, Belgium, the Trentino & all the Hun Colonies we'ld still have lost the war if we leave things as they are in the east – or rather we'ld have lost the next war which is much the same thing.

The present newspaper talk of trouble in Austria is not, I think, the same sort of rot as they always spit out about riots in Berlin etc. There won't be a decent revolution in Germany for a long time – probably never though there might be friction between Prussia & her vassals which would be awkward for her. Austria – Hungary however has 50% of her population who are neither Austrians nor Hungarians and now that they're a bit hungry they're remembering it (that isn't meant as one of Noah's jokes).

If only the government would talk a little less about the nobility of our aims and explain a little more why we can't let Germany by her annexations increase her population from 60 to 120 millions we'ld have more chance of winning this war in such a way that we won't shortly need another.

I'm afraid it's no use your expecting ever to see me on leave from here unless I'm unlucky enough to stay here for the rest of the war. They are still working through the people who came here in 1915 i.e. who left England in July 1915. As I left in Jan 1917 I've 18 months of the list to work through – which probably will mean two or three years i.e. the probable duration of the war.

Noel Pemberton Billing

In 1918 Noel Pemberton Billing was the Member of Parliament for East Hertfordshire. He was homophobic to an extreme and quite paranoid that homosexuality was infiltrating English society and was a danger to the country during war. He claimed that the Germans were blackmailing tens of thousands of British "perverts" and were luring men into homosexual acts just so that they could then blackmail them. His prejudice went a bit too far when he extended it to include lesbians, even making suggestions about the then prime minister's wife Margot Asquith. Things came to a head in a sensational court case for libel after his journal Vigilante published an article suggesting that the actress Maud Allen was a lesbian and in association with conspirators. He won the case and, his popularity undiminished, went on to be re-elected to parliament in the next election.

It is a pity that Noel Pemberton Billing is primarily remembered for the court case. In 1903, aged 22, having fought in South Africa in the Second Boer War and been invalided out, he opened a garage in Kingston upon Thames. His real interest, however, was aviation and over several years he tried different ways of getting into that field. Finally in 1913 he founded an aircraft business Pemberton-Billing Ltd and started the construction of his flying boat design, which came into its own a year later when the war started. He was an early advocator of the creation of an air force unattached either to the navy or the army.

But if I can get to France all will be well.
Please thank Honor for her letter which I'll try and answer soon.
With much love to you both.

You're very loving,

J.S. X

June 30th

My Dearest Mother,
Many thanks for the birthday letter which I got two or three days ago also for the cuttings of the Billing trial which came earlier in the week. What an extraordinary affair it is. I suppose Billing may be a bit off his head but the idea that the Bosches try to blackmail any of our prominent men whom they can is quite plausible. It's the first three days of it I've got and I'm wondering how it finishes up.

I saw the ADW again yesterday for a moment and reminded him that he'd try and find out for me how best to get to France. He said he'd asked his boss & had been told that it would have to stand over for the moment though doubtless I should get an opportunity later. That doesn't bring one much forrader.

I'm afraid I have no chance of leave from here for a couple of years. If Colin thinks he'll get one this year he's optimistic. He certainly has no right to. It's only 18 months since he was home and the people now getting leave are those who have been away three years – those who left England at the same time as Colin but didn't have his luck in getting away with one of the first leave parties. My only chance of getting home is to get transferred to France.

I'm quite optimistic about the general situation these days. Till now the Austrian offensive was always an unpleasant thing to look forward to but now that it's come and gone and has done nothing everyone feels much more stable. Next year I suppose we shall do shunts of the kind the Bosch has been doing this year – pretty big but just not big enough – and 1920 ought with luck to see us over the Rhine and anywhere we want to go. Its a longish business but six or seven years isn't much for a war of this magnitude. I always feel sorry for the people who got their commissions just at the beginning of the Hundred Years War.

(IWM Q31775)

A British soldier looking over the Macedonian countryside at sunset.

I can imagine that those pictures you saw of the Doiran front will have been very beautiful. I often longed to be able to paint when I was there. Looking across the Lake on a clear winter day one got one of the most splendid views possible. There'ld be a cloudless blue sky and the lake the same colour and behind it the great wall of the Belesh Dagh (or Belashitsh Planine – one's the Turk & the other the Serb & Bulgar name) with three quarters of it covered with snow.

Where I am now the immediate surroundings haven't any special magnificence. It's all pretty high and is rather rolling. But we do at times get lovely views particularly about sunset or in the early morning. It's then that you see Olympus away to the south and when it specially clear Ossa behind him & to the left. We can't see Pelion.

There's a story in Le Fanu's 70 years of Irish Life, which I've recently been re-reading, of a fellow bursting into tears as the river steamer passed Greenwich Hospital because it reminded him of his poor dear fathers stables in County Galway. I couldn't help thinking of that story when I thought the other day how Olympus is almost exactly like Binion. But it is all the same!

I've just got hold of a paperback copy of 'Diana of the Crossways'. After trying various paragraphs in the first chapter I decided to give that one a miss and went on to the second. I dare say I shall quite like it in the end.

Any old paperbacks you may have would be extraordinarily welcome. We're a very small colony here and our pooled libraries don't go very far.

When the war's over I'm going to buy a typewriter and make Betsy learn shorthand and then sit in a comfy chair and dictate books on Modern European History. I think that would be an ideal way of earning pennies – provided one earned enough.

With much love to you both.

Your dearly loving,

J.S. (X)

John's own sketches

July 14th 1918

Dearest Mother,
I've been spending quite a lot of the afternoon in studying Turkish but some things are beyond a joke. What do you think of the sentence "the sister-in-law of my grandmother is my father's uncle's wife and is related to us". Even that one can stand alone but when I found a whole exercise bringing in nothing but names of relationships I thought it time to move along. As far as I can make out a Turk can be related to people in 48 different ways without getting further away than a first cousin.

At the present moment there's a thunderstorm going on & a pretty high wind with lots of rain. This mess is only sun proof and is quite capable of blowing away altogether but I hope it won't. I'm afraid this will be rather a messy letter, but I've no non-indelible pencil.

At that point I gave up the attempt and now it's rather late. A fellow I met last year passed through here & I've had him in.

Very many thanks for the Homer, which arrived a few days ago. I read the first book almost at once & since then have done part of the twelfth – where Hector is trying to capture the Greek trenches & then burn the ships. He's still a bit tied up in the wire.

I've not yet taken over my new area & may now very probably have to wait a little while though theoretically the move might come any moment.

I'm sorry this is such a scrawl. It was started under difficulties & now I ought to be getting into bed.

With much love to you both.

You're very loving,
J.S. (X)

July 21st 1918

My Dearest Mother,
Life doesn't vary very much in Macedon. I've had a burst of enthusiasm over Turkish and have done quite a lot during the past week. Its because I'm alone again that I'm able to do it. When there are two of you, you always waste any spare time you have in talking. Unfortunately I don't get very much opportunity of talking Turkish nowadays but if I can get through most of the grammar and syntax now it will be a great advantage when I

The Final Allied Offensive

In the first half of 1918 there were three significant events that affected the British Salonika Force, two positively and one negatively. A new French Allied commander arrived, combining freshness with a good understanding of the Balkans; the Greek army finally deployed alongside the Allies, taking over the eastern sector of the front the British had held for over a year along the River Struma; and twelve British battalions were redeployed to France, to make up for heavy losses incurred there, placing an even greater strain on our resources.

Fortunately for the Allies, the Bulgars continued to hold their strong defensive position along the high ground on their southern border, making no attempt to launch attacks to force the Allies back towards Salonika. They had no wish to extend their military alliance with Germany beyond their own borders. Had they done so and had Salonika fallen, with Greece coming over to the German side and the creation of a submarine base at Salonika threatening the entire Mediterranean, the whole war might have lasted for two or three years longer.

A new Allied strategic plan was drawn up for a full offensive operation. The French and Serbian Armies would launch strong attacks against the German defensive lines on the southern border of Serbia, with the aim of driving a wedge between the Bulgars and the Germans, and at the same time cutting off the Bulgars' main supply routes. Three days later the British would attack the strongly held enemy positions west and north of Lake Doiran area, with XII and XVI Corps respectively, each corps having a Greek division under command.

The first phase was launched on 15th September. The Serbian and French forces penetrated the main enemy defences and advanced strongly on a twenty five mile front. The British attack would therefore put additional pressure on the Bulgars, and prevent them moving reinforcements to their right flank. On 18th September our assault was launched.

In almost impossible terrain for an assault against such strongly fortified and defended high ground around Lake Doiran, our operation failed, despite incredible bravery on the part of our infantry. In order to maintain the pressure on the enemy, the British were ordered to attack for a second time the following day – again with no success and very heavy casualties.

To the west, the Serbs and French forged on and by 21st September had cut the vital Bulgarian communications on the Vardar. The Bulgars were ordered to withdraw from their front line – including their Doiran positions. The Allied plan had succeeded.

In the two days fighting the British suffered nearly 4,000 casualties – killed, wounded or missing. A very high sacrifice by very brave men.

do start talking again and it will also give me an excuse for a trip to Turkey after the war to study the language.

One has many different ideas of what one will do after the war. I'm rather off India, I think, because it's getting too democratic. I don't mind being in an ordinary country like England where one man is as good as another and I don't mind being one of a ruling caste in some other place, but I don't want to be one of a ruling caste that is gradually losing its power & dignity.

I thought a while ago of going to Palestine but it'll be awfully overrun with Jews. It would be interesting work opening it up with roads and railways but my methods are a little rough & might cost a pound where another fellow could do the work for 19/- & so I shouldn't get on with the Jews.

My latest idea is to leave engineering alone for a bit and go in for getting interpreterships. I could take French in a month or two and probably by the time I'm out of Macedonia I'll know enough Turkish to make it worthwhile to finish it off thoroughly but what I want to go for chiefly is Polish and Roumanian. If we win the war they'll be powers nearly as big as Italy and there'll be very few army officers who'ld know their languages. Roumanian is a latin language & so shouldn't be too difficult. Polish may be a bit harder but I dare say it won't be too bad provided one can learn to pronounce Przemyśl. One would run quite a good chance of some semi-diplomatic job or military instructorship there for English influence ought to be very strong there if we really set them up properly. Betsy & I could have great times at their Gilbert & Sullivan capitals and Peter would become a dreadful little cosmopolitan. Think of the Winchester scholar who could talk Polish and Roumanian. It'ld make William of Wykeham turn in his chantrey. You & Honor can come out and I'm sure will be able to give you excellent winter sports.

One would be in England fairly often and anyway I'd have to come back to do advanced construction courses and promotion exams & things. If I seem stuck in England for a bit at any time I could take up Norwegian, Swedish, Danish, Dutch or Flemish none of which are hard I believe if you know English & a smattering of Bosche, but those countries don't interest me particularly.

I haven't bothered with Greek at all here though now I've more Greek labour than Turkish I think. All I know is καλ'ημερα (*good day*), καλ'ησπερα (*good evening*) and καλανυκτα (*good night*). The first syllable of ημερα and ησπερα are hardly pronounced, the accent coming on the second which are

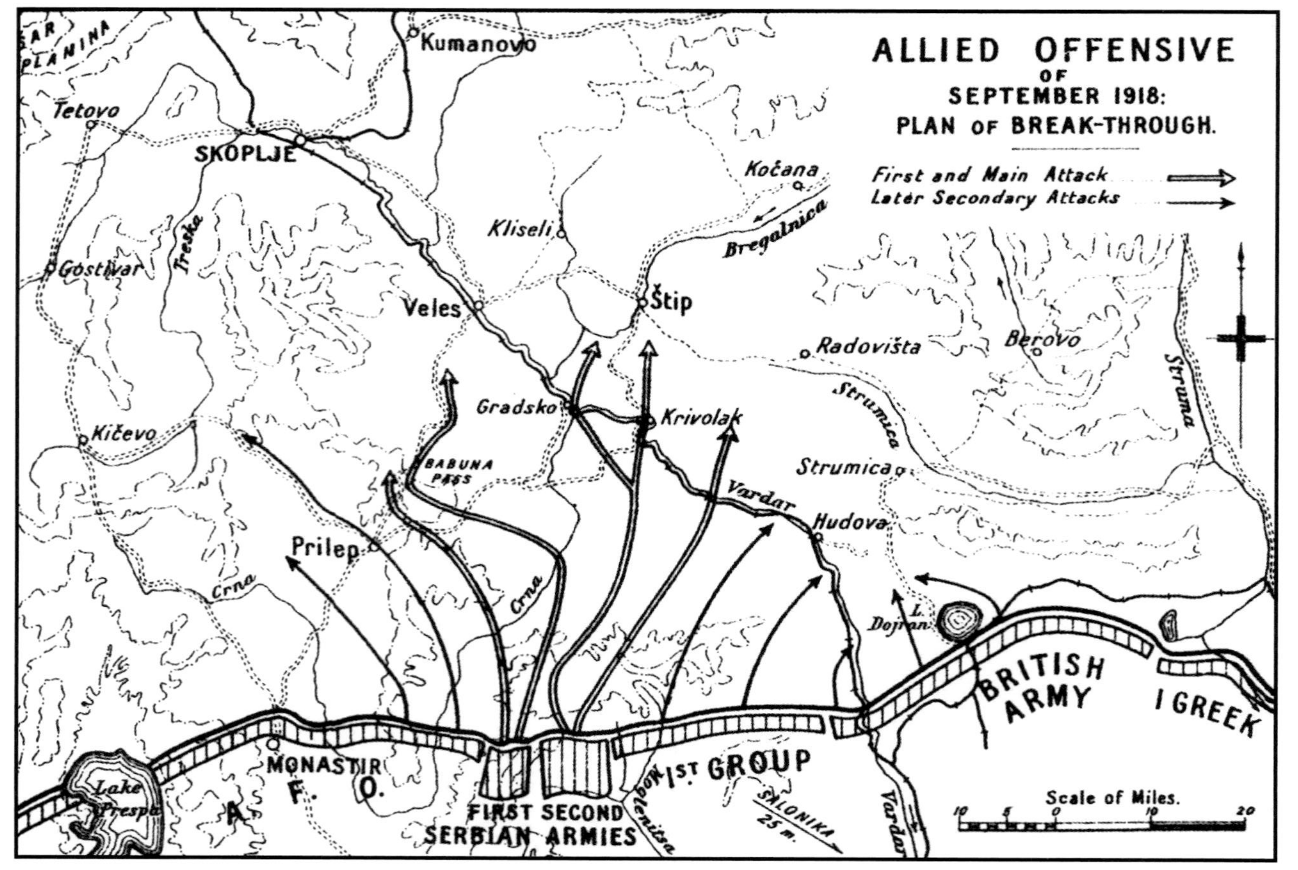

(The Official History of the Great War: Military Operations Macedonia, *Cyril Falls, 1935*)

Allied Offensive of September 1918 – Plan of Break-through.

pronounced to rhyme with mare, pair νυκτα is pronounced nykta. Upsilon being like our y.

I'm waiting for the wireless to come through. I'm much excited by yesterdays in which the French counteroffensive had got a mile from Soissons. I at once wrote a Belloc article & pinned it up with a map. I've done that a good deal this year & I don't generally find much in Land and Water that hasn't already appeared in the Macedonian News. My respect for Belloc therefore grows since he comes to most of my conclusions.

There's only one thing which would improve Belloc's articles. He ought to have got his manuscript, maps & all onto a board 18 inches square, & short of drawing pins at that. If he were paid for every line he left unwritten instead of for every one he wrote he could be just as instructive & would use a fifth of the amount of paper. I sympathise with him however, for I'd write at much longer length if I had a bigger board and were not afraid of boring the Sappers.

Belloc of course will be in the seventh heaven now at having this counter-attack to write about.

I'm going to be a Belloc in the next war. His methods are perfectly easy but at the moment they're unique. He's the only military critic who can intelligently read & explain a map. Why the others don't do the same thing I can't imagine.

Leave is running better now. In officers they've got through the original people who came out in 1915 and are at those who came out in January 1916 i.e. a year before me. Perhaps mine may come in about a year now. It'll be jolly if it's in the summer and we can all get up to the Lakes. Honor will have to get a special leave too.

With much love to you both.

You're very loving

JS

The Pursuit into Bulgaria

At noon on 22nd September an exultant signal from the Allied Commander in Chief announced the news of the enemy retreat on the whole front from Doiran to Monastir, with orders that it must be turned into a rout by unceasing and resolute pursuit. This signalled the start of one of the most remarkable and little-known actions of the war – the switch from two years' static deadlock across the whole Salonika front to mobile warfare of the most intense, chaotic and one-sided nature.

The retreating Bulgarian units were in disarray, suffering very heavy casualties from Allied fighter aircraft bombing and machine gunning them as they were channelled through the narrow defiles of the mountain passes in their rush north.

Despite the appalling condition of the roads (needing constant repairs round the clock) the co-ordinated Allied pursuit, across a wide front, succeeded in outflanking and isolating large sections of the Bulgarian forces, which were unable to reinforce each other. To the west the Serbs forged ahead with a vengeance and relentless ferocity, to liberate their own country.

The Bulgars, verging on open mutiny, capitulated unconditionally. An armistice was signed in Salonika on 29th September, twelve days after the Allied breakthrough, effective from noon on 30th September. This was a magnificent achievement by the Salonika Allies, after an extraordinary three year chapter of the First World War.

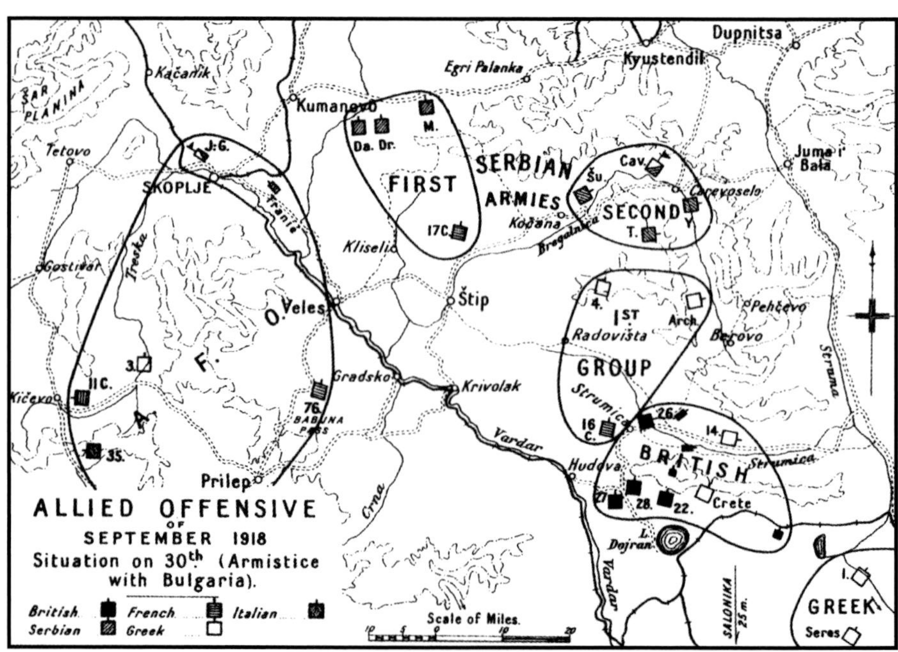

(The Official History of the Great War: Military Operations Macedonia, *Cyril Falls, 1935.)*

Allied Offensive of September 1918 – Situation on 30th (Armistice with Bulgaria).

286th AT Coy RE
B.S.F.

October 24th 1918

My Dearest Mother,
Since last I wrote I've been through many changes. When the Bulgar retreat began the 420th Coy was pushed up & was one of the many Coys working on a long length of road which had to bear an enormous amount of traffic from railhead on. We were at railhead and the change there in a day or two was wonderful.

The day we arrived there were just a few tents which had been pitched that day & some heavy guns that had not yet been got forward. We had splendid firework displays the first two nights with all the Bulgar dumps blowing up on the hills the other side of the lake.

Two days later what had just been a passing place on a single-line railway had become a great goods yard with long sidings, between which we were putting roads as fast as we could get stone. There were camps everywhere – British units, Macedonian labourers, Turkish Prisoners of War. Wells were being driven, steam pumps going & a piped water-supply was spreading itself out. The traffic on the road was prodigious and one swallowed clouds and clouds of dust. Everyone was working full pressure & the announcement of peace only seemed to increase it.

The weather broke and almost immediately afterwards on the 6th at about 10.30 I got one message telling me to take command of the 286th Army Troops Coy R.E. and a copy of another saying this company was to move at once or sooner with a British Labour unit & a Macedonian Battalion of 350 men.

I got to the Company just before lunch with my kit, having borrowed a car, & found everyone packing. We were moving by lorry, had about 40 of them, but as they rolled up in driblets it was 5 o'clock before we got away. I was on the front of the first lorry. I had a Macintosh & fortunately had a serge and not a drill jacket on for underneath I had only the thinnest of cotton shirts. It rained or drizzled a lot of the way and going through the passes it was bitterly cold.

The OC of the Labour Coy sat with me. I'll remember him all my life for he had a bottle of whisky & a blanket and I had about 3 quarters of each I think.

In the immediate aftermath of the victory over the Bulgars, John's morale was clearly high. Out of the blue he had been given command of a company, in the most chaotic situation. Things were moving at a fast pace as the pursuit into Bulgaria accelerated. Much engineer support was urgently needed to keep the roads open, and that initially took him and his unit 15 miles across the border with Bulgaria as far north as Strumnitza.

At this stage of our research, after reading through many pages of unit war diaries, it was a delight to find ones in a handwriting we immediately recognised, written so clearly.

Extracts from 286th Army Troops Company RE War Diary

'**7th Oct:** … Sappers, Labour Coy and Macedonians began shovelling mud with a view to further progress. … Fresh lorries, as they arrived, increased the working party. British rations were on the first lorry and breakfast was given as the men arrived … Macedonian rations did not arrive. ½ loaf of bread issued to each man from reserve British rations. Most of these had spent night on open hopper lorries and had not eaten for 24 hours. They were wet through.'

'**8th–14th Oct**: Average labour was R.E.110, 95th Labour Coy 100, Macedonians 350, A.S.C. limbers 35… Road was got open for through traffic again and was kept open but had to be very carefully watched …'

'**15th Oct:** Orders received that 35 lorries would report same evening and company would move at dawn 16th to Doiran rest camp to entrain for Guvesne at dawn on 17th. All tools including quarry tools to be taken and all British & Macedonian labour.'

'**17th Oct:** Began to entrain … Told to detrain as another train had come in and first train given to company was wanted for carrying machinery … Entrained in fresh train.'

'**19th Oct:** Company began work on Decauville Railway … This was in process of construction by the Greek Army. O.C.Coy had verbal orders to "butt in" so as to expedite work. Chain of command was approximately as follows: Subalterns of company were under Greek Engineer Coy Commanders, O.C.Company was under Greek C.R.E. Major Vrontamitis who had under him the 1st Field Company of the 1st Greek Division and two engineer companies of Greek Corps Troops. Major Vrontamitis was under Colonel Vary, a French Infantry officer with the French Military Mission with the Greek Army and who had as an Adjutant Captain Lemoine a French Engineer Officer. O.C. 286th Company R.E. (*John himself*) was under Capt Lemoine's orders. Lt Col Taylor RE, ADW Seres Road, was not responsible for the Decauville or road, but gave advice to Capt Lemoine.'

(National Archive WO95/4803)

At about 1:30 a.m., 4 kilos or so from our destination I met the A.D.W. and we started scraping mud from the road to get lorries on further. I had about 10 then of the original 40.

We soon stopped, however, and after ordering parade for 6 a.m. I got into a lorry & though very wet & in a clammy Macintosh I slept soundly on the top of three packing cases all of different heights.

At 6 we resumed mud scraping & about 7 the cooks had got breakfast going so we knocked off for that. I'd brought the cooks & rations on the first lorry so that I at least should not be stranded. The hot tea & fried bacon were very lovely. I'd no knife & fork but I sat on a stone on the side of the road & munched the bacon sandwich-wise between two splendid slices of bread. In the course of the day most of our lorries had rolled up and the hair pin corner which was our immediate objective was made passable soon after lunch. So we tramped in the rain up to our camping ground & pitched bivouacs. There was a small R.E. detachment already there, opening a quarry for me, and I shared the officer's tent for that night. My valise was wet & my pyjamas & everything else but it was topping to get into bed. The Macedonians, poor devils had many of them been in hopper-lorries. They must have been frozen to death. Some of their tents arrived but no rations. We were able however to give them some bread to keep them going.

We had a week or so in Bulgaria. We spent the first day or two digging lorries out of the road & then got it safe for traffic. On the 15th I moved again. One day's lorry, one of train and another of lorry brought me here where I'm helping Greek Sappers to make a light railway. They're supposed to be doing the job with us under them but at the same time I get strafed by our people for every mistake they make. They're a little inclined to resent our presence and I don't blame 'em. So it's a position which needs tact.

I get on well with them individually and quite like them but I'm not sure that they really relish being strafed by my supervisors & by Frenchmen as well as by their own. I'm under a Greek Major who's under a French Captain who's under both my Colonel and a French Colonel on the Greek Staff. The railway however is getting made in spite of everything.

I'm very glad I know a certain amount of French.

It's rather nice having a company of one's own. I wish it were a Field Coy but really, when there's anything doing, it's wonderful how interesting the L of C can become.

I've got quite a nice lot of officers & quite good senior NCOs & at last I've a car of my own, even if it is only a Ford van.

(King's Own Royal Regiment Museum, Lancaster)

Looking north from the summit of the pass over the Strumnitza Valley. Sketch by a member of 2nd Battalion, King's Own.

I've just had your letter which you wrote before leaving Coniston. Marshall should be shot for draining Tarn Hows.

I don't know when leave will re-open, but I think that now, even if I get the chance of it, I'll wait. Its good experience having a Company and it might be very useful when peace comes to be able to say I'd had no leave for over two years. I could claim it then & could get to England & see the War Office & could probably wangle to stay at home if I wanted to.

I've now run entirely out of paper so with love to Honor I'll say Goodnight.

Your loving
JS X

You'll find the end of this letter on the other side of this sheet. I didn't notice I hadn't used this side I don't know really however that there's very much more to talk about. I'm very homesick now and again, especially while I'm dressing. I suppose it is that getting out of bed is so beastly all the world over, that doing it here reminds one forcibly of home.

Dec 15th 1918

My Dearest Mother,

I should have made my last letter a Christmas one but I haven't fully realised that the time is so close. But perhaps this one won't arrive so very late and it carries all my love to you both and my dearest wishes for both Christmas and the new year.

We're having lovely weather now, cold but sunny, after rather an unpleasant autumn, which we noticed perhaps more than usual as we were doing so much moving about, which meant we could never make a camp at all comfortable.

The weather broke about the beginning of October. We left Doiran for Strumnitza on the 6th & had it pretty wet up there. We were right up in the clouds whenever there were any & there generally were. We were several days before we saw the Strumnitza valley just at our feet

Then we trekked Oct 15th – 17th after which we had 6 weeks or so on the Struma plain near Yenikoi in a place without a vestige of protection from the north winds & in a completely flat camp which easily became a lake. It was pretty beastly under canvas though the two blizzards we had

Looking across the River Struma and the Struma Valley to the Bulgarian defensive line (until 21 September 1918) on the high ground. Painted by William T. Wood from *The Salonika Front*, by A.J.Mann 1920

fell as rain where we were, the snow line being a couple of hundred feet or so above the plain, which is ten miles across & absolutely flat.

Now we're at Janesh (Yanesh or Janes however you like to transcribe it). It used to be the Corps HQ for the Doiran Front in the old days. We're in a steep little hollow in the hills, with plenty of trees and we're gradually making ourselves comfortable. We're still more or less under canvas but we've got the Officers' and Mens' cookhouses built, the mens' dining shelter, a corrugated iron building about 60 ft by 16 ft is nearly finished and we got into our own mess two days ago. Its made of curved sheets of corrugated iron with a layer of earth outside (in sandbags) to retain the heat. The curved sheets give it a horseshoe shape in cross-section. It's about 15ft by 9 sandbag walls at the ends except for the fireplace which is brick & stone with mud mortar. That's at one end & a door & window at the other, with a fan-light over the door. The inside is white-washed so that it's nice & light. The break in the sandbags made by the chimney leaves rather a blank- looking panel but we're going to have a picture there as soon as Allner has painted it.

I've got quite an easy time here. I run round in the car, taking a glance at how various jobs are going on but I can manage pretty well as many joy-rides as I like.

Osborne & I have been running around the country trying to find turkeys or geese without success. Yesterday we gave it up & decided on chickens. We could probably have got them nearer but we went to Vurlan my own old Turkish village which is about 30 kilos away, mainly over my own tracks which weren't finished enough to be reliable in winter. We got there, however, and I had a look at my old dug-outs. Alas! my old arm-chair, my shelves & most of the other timber had gone – firewood for the village, I suppose.

We went on into the village, probably the first car to have been there since I was last there in Wyman's old bus. I made for a crowd of small boys who all ran away. However I got out and found a fellow quite close who used to work for me. I asked him where Hassein Hassan was & he brought me along. I waited at the gate of the house & Hassein appeared. When he saw it was me he gave me a great smile of welcome & I was awfully glad to see him again. I broached the subject of turkeys & geese, but, as I expected, there were none in the village so I asked for chickens.

After a little more chatting he went off with Sali Tokmakgi (i.e. Sali the Hammer man, who used to drive in my iron-pickets for my entanglements) to get the chickens. With Hassein had come his father and several other

Macedonia after the War

The First World War did little to change the historic complexity of Macedonia's position and status in the Southern Balkans. Before and during the war Macedonia was effectively under the control of the three countries that it spanned – Serbia, Bulgaria and Greece. For many years thereafter it continued to be a nation without a state, defined only by its ethnic ties and traditional geographical area.

For the Greek Macedonians – John's village friends – their worst fear gradually became a reality. Their traditional village, town and regional place names were progressively changed to Greek names; so also were the surnames of ethnic Macedonians. For example, John's village of Vurlan became Anavrito. The process, which was called Hellenization, was effectively completed in 1927 when the Greek government issued a legislative edict declaring that 'there are not any non-Greek people in Greece.'

Meanwhile it was the Serbian Macedonians who continued the struggle for Macedonian independence. In 1929 Serbia became the Kingdom of Yugoslavia. Its southern province covered the historic and geographical area of much of Macedonia. During the 1920s and 1930s this area of the Balkans was subjected to a confusing period of internal and regional guerrilla warfare, master-minded by the Macedonian nationalists. In 1934 the Yugoslav Comintern issued a special resolution in which, for the first time, directions were provided for recognising the existence of a separate Macedonian nation and language.

During World War II Yugoslavia was occupied by the Axis Powers from 1941–45. Harsh rule by the occupying forces encouraged many Macedonians to support Tito's Communist resistance movement, resulting in the German forces being driven out of Macedonia by the end of 1944.

In 1944 it was peacefully agreed that the People's Republic of Macedonia would become one of the six republics of the Yugoslav federation. On 8 September 1991 Macedonia finally became the independent state that it is today.

old gentlemen, who then asked us to come in & sit down. So we went into the court-yard and onto the veranda which all Turkish houses have and I was given the seat of honour on an up-turned wicker basket. Osborne shared a sort of ledge with some of them and the remainder completed the circle squatting on the floor. They brought us excellent coffee & rolled local cigarettes for us and presently Hassein brought each of us a wooden spoon that he'd made. There was another half-made he'd been working at. It's a topping little spoon, beautifully rounded, all done with an adze except perhaps the last smoothing. It's about table-spoon size.

They were very keen to know where I'd been since I left them & appeared greatly interested. They also asked me almost as soon as we sat down who Macedonia would belong to after the war – Greek? Bulgar? Serb? Franxsa? Inghiliz? I shrugged my shoulders & said I didn't know. Perhaps the Greeks.

A sort of wail went up from them all. The Greeks Gendarmes would drive them all away. Greek no good. Bulgar was good. Serb no good. Franxsa no good. Inghiliz give plenty work, plenty food, plenty money.

It's an absolute crime to leave people like that at the mercy of the Greeks.

They asked with great interest when I would be in England again. I said I hoped in about a month and they all congratulated me very warmly and agreed that two years was the deuce of a long time to be away from home.

It was getting late. We hadn't started till after lunch and I wanted to get back to the metalled road at Kukus before it was quite dark as the tracks were a bit cut up, so we made a move. They'd got 8 chickens in one house & 12 in another & we took Hassein along in the car while Sali & some others followed (we'd paid ceremonious adieus to the old gentlemen). Another fellow rolled up with 3 more just as we were leaving.

I don't suppose you've ever travelled in a car with 23 live fowls round your feet, tied together by the feet in pairs & fours except for three who were stuffed in a sandbag, the string supply being exhausted. They kept our feet nice & warm.

I'm awfully glad we went there. It was almost like going home again. They seemed so genuinely glad to see us. The Turk may be 'unspeakable', but he's got topping manners and when he does go & do a massacre one can quite see his point of view & sympathise.

When I get my leave I'm going to try & get to Chatham as soon as possible for an advanced construction course, and if it's practicable I'll try & get some Turkish from this new School of Oriental Languages they've got in London. Then I'll be in a position to agitate strongly for a job in some place inhabited by Turks. I'm not attracted by India nowadays. There'll be

(IWM Q31575)

Officers versus other ranks football match at a camp outside city of Salonika more pioneer work to do in Turkey and though more out of the world in one way yet it will be easier to get home from there. It would be quite practicable to get home every other year at least, preferably in the hot weather, and Betsy & Peter could get home if they got run down at all.

You & Honor will have to come out to us some spring or autumn & then if I could get leave we could do Constantinople, Athens, and as many other places as you'd like – even Vurlan perhaps, though it might be rather a dangerous place in peace-time.

We're just going to have lunch, after which I'm going to watch a footer match against the 140th AT Co R.E.

I'm longing to hear how you celebrated Nov 11th.

With all love to you both,

Your very loving,

J.S. X

Would you let Betsy see this letter. It will save me enthusing twice on the subject of Vurlan.

30.12.18

Dearest Mother,

This letter will be crossing on the same boat as I do, I suppose, tomorrow or the next day, but from Taranto it will go rapide and so get to you 3 or 4 days before I arrive.

I'm quite enjoying my trip. I had to report at the leave camp on Monday 23rd but as the train wasn't going till 26th I got permission to go away again & report at the train on the day. I stayed Monday night in Salonika with the 37th Co, dining at the Officers' Rest House & having quite an amusing evening there round a billiard table. On Tuesday I bought a few things and then lunched at the 60th General Hospital. My friend Miss Sorensen is now Matron there, so I felt very grand as her guest. We had a picnic afterwards at Hortiack which was quite good fun. We remembered everything except the tea, but did quite well by emptying a tin of condensed milk into the kettle. It's a great thing to have a car.

I got back to the company a little late for dinner and had a topping day for Christmas. Osborn & I went to church at 10 o'clock & it was one of the jolliest services I've known. It's an old Greek church with every bit of its surface covered with paint – saints all over its roof and everywhere. The

(King's Own Royal Regiment Museum, Lancaster)

Royal Engineers Christmas Card for 1918 and New Year 1919.

artists mayn't have been Academicians but the effect is very nice. They had a portable harmonium with quite a good tone & several violins. The sermon was good for a wonder and we had music with all the hymns & chants. The second service being distinct, with a five minutes interval, we got O come all ye faithful twice to my great delight & we had hymns all through the communion, including "And now, O Father mindful of the love".

The mens' dinner got started soon after one. We'd just got our dining room complete the evening before & quite a nice room it was. We went round & I had to make speeches in the Sergeants Mess (where we were given very stiff whiskies to drink) and in the Sappers Mess (where they gave us beer). They cheered us and drank our health and all that sort of thing and we got away to our own dinner.

The A.S.M. had presented us with a Turkey and a most excellent one it was. We're very lucky in our cook & he gave us a splendid meal. I'm afraid that no officer remained awake the entire afternoon, though I held open my eyes till just before tea.

About 7.30 the men's concert began. We drifted in about 8. It was quite a good show. We'd been meaning to leave before the end but as the Sergeant Major was finding it a little hard to get silence kept at the back of the room we decided to stay and give him moral support. The men were very well behaved really though of course we'd been generous with the beer. I must say that as long as they get drunk like gentlemen I think a good wholesale burst at Christmas does them good.

About the middle the Sergeant Major proposed the toast of the officers, so I had to make another speech. I got through all right by being fairly short & to the point & giving them the toast of the Corps of Royal Engineers.

What wasn't fair was that at the end just before "The King" the C.S.M. got up and said he'd ask me to say a few words before I went away. I shouted out a few sentences and they went down quite well. It was the best Christmas I've known on service.

At 5 a.m. on Boxing Day I had to get up and by 6 I was away in the car. I got down to the station in two & a half hours & sometime in the morning the train started. We got tea at Katerini and dinner at Larissa.

The next morning we had wonderful scenery past Lamia, through to Bralo where we left the train. Bralo is in the plain of Doris & in the afternoon two of us went & saw the remains of a Dorian fortified village, which guarded one of the passes. It was most interesting from a constructional point of view. We decided their way of building made a wonderful wall but that a modern contractor would lose money if he cut his stones that way.

In Memory of John's comrades in arms
British Salonika Force 1915–1918

Killed in action and died of wounds	4,096
Missing	1,584
Prisoners of war	1,194
Wounded	16,888

(Official History of the War: Macedonia Vol 2, *1935)*

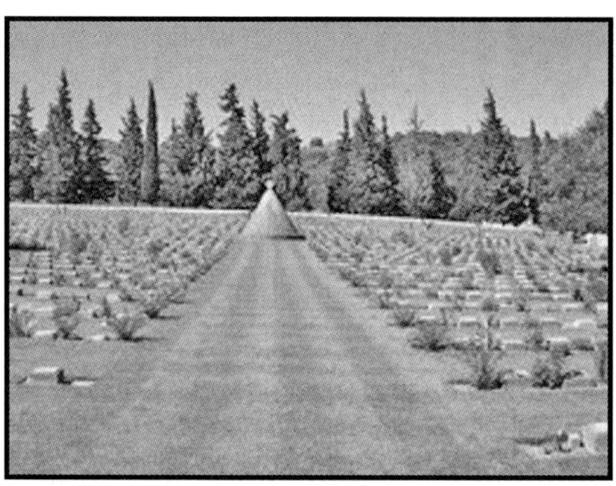

The Doiran Military Cemetery was formed at the end of 1916 as a cemetery for the Doiran front. The graves are almost entirely those of officers and men of the 22nd and 26th Divisions and largely reflect the fighting of April and May 1917 (the attacks on the Petit-Couronne), and 18–19 September 1918 (the attacks on Pip Ridge and the Grand Couronne).

(Commonwealth War Graves Commission)

The Doiran Memorial stands close to the western end of the line held by the Commonwealth forces.
It marks the scene of the fierce fighting of 1917–1918, which caused the majority of the Commonwealth battle casualties.

We dropped in to tea with some Sappers there and left between 12 & 1. We again had to get up at an un-earthly hour and about 7 our lorries started for Itea, on the Gulf of Corinth where I now am. Its a wonderful road with zigzags which would make the Canx-Glion road look like a straight line.

We're about 6 miles from Delphi, & yesterday some of us walked up there. It was a bit of a pull but was thoroughly worth it. We saw the oracle & I asked her all about it. She replied , "Τον δε άπομειβομενος προσεφη ποδυς ώκυς 'Αχιλλευς" (*"And Achilles fleet of foot made answer and spoke to him." Homer, The Iliad, Book 1, line 84).* I said "That's all right but, Pythia, Apollo is the man I want to hear" *(Apollo is the god of Delphi and the source of the oracle; Pythia is the priestess of Apollo through whom he speaks)* "Ah right" said she "put him in. He'll scan nearly as well". So I put him in & waited in hopes of hearing more & said "Do you really mean what you've told me?" "Perhaps" said she.

The temples were quite interesting from a constructional point of view though only the ground plan is really left. The theatre is very fine & is almost complete except for the stage. The museum has quite a lot of good things and the Auriga is lovely. He's the first thing you see when you open the door.

I've got a few photos but they were sold out of most of the good things, including the Auriga. I may be able to get one in the town here.

They've just stuck up the results of the General Election. Everyone was rather disappointed. They thought it was something important, such as when our boat will go. I'm glad old LG has brought it off well.

You'ld love this place. When I'm chief engineer on some Turkish railway we'll do a trip through all this part one holiday.

Best of love to you both. I'll wire you from Southampton and hope you'll be able to meet me at Waterloo.

Your loving

J.S. X

How the Salonika Campaign helped to bring the First World War to an end

On 3rd October Field Marshal von Hindenburg made the following statement to the German Chancellor: "As the result of the collapse of the Macedonian front, and the weakening of the reserves in the west, which this has necessitated, and in view of the impossibility of making good the very heavy losses of the last few days, there appears to be now no possibility as far as human judgement goes, of winning peace from our enemies by force of arms... In these circumstances the only right course is to bring the war to an end.'

In his memoirs General Ludendorff wrote: 'The events that from 15th September onwards took place on the Bulgarian front sealed the fate of the quadruple Alliance'

FINISH JOHNNY!
GREETINGS FROM THE
SALONIKA ARMY
XMAS - 1918.
8th Field Survey Coy. R.E. No. 529.

What happened to John after the War?

John Baines continued to serve in the Royal Engineers after the war. Promoted to Major in 1929, he was posted to Egypt as Staff Officer RE, before being appointed Chief Instructor RE Wing at the School of Anti-Aircraft (AA) Defence as a Lieutenant Colonel in 1934.

Soon after that he was promoted to Brigadier to command 54th AA Brigade, before becoming CRE Gibraltar in 1937 and then OC of an Air Defence (Searchlight) Brigade in 1939.

After 25 years of service, John left the army in 1940 and became an assistant master at Rossall School in Lancashire from 1941–45. He then attended London University, graduating with a History BA in 1947. His last appointment was as an assistant master at Academy House, Crieff, from 1949.

John Stanhope Baines died on 11th August 1951, aged 57. Dearest Mother died on 27th June the following year aged 89.

Appendix I

TRIBUTE TO THE BRITISH SALONIKA ARMY

From the Times of late October 1918

We publish to-day a letter from the BISHOP of LONDON pleading that in our congratulations to the British Army on its magnificent victories the Salonika forces should not be forgotten. Few of us at home have any conception how much our praise, and when necessary our criticism if only it is sympathetic, means to the Armies at the front – how much it sustains them in their trials and spurs them to fresh efforts for victory. In that regard our Army in France has been well served, and moreover its soldiers have had opportunities of coming back amongst us and learning how much they are in our minds. Not so the Armies in what have been irreverently called the "side-shows" – and most unjustly – for the firmest "Westerner" is now ready to proclaim that without our Eastern campaigns his victories could not have been so decisive. These men in our Eastern Armies have had the dust and toil without the laurel of the race to victory. They have had few chances of coming home and renewing their enthusiasm in our interest and praise; their work – through no fault of the correspondents – has been ill reported; and too often the suggestion has been made that their work was all being wasted. Especially is this true of the Salonika Army. The Serbian Armies have done magnificently, but it is no disparagement of their achievement to recognise that it would have been impossible without the help of the British Army under GENERAL MILNE. It is, as the BISHOP of LONDON says, not generally known that the initial success of the Serbian flanking movement was due principally to the success of the British on the right in making the enemy believe that theirs was the main attack. Moreover, after the Serbs had got going, theirs was, in fact, the principal attack so far as downright hard fighting went. It was, again, the British Army that first entered Bulgaria over the Belashitza range and into the Strumnitza valley. Add the malaria, and we begin to get some measure of the quality of the British Army in Macedonia.

Our Army in Salonika. A Gallant Force
Testimony of the BISHOP OF LONDON

To the Editor of the 'Times'
Sir, – I have completed the task entrusted to me and have reached here at Sofia the 'ultima Thule' of my expedition. Assisted by glorious weather, and helped at every point by the never-failing kindness of the Commander in Chief, I have addressed every fighting unit of the Salonika Army still left in Macedonia or Bulgaria. I have read them the King's message of congratulations which was cheered with equal enthusiasm in the valleys of Macedonia or the rocky fastnesses of Bulgaria. I have given each brigade a message from home of love and affection, and, as in duty bound, have added to each and all to the best of my power a message from God. St Paul, who toiled not in a motor car, along some of the many roads on which I have travelled, would have been ashamed of the 108th Bishop of London if he had not at least attempted the last. From first to last, my threefold message has been received with a touching welcome by the whole Army, from the Generals to the youngest private.

But now, before I turn my face homewards, I want to say a word, Sir, through your paper to my fellow-countrymen at home. We have not appreciated at anything like its full value the fortitude, courage, and wonderful success of the Salonika Army, and they have a sore and disappointed feeling they are neglected and despised. A music-hall song, which ought never to have been allowed to be sung: – "If you don't want to fight, go to Salonika" has been gall and wormwood to those who had almost reached the limits of endurance before. The few who have got home on leave found the opinion common among their friends that they have been spending their time a few miles outside Salonika, with frequent opportunities of visiting on most evening the cafes in the town.

Now what are the facts of the case? To start with, large numbers have had no leave for three years, and are in many cases greatly distressed as to what is happening in their homes; so far from spending their time near Salonika, the lines which they have had to hold have been 60 miles from the town, and most of the soldiers have not been able to visit Salonika at all. Malaria and influenza have been so rife and universal that I found on arrival, on October 16, that there were 31,000 sick in the doctors' hands, nursed by 1,600 of our splendid nurses, whose services are beyond praise. I have examined in detail on my way here the positions which were opposed to them and I have never seen positions of such terrible strength. From the summit of the Grand Couronne, which is 3,000 ft. above the plain, a full view could be obtained by the Bulgarian Army of Salonika harbour, and every road of communication which led from it to the British lines.

In spite of this, and the fact that their numbers, always comparatively small, had been depleted by sickness, they carried out the attack so elaborately planned with consummate courage. No one wishes to deprecate the magnificent dash of the Serbian flank attack on September 9, or the onset of our Greek allies, but what is not generally known is that this was only made possible by the great bulk of the enemy's forces being gathered opposite our lines by elaborated camouflage and feint attacks from September 1 onwards. In this operation one brigade alone lost very heavily indeed. But it was not until September 18 and 19 that the great attack came which decided the issue. The Grand Couronne and the Pip Ridge, which had frowned down upon our men for three years, were stormed by direct assault to draw away attention from the flanking movement of the Serbs and French. Every man, as he went up, went up humanly speaking to certain death, but not one turned back. One sergeant was found dead 20 yards from the summit, and a very great proportion of those who attacked were killed or wounded. But this sacrifice was not in vain. They had held the main body of the Bulgarian Army long enough for the flank attack to succeed. The retreat began; our flying men swept over and attacked the retreating enemy in the deep gorges through which alone they could attempt to escape, and the fact that I was able to motor through Bulgaria at night, alone with my chaplains, within a month after the battle, and should be writing this as quietly in Sofia to-night as I should be in London, will attest to the completeness of their victory. But they have won a moral victory as well. They are leaving Macedonia now for enterprises of which I must not speak, but the Governor-General of Macedonia endorses the opinion of the whole of Macedonia that the best piece of propaganda for the British nation has been the conduct of the Salonika Army. They are leaving with the enthusiastic affection of the whole country. The clean-limbed, clean-living, courteous British soldier who saved them during the fire, and who has never interfered with their women folk or their goods, has won the heart of his Allies at the same time as he has been the first to make his enemy surrender.

May I plead for full justice to be done at home to the work of the Salonika Army?

Yours faithfully,
A.F. LONDON
Sofia, Oct.24.

Appendix 2

L'EPINETTE OPERATION

Extract from 'A Short History of the 6th Division Chapter IV – Armentieres 1914–15

The next few months were uneventful ones, the only incidents worthy of remark being a visit from the King on the 2nd December; a minor operation by the North Staffordshire Regiment on the 12th March, resulting in the inclusion in our line of the unsavoury Epinette Salient. The minor operation at L'Epinette was a very well-planned night affair, whereby the 17th Infantry Brigade advanced their line 200–300 yards on a frontage of half a mile. It was carried out by the 1st Battalion North Staffordshire Regiment and 12th Field Company, and Sir Smith-Dorrien (Army Commander), in congratulating the regiment, mentioned particularly Lieuts. Pope and Gordon for fine leading.

Extract from 1st Battalion North Staffordshire Regiment War Diary 1915

10th March
3.45 a.m. Firing of guns and rifles on extreme right. Sentry woke me up and all stand to. Coys start demonstration at 4.30 a.m. All quiet by 5.10 a.m. Germans unimpressed. At 7.15 a.m. our big guns opened and continue bombarding for half an hour. Incident and 7th Division captured German trenches. At 1.30 p.m. orders received to strike? vigorously for half an hour. Dug out in front that night putting out saps. Relieved 7 p.m. At 11 p.m. C.O. to Bde Office. Returned with scheme for attacking L'EPINETTE. C.O. writes up all the detail bomb throwers, wire cutters, storming parties, co-operation of guns, digging parties, parties for filling up communication trenches, etc. Two objectives 5 houses on left to C Coy, houses on road to D Coy, B Coy 'Water Wash' Farm and houses on right, A Coy in support of right.

11th March

Fine morning. [Very busy, writing orders, arrange details] send for tools from Bde also 47 wire cutters. [Pack up sentries, but leave one sentry for day to look after stores, etc.] Went up to the trenches in afternoon to look at everything and show O.C.Coys and platoon Sgts exact approaches to houses, etc. Men to carry 220 rounds and two days rations. Start at mid night. Rum issue at 11.00 p.m. Took houses without much opposition. [General Harper wished us good luck and 2nd Army wishes 'Best luck and good wishes to the N.Staffords']. Lt Gordon wounded by bomb in the knee and several men. Lt Pope gets into farms in half an hour with no casualties. Patrols did good work in cutting wire. [Cpl Pain, Trotter, Maddox, McNicol work well].

12th March

Reported all farms taken at 2 a.m. RE parties attached to all parties. Lt Oxley hit in stomach. Our artillery bombarded enemy's trenches at 5.15 a.m. [At 4 a.m. C.O. and self went round left trenches and No 5 house (as on sketch)]. Enemy tried to counter attack by coming up communication trench with bombs. Lt Dale went out to meet them and got a bomb at him killing two men and wounding him. Later he died of wounds. Houses loopholed, dig hard, RE help and digging parties. Major Wyatt (2nd in Command) commanded right part (B & A Coys). Enemy fired a good deal. At 1.40 p.m. enemy's guns opened and shell for ¾ hour. Our guns did not open for a little then bombarded their trenches. Up to 12 noon casualties were 4 officers, Gordon, Daley*(?)*, Whittington*(?)* Wounded, Dale died, 1 man killed, 33 wounded.3 p.m. more shelling. 4 p.m. more shelling. C Coy report over 40 casualties. No 5 house untenable. Wire Bde for additional s.bearers. Working parties of 200 men came up. We relieved C Coy by A Coy, D by B Coy. REs and Leinsters help us with wounded all night. 2/Lt Manyon*(?)* killed, 2/Lt Paget wounded. Bomb throwers of Germans attack again, but opened m.gun on them and killed 17 out of 20, 3 prisoners. They are Saxons *(?)*139th & *(?)*113th Regts also Pioneers with solid bombs.

13th March

Bad night. Heavy guns out of action. 4 a.m. Heavy firing by E.Yorks on left but nothing. Enemy bombarded between 12–1 p.m. Total casualties up till noon 6 officers 84 o.ranks. More shelling, very heavy by enemy's guns. Very accurate in trenches. 2/Lt Hill(?), 2nd Hants Regt wounded.

Relief at 7 p.m. and 10 p.m. Got back midnight all in. Total casualties 131 as follows 7 officers, two of them killed, 103 men wounded, 21 killed.

14th March
Bde and Corps very pleased. Men worked well and all the officers. Copy of wire received from Sir Horace Smith-Dorien:

'I have just read the full report of the capture of L'EPINETTE. It reflects great credit on the 17th Bde especially on the 1st North Staffordshire Regt and the leading of Lieuts Poe and Gordon of that Regt and on 12 Coy R.E. and supporting artillery. Should like all thanked on my behalf.'

(National Archives WO95/1613)

Extract from 'I Was There' – letters by Denis Oliver Barnet, 2nd Bn Leinster Regiment

© *Paul Foster*

St Pathrick's Dhay (17th March 1915)

P'rhaps I've now got time now for a bit of a letter, and can tell you a little of what's been going on to prevent me from writing these days. I may tell you that, even if I *had* written (which I couldn't), I could not have got a letter any further than my own pocket.

Someone tells me that he's seen in a paper that we've '*advanced 300 yards on an 800 yard front*'. That is true.

Some 10 days ago, we together with another battalion (which easily had the worst part to do, and did it very well), took the village of ---- [*Epinette*] which lies just in front of the main German fire trench, and which they had connected up with saps and entrenched pretty strongly, loopholing the houses, and so on. My share was to advance on the flank of the village, and '*dig in*', under the Divil's own rifle and machine gun fire, within 200 yards of the Allymans.

The assault was a surprise affair and began at midnight. It was a real surprise for the Dutchman, and most of the houses were unoccupied. We took them all – our crowd having practically no fighting to do – and entrenched round about them. Just before dawn, when we thought they might think of counter-attacking, our guns basted the German trenches with shrapnel at top pressure, and if they ever meant to attack, they decided not to. In the meantime, I was digging like blazes, as I knew we should have to hold the unfinished trenches during the following day. When day broke, they began to shell, and that was how we got our casualties in the new lines. In fact we got it in the neighbourhood of the neck! However, we stuck it all right, and that evening, when twenty Bavarians crawled up with bombs, we shot eighteen and took two prisoners. It was not our show, but a fine bit of vigilance on the part of the battalion concerned.

Ever since, we have hung on to the advanced line, making it better every night, being sniped at pretty continuously and being shelled in the intervals. The trenches are now perfectly excellent, and we can defy an attack or any amount of shelling, as we have made dug-outs and all conveniences. But I can assure you that enduring out those days and nights, especially the nights, in little rabbit scrapes, bringing material up the roads with the searchlight on, putting up wire, and the continuous dig, dig, dig at the parapet, has been work which I am glad is finished. The RE have been magnificent, and so have our own men.

Extract from 12th Field Company RE War Diary 1915

N.B. Lt J.S.Baines was OC 3 Section

11th March

During night took part with NStaffs in attack on L'Epinette. Paraded at 10 p.m. and reported at 11 p.m. to OC NStaffs at BARRIER on L'Epinette road. Distributed company as follows: Lt Turner and 10 men of No 1 Section with right assault column, the remainder of No 1 Section accompanied the working parties of right column. Lt Jackson and 10 men of No 2 Section with working parties of left column. No 3 Section followed right column to start on consolidating new line. No 4 Section assisted in consolidating left of new line. Capt Noble supervised working parties of 2 London Regiment who worked on new lines between BARRIER and L'EPINETTE. Both assaulting columns encountered barbed wire entanglement but this was not of a formidable nature and was successfully cut through. As soon as all buildings on new line had been reoccupied all sappers assisted in strengthening the houses and joining up between the houses. The Company had 2 men wounded and 1 missing during the operation.'

12th March

All sections all night of 12/13 at L'EPINETTE. Whole of new line now wired, barricades built on road at No 5 House; shelters put in trenches and communications improved.

(IWM WO95/1599)

Appendix 3

WINCHESTER COLLEGE REFERENCES

With thanks to the Warden and Scholars of Winchester College for the use of archive material

1. Montague John Rendall – Headmaster 1911–24

Montague Rendall, a Harrow scholar, joined the staff in 1887. In 1899 he became Second Master, and then Headmaster in 1911. So John Baines knew him well throughout his time at Winchester and was certainly taught by him, referring to him in a number of his letters.

Short extracts from his obituary in the Wykehamist dated 7th November 1950 provide a good picture of this inspirational man:

'It was soon realised that he was an exceptionally forceful and gifted teacher, as well as a scholar of rare quality … Only those who were at Winchester in the last century can recall his energy on a "Penny-farthing", and the lightheartedness with which he coasted down St Giles' Hill … His lavish and generous hospitality was always memorable. He loved to fill his house with guests and to preside at a crowded dinner-table … To a junior indeed he might appear aloof and awe-inspiring; it was only later that boys realised how deep was his affection for them even when his disciplinary measures were most stern.'

However, in the context of this book, it is the following extract from his obituary that is the most poignant:

'His period as Headmaster was clouded by the 1914–18 war. He felt the loss of young lives intensely, did all he could to mitigate the lot of those serving, and delighted many of them by Christmas booklets containing "snaps" of well-remembered scenes and figures. In his last two years of office, for which he was specially asked to stay on beyond the normal retiring age, he saw War Memorial Cloister completed. The conception of a memorial that should offer neither increased facilities nor improved accommodation had been his own, and he was responsible for the wording of the great inscription – his "prose poem" as he called it – and for much of the detail, which he supervised with loving care.'

Surprisingly, the obituary did not mention that the photographs in the Christmas booklets, sent to Wykehamists on active service overseas, were all taken by 'Monty' Rendall himself. He was a keen amateur photographer.

Winchester,
December, 1917.

I send you a few of my photos, taken chiefly in 1917, to carry a message of love and trust from Winchester, for which you are fighting.

Our thoughts are with you always, and we do not forget you for one day.

My Christmas Card does not expect an answer.

M. J. R.

2. Killed in Action

SECOND LIEUTENANT FREDERICK ATHELSTON FANSHAWE BAINES
King's Royal Rifle Corps

F.A.F.BAINES
College 1909–14

SECOND LIEUTENANT FREDERICK ATHELSTON FANSHAWE BAINES (COLL., 1909–1914) was born on February 2nd, 1896 – son of A.A Baines Esq.,(B, 1867–1872), of Westmeston, Lewes, Sussex – and entered College from Cordwalles School. He left Winchester for Sandhurst in October 1914, and in February 1915 was gazetted to the King's Royal Rifle Corps. He went to France on May 18th, and joined the 4th Battalion at Poperinghe. The next day they were called up to regain some trenches near the Ypres-Menin Road which had been lost in a gas-attack some hours before. He was killed leading his company in the early morning of May 25th near Bellewaarde Wood, in the attempt to retake that position.

A stained glass window has been erected to his memory in Westmeston Church.

LIEUTENANT FRITZ PORTMORE CRAWHALL
King's Royal Rifle Corps

F.P.CRAWHALL
College 1908–14

LIEUTENANT FRITZ PORTMORE CRAWHALL (COLL., 1908–1914) was born on August 15th 1895 – the son of Rev. E.I.L. Crawhall, of Herriard, Basingstoke – and came to Winchester from Mr. Carter's school at Maidenhead. After a year at Sunnyside he stood for election to College and was placed first on the Roll. He became a School Prefect in 1913, captained College VI for two years and played in 2nd XI (Association). In 1914 he was elected to a Scholarship at Merton College, Oxford. At the outbreak of war he was in camp with the Winchester O.T.C., in which he held the rank of Colour-Sergeant, and obtained his commission within a few days in the 6th Battalion King's Royal Rifle Corps. He fell in action at Givenchy-lez-la-Bassée on March 10th 1915, during the battle of Neuve Chapelle.

SECOND LIEUTENANT VERE HERBERT SMITH
Rifle Brigade

V.HERBERT SMITH
B 1906–11

SECOND LIEUTENANT VERE HERBERT SMITH (B, 1906–11) was born on December 17th, 1892. He was the son of N. Herbert Smith Esq., of The Hall, Hickling, Norwich and before coming to Winchester was with Mr. C.E. Stanford at St. Aubyns, Rottingdean. He was two years Head of his House and Senior Commoner Prefect his last half; he played two years in O.T.H. VI (captain in 1911), one year in Association XI, rowed in School IV and won Steeplechase. Early in 1912 he went up to New College, Oxford, where he took his degree with First Class Honours in Jurisprudence.

At the outbreak of war he applied for a commission and was gazetted to the Rifle Brigade; he had previously had seven years experience with the O.T.C. He went to France to join the 3rd Battalion in February 1915 and was killed by a bomb near Neuve Chapelle on March 21st, 1915, while inspecting rifles in a front line trench. The Vere Herbert Smith School History Prizes were founded by his uncle in 1916 to his memory.

SECOND LIEUTENANT BERTRAM ANTONY MEDLEY
Highland Light Infantry

B.A.MEDLEY
Coll 1908–14

SECOND LIEUTENANT BERTRAM ANTONY MEDLEY (COLL., 1908–1914) was born on February 23rd, 1895 – son of D.J. Medley, Esq., Professor of History in the University of Glasgow – and came to Winchester from Cordwalles School. He was a School Prefect and a member of College XV his last year, and took a prominent part in the proceedings of Natural History Society, being especially interested in botanical work. He won the Duncan Prize for Reading in 1914 and had intended to go up to Balliol College, Oxford, in the following October.

He was gazetted that same month to the Highland Light Infantry and went to the front in April 1915. During the operations of September 25th, 1915 (Battle of Loos) his company of the 2nd Battalion was one of those leading the attack at Givenchy. After taking several lines of trenches they were bombed back to their former position; Mr. Medley fell severely wounded, but refused to be moved until all his men had been got away. The ground shortly afterwards fell into German hands and it is presumed that he died of his wounds.

His name appeared in Lord French's Despatch of January 1st 1916.

3. Other Obituaries

Charles William BEART, K 1907–1912. Born 1894, the son of Frederick Robert Beart and Violet Baumgartner. In both Lords XI and Assoc XI. Joined the Durham Light Infantry in 1914 as 2nd Lieut; ADC 1915; GSO3 1917; Brigade Major 1917–1919; wounded, MC, despatches twice, Croce di Guerra; Adjutant 1919; 2nd in command of Battalion 1919; Lt Col 8 Battalion BEF and MEF, 1940–1942; Brigadier, East Africa 1942; AAG and WO 1943; wounded, OBE, despatches twice, retired 1947. Died in Feb 1972 and his obituary says that he took up ranching in Argentina and became a successful fisherman.

Leonard Treise MORSHEAD, E 1908–1913. Born 25 Sep 1894, the son of another Wykehamist, Leonard Frederick Morshead, CSI, and his wife Sybil Brownlow Hill (the daughter of another Wykehamist). A successful sportsman at school, Lords XI 1911–1913, Rackets Pair 1913, Commoner XV and VI 1912. Joined the Royal Engineers in 1914, rising to the rank of Captain and Adjutant. Served as a GSO 3; mentioned in despatches 3 times. Member of the 1922 Everest Expedition. Married Marjorie Ridley 3 Dec 1921. Died 27 Aug 1931.

Frederick William Leopold McClintock PARKER, College 1911–1915. Born 1898, son of Mr Justice Frederick Hardyman Parker. RMA 1916, 2nd Lt RE 1916; despatches; QVO Sappers and Miners, 1919–1922; Waziristan FF 1921–1922; Jesus College, Camb 1922; SME Chatham 1923; QVO S and M 1924–1929; Capt 1926; psc 1931; staff capt 1932–1935; Major, S and M, 1936–1939; GSO2, BEF 1939–1940 (despatches); GSO1 UK 1943, NW Europe 1944–45, Colonel; CBE; Commandant, QVO S and M 1946–47, HQ BAOR 1948, retired as a Brigadier 1950. Died Jul 1989.

William Leonard ROSEVEARE, K 1909–1913. Born 11 Dec 1895, the son of Professor William Nicholas Roseveare and Ethel Mary Bushell. Two brothers in the school, Richard (Coll 1910–1915) and Harry (I 1916–1918). Prize Cadet at RMA in 1913, first in the class. Joined the Royal Engineers in 1914; served in the Signal Service throughout the war. Mentioned in despatches and MC. Served in India from 1921 to 1923, and then in the Irrigation Dept in India and Burma from 1924. Retired as a Major in 1929. Stayed in India, working for the Indian Service of Engineers. Married Marjory Constance Webb 20 Dec 1919. Died 4 May 1976.

John Amherst SELBY BIGGE, College 1905–1911. Born 1892, son of Sir Lewis Amhurst Selby-Bigge. Played in College VI, went on to Christ Church, Oxford in 1911 and then to the Slade School in 1913; 2nd Lt RASC 1914; Macedonia; Intelligence Corps 1918; advisor in censorship to Greek Government; engaged in farming, business and painting, in Austria and France, 1935–1941; with BBC (European News) 1942–43; British Red Cross, 1944–45, BBC 1944–45. Died in 1973.

George Robert Sabine SNOW, College 1910–1915. Born 1897, son of Thomas Snow. Prefect of School, College VI. 2nd Lt RFA, 1915; Scholar at New College, Natural Science, BA 1921, BSc and MA 1925; fellow at Magdalen College, 1922, engaged in research about plant physiology; FRS 1948. Retired to Budleigh Salterton and Gascony, died August 1969.

4. Lieutenant Colonel D. BURGES VC DSO (B.1887–91)

Lt Col Daniel Burges was among those who dined with John Baines at the Salonika Old Wykehamist dinner on 5th February 1918. At the end of that year, in the final stages of the offensive against the Bulgarians, he was awarded the VC for his gallantry as CO 7th Battalion South Wales Borderers. He was one of four Old Wykehamists VCs in the First World War. His citation reads:

For the award of the Victoria Cross – Major (Temporary Lieutenant Colonel) Daniel Burges, The Gloucestershire Regiment, comd 7th Bn, South Wales Borderers:

For most conspicuous bravery, skilful leading and devotion to duty in the operations at Jumeaux (Balkans) on the 18th September 1918. His valuable reconnaissance of the enemy first line trenches enabled him to bring his battalion without casualties to the assembly point, and from thence he maintained direction with great skill, though every known landmark was completely obscured by smoke and dust.

When still some distance from his objective the battalion came under severe machine-gun fire which caused many casualties among company leaders. Lt.-Col. Burges, though himself wounded, quite regardless of his own safety, kept moving to and fro through his command, encouraging his men and assisting them to maintain formation and direction. Finally, as they neared the enemy's position, he led them forward through a decimating fire until he was hit again twice and fell unconscious. His coolness and personal courage were most marked throughout and afforded a magnificent example to all ranks.

Index